THE VICTORIAN NOVELIST: Social Problems and Social Change

WORLD AND WORD SERIES
Edited by Professor Isobel Armstrong, University of Southampton

Literature and the Social Order in Eighteenth-century England
Stephen Copley

English Humanism: Wyatt to Cowley
Edited by Joanna Martindale

Restoration and Revolution
Edited by William Myers

THE VICTORIAN —NOVELIST:— Social Problems and —Social Change—

Edited by Kate Flint

CROOM HELM
London • New York • Sydney

© 1987 Kate Flint
Croom Helm Ltd, Provident House,
Burrell Row, Beckenham, Kent BR3 1AT
Croom Helm Australia, 44-50 Waterloo Road,
North Ryde, 2113, New South Wales
Published in the USA by
Croom Helm
in association with Methuen, Inc.
29 West 35th Street,
New York, NY 10001

British Library Cataloguing in Publication Data

Flint, Kate
    The Victorian novelist: social problems and social change.
    — (World and word series).
    1. Great Britain — Social conditions —
    19th century — Sources
    I. Title   II. Series
    941-081   HN385

    ISBN 0-7099-1023-1
    ISBN 0-7099-1093-2 Pbk

Library of Congress Cataloging-in-Publication Data

The Victorian novelist: social problems and social change
    (World and word series)
    Bibliography: p.
    Includes index.
    1. English fiction — 19th century — History and criticism.
2. Social problems in literature. 3. Literature and
society — Great Britain. I. Flint, Kate. II. Series.
PR878.S62V53 1987   823'.8'09355   87-20027
ISBN 0-7099-1023-1
ISBN 0-7099-1093-2 (Pbk.)

Typeset in 10pt Baskerville by Leaper & Gard Ltd, Bristol, England
Printed and bound in Great Britain by Mackays of Chatham Ltd, Kent

General Editor's Preface

The *World and Word* series, as its title implies, is based on the assumption that literary texts cannot be studied in isolation. The series presents to students, mainly of English literature, documents and materials which will enable them to have first-hand experience of some of the writing which forms the context of the literature they read. The aim is to put students in possession of material to which they cannot normally gain access so that they may arrive at an independent understanding of the inter-relationships of literary texts with other writing.

There are to be twelve volumes, covering topics from the Middle Ages to the twentieth century. Each volume concentrates on a specific area of thought in a particular period, selecting from religious, philosophical or scientific works, literary theory or political or social material, according to its chosen topic. The extracts included are substantial in order to enable students themselves to arrive at an understanding of the significance of the material they read and to make responsible historical connections with some precision and independence. The task of compilation itself, of course, predetermines to a great extent the kind of connections and relationships which can be made in a particular period. We all bring our own categories to the work of interpretation. However, each compiler makes clear the grounds on which the choice of material is made, and thus the series encourages the valuable understanding that there can be no single, authoritative account of the relationships between word and world.

Each volume is annotated and indexed and includes a short bibliography and suggestions for further reading. *The World and Word* series can be used in different teaching contexts, in the student's independent work, in seminar discussion and on lecture courses.

Isobel Armstrong
University of Southampton

Contents

Introduction

> The condition of England, on which many pamphlets are now in the course of publication, and many thoughts unpublished are going on in every reflective head, is justly regarded as one of the most ominous, and withal one of the strangest, ever seen in this world.[1]

Carlyle, introducing *Past and Present* in 1843, proclaims both the current fascination with threatening social issues, and the extraordinary difficulties involved in making sense of them. The fiction of mid-Victorian Britain which addressed itself to questions of urban and rural poverty formed part of an attempt at understanding contemporary society. It warned of horrors, whether of typhoid or lung disease in the Manchester slums, or of fetid water and crowded garrets in London. Together with fiction set in the recent past, like Charlotte Brontë's *Shirley* (1849), or Dickens's *Barnaby Rudge* (1841) and *A Tale of Two Cities* (1859), it echoed contemporary fears about the animalistic qualities of mob violence. Such literature did not exist in isolation. Around it lay a vast number of government reports — the Blue Books; newspaper and periodical articles and letters; pamphlets, and exploratory surveys conducted by individuals. The proliferation of information in the 1840s and early 1850s about social conditions, and demands for legislation and other forms of action to improve them, directly coincided with the main body of social problem fiction. Although novelists later in the century, such as George Gissing in *The Nether World* (1889) and Arthur Morrison in *A Child of the Jago* (1896) also incorporated shockingly graphic detail about slum conditions, they did not share the didacticism, and the tempered optimism about regeneration and amelioration, which characterised the earlier work.

This was popularly thought of as the age, as B. Love put it in *The Hand-Book of Manchester* (1842), of the '*diffusion of knowledge*'.[2] Readers and writers could not fail to be aware of the written contexts in which novels were produced and consumed, and this collection of material attempts to restore some of this inseparably connected material.

The government commissions, and other reports, testified to a belief in the necessity for detailed knowledge, not only allowing

1

the causes of domestic, industrial and agricultural hardship to be recognised and remedied, but with the aim of instilling principles of compassionate responsibility. Such a belief was shared by the newspapers and periodicals which printed and commented closely on their findings. In gathering their information, they not only accumulated facts and statistics, but experimented with various angles of vision from which to inspect society. There was the detailed recording of individual testimonies by government commissioners or, less officially, by Henry Mayhew; or, as in Hector Gavin's *Sanitary Ramblings* in Bethnal Green (no. 27), the notation, street by street, sometimes dwelling by dwelling, of drainage and water supply. Yet such minutiae were balanced by looking, as it were, through the telescope rather than the microscope, observing from a distanced, aerial vantage point, such as might be obtained from the railways whose viaducts sliced through the inner London suburbs, or from the observation eyries erected by the Metropolitan Commission of Sewers on high points which scanned the East End slums, or from a balloon. Whilst the overall impression given by this mass of collected observation is one of vast and frightening misery, the very repetitiveness of the details induced a process of familiarisation through reiteration. The threat of the strange was thus tempered through knowledge: to know *of* terrible social conditions was a necessary prerequisite not just for legislation and for specific philanthropic efforts, but represented a means by which one's reactions could be contained, one's fearfulness given names and boundaries. Additionally, the more that was known about society, the easier it became to see it as an interconnecting whole: the model of society promoted by Herbert Spencer; the social and moral web which George Eliot uses to structure *Middlemarch.* When Dickens enquires: 'What connection can there be, between the place in Lincolnshire, the house in town, the Mercury in powder, and the whereabout of Jo the outlaw with the broom ...?' (*Bleak House,* Chapter 16), his rhetoric both draws on, and helps to create, an awareness that processes of cause and effect permeated the entire social system.

The passion for quantification derived from methodically classified facts — on the surface, the most rational and ordered means of social investigation — is exemplified in the growth of statistics as a science: the Board of Trade set up a Statistical Office in 1832, the British Association founded a statistical section in 1833, and later the same year, Manchester and London both founded statistical societies. Figures rendered hardship more tangible. Moreover, they both derived their authority from, and helped to underpin, the theories of political economy, which allowed impersonal market forces, rather than considerations of human compassion, to determine the direction of commercial development. However, the accumulated bulk of official volumes and the studied impersonality of some of their contents prompted commentators, by the 1850s, to satirise these 'ponderous blue books measured by weight' in terms similar to the invective Dickens pours upon paper as a substitute for action in *Bleak House*. A piece by Henry Morley, in *Household Words* in 1850, 'The Penny Saved; A Blue Book Catechism', adds gently to the scorn:

> *Rising Young Operative*, 'Please, father, what is a blue-book?'
> *Paternal Operative*, 'A blue-book is a thick heavy catechism done up in blue covers.'
> 'What is it for?' — 'Why, when Parliament sets some of its Members to inquire about a subject, and hear evidence quietly in a room for to get at facts, they print the evidence and so on, and send it to all the other members, so that they may read and know the facts.'[3]

Dickens's satire was, in the long run, as he wrote to Charles Knight in 1855, directed at those who:

> see figures and averages, and nothing else — the repre-sentatives of the wickedest and most enormous vice of this time — the men who, through long years to come, will do more to damage the real useful truths of political economy than I could do (if I tried) in my whole life; the addled heads who ... would comfort the labourer in travelling twelve miles a day to and from his work, by telling him that the average distance of one inhabited place from another in the whole area of England, is not more than four miles.[4]

Parliamentary measures based on such investigations, com-plained the *Westminster Review* in 1853, were likely to be 'addressed only to the present and patent evil ... leaving the root of it untouched'.[5] More pertinently to the fiction of social prob-lems, other commentators expressed anxiety about the dehumanising effect of amassed figures. Carlyle might have lamented his 'want of statistics' in writing *Chartism* and sent to

3

Edwin Chadwick for some specific details, but in the book itself, his attitude towards statistics becomes one of mockery: 'with what serene conclusiveness a member of some Useful-Knowledge Society stops your mouth with a figure of arithmetic!'[6] His own method of history, stressing everyday details rather than a procession of great men, both drew from, and gave status to, the developing interest in the history, as well as in the present state, of social concerns: an interest reflected in the growing popularity of genre paintings, in George Eliot's demand: 'let us always have men ready to give the loving pains of a life to the faithful representing of commonplace things' (*Adam Bede*, 1859, Chapter 17). When Elizabeth Gaskell claimed 'I know nothing of Political Economy, or the theories of trade' (*Mary Barton*: Preface), she should not so much be thought of as proclaiming complete ignorance about the ideas which informed free-trade economics — this would seem improbable, for one with her interests and connections in Manchester of the 1840s and early 1850s — but as protesting the far greater importance, both to her fiction and to her understanding of contemporary conditions, of compassion, comprehension achieved on an individual, untheoretical level, and human love. Dickens's antagonism, to the short-sighted Mr Filer, who 'can prove it, by tables', in *The Chimes*, has a similar basis in a belief in the importance of describing problems in terms of their effects on specific women, men and children rather than as statistics and units. That the novelists fed off the documentary material available to them and to their readers is in no doubt. This fact was readily remarked on by contemporary commentators. Recently, the research of Sheila Smith, Martin Fido and Anne Humphreys, in particular, has illuminated the precise use made of Blue Books, of reports of parliamentary speeches, of private surveys, and of Mayhew's researches.[7] The power, and perhaps, for many, the overwhelming sense of helplessness and confusion produced by immersion in such evidence is felt by Lancelot, the hero of Kingsley's *Yeast*:

> So Lancelot buried himself up to the eyes in the Conditions-of-the-Poor question — that is, in blue books, red books, sanitary reports, mine reports, factory reports; and came to the conclusion, which is now pretty generally entertained, that something was the matter — but what, no man knew, or, if they knew, thought proper to declare. (Chapter VIII)

The Sadler Committee of 1832, with its exposure of the horrors of infant labour in factories, lay behind much popular 'Ten Hours' poetry, voicing the demand for new factory legislation,[8] and its findings were incorporated into Douglas Jerrold's lost play *The Factory Girl*, and Frances Trollope's novel, *The Life and Adventures of Michael Armstrong, the Factory Boy* (1840) and Charlotte Elizabeth Tonna's *Helen Fleetwood* (1841). Press discussions over the New Poor Law, in 1834, ensured a non-fictional prose context for *Oliver Twist* (1838) and Frances Trollope's *Jessie Phillips* (1842-3). The dependence of Disraeli, in *Sybil* (1845) and Kingsley, in *Alton Locke* (1850) and in *Yeast* (1848: *Fraser's Magazine*; 1851: volume publication) in particular, on written evidence which they added to their personal observation, has already been well documented (nos 15, 17, 18, 23, 24, 25, 34, 35 and 36): showing that it was derived from a wide variety of commissioners' evidence and, in the case of Kingsley, from Mayhew's *Morning Chronicle* reports as well. Even Elizabeth Gaskell, who, through the interest she took in the area of Manchester served by her husband's chapel, probably had the greatest first-hand knowledge of poverty, used the records of the Manchester Unitarian Mission Society to support her evidence (no. 3) when she wrote *Mary Barton* (1848).

The growing number of government reports, and the increased amount of public attention which was simultaneously paid to matters of housing and sanitation joined with the sheer fascination at the paradoxical spectacle of the industrial city, magnificent and productive, crowded, anonymous and dangerous, to stimulate fiction which dealt with working-class social and political life. Moreover, the presentation of the Chartist petitions in 1839, 1842 and 1848, together with the massed members of the working classes attending Chartist meetings, the rhetoric of the speeches delivered at them, and press reports which played up their unruliness, fed middle-class apprehension about the potential for violence inherent within the working classes if nothing was done about their living and working conditions. Chartism, hazily defined, provides a convenient fictional focus for *Mary Barton*. In her Preface to the novel, and in correspondence of the time, Gaskell disclaims that she is capitalising on the recent events on the continent, yet the disturbances in France in 1848 undoubtedly added to the novel's topicality, and added to apprehension of widespread disturbances in England.

As has already been mentioned, Dickens, in *Hard Times* and *The Chimes*, notoriously satirised over-dependence on facts. But he was far from immune to the individualistic, humanitarian contents of the Appendices to Blue Books. In the conclusion to *American Notes* (1842), when he is complaining about the deficiencies in public health, he claims that 'There is no local Legislature in America which may not study Mr Chadwick's excellent Report upon the Sanitary Condition of our Labouring Classes, with immense advantage' (Chapter 18). When addressing the Metropolitan Sanitary Association in 1851, he recalled how

> twelve or fifteen years ago some of the first valuable reports of Mr. Chadwick and Dr. Southwood Smith, strengthening and much enlarging my previous imperfect knowledge of this truth, made me, in my sphere, earnest in the Sanitary Cause.
> Joining this gathered information together with the evidence of his own eyes and nose, he became convinced that 'even Education and Religion can do nothing where they are most needed, until the way is paved for their ministries by Cleanliness and Decency'.[9]

In the *Examiner* in the 1840s, and later in his own periodicals, he cites or discusses a variety of works on imprisonment, as Philip Collins has pointed out: texts such as Wakefield's *Facts relating to the Punishment of Death*, Captain Maconochie's and Archbishop Whateley's pamphlets on convict management, secondary punishment and the marks system; Hepworth Dixon's *London Prisons*, the Reverend Field's *Prison Discipline*, and official reports by the police and by prison chaplains. The catalogue of his library at Gad's Hill shows, among other things, his interest in metropolitan graveyards (no. 22).[10]

Most contemporary critics tended to regard the over-use of second-hand evidence with disapproval. Thus W.R. Greg, whilst admittedly probably biased in the line he took through his associations with the manufacturing interest, complained, when he reviewed *Sybil* in the *Westminster Review*, that Disraeli's knowledge of working-class life had been derived

> entirely from published reports, which he had not even preliminary information enough to read aright ...
> Accordingly, he has done exactly what might be expected from a novelist who thought only of his novel, — he has selected a few of the coarsest and most questionable

pictures contained in the reports referred to, relating to peculiar and exceptionable cases, and resting on the testimony of a class of witnesses whose whole tone breathes inaccuracy and exaggeration.[11]

Certainly, Disraeli was selective in his writing-up of evidence, but Greg misses the point. Novelists may indeed have chosen and arranged their material with an eye to the dramatic, to add narrative and descriptive excitement to their fiction, in order to enhance its readability and marketability. But such shock tactics were employed deliberately, not to create Gothic frissons for their own sake, but to publicise dreadful social conditions, and, beyond this, to stimulate a belief in the need for action. For this to carry full weight, it was important that they should be perceived to be founded in fact, however selective their use of material might be. Disraeli's publishers explicitly claimed that the truthful weight of contemporary investigators lay behind him in the advertisement for *Sybil*: 'there is not a trait in this work for which he has not the authority of his own observation, or the authentic evidence which has been received by Royal Commissions and Parliamentary Committees.' None the less, as Brantlinger has pointed out, if fiction drew from Blue Books, so it was a frequent rhetorical practice to speak of the latter as though they were stranger than fiction. The *Quarterly Review*'s critic said of the 1842 Report on Women and Children in the Mines that it 'disclosed ... modes of existence ... as strange and as new as the wildest dreams of fiction',[12] and the *Spectator* commented of the same report that 'it discloses scenes of suffering and infamy which will come upon many well-informed people like the fictions or tales of distant lands'.[13] The *Morning Chronicle*, on 18 December 1849, during the period that it was publishing Mayhew's pieces, quoted a tribute paid by its rival, the *Sun*, that these were 'revelations so marvellous, so horrible, and so heartrending, that few histories can equal, and no fiction surpass them'.[14]

The class bias shown by Greg cannot be entirely discounted: those interviewed by commissioners and others may well, to some extent, have given answers which they felt were expected of them. Mayhew's Thames dredger is a prime example of this (no. 31), claiming that he has never found money on a drowned man, when Mayhew's introduction makes it entirely clear where these fishers for corpses gain the bulk of their income. But the sheer volume of evidence, much of it numbingly depressing in its reiteration, makes it impossible to believe that the tens of thousands of the poor who were interviewed were uniformly mendacious. The mid-century social problem fiction fulfilled a function which went beyond that of exposing and controlling: it provided a sense that one was bridging, if only temporarily, the chasm of class division. However, it can equally well be argued, as Gertrude Himmelfarb has done, that the repetition of the metaphors of the 'two nations', of the poor as a 'foreign country', of the slums as 'dark and unknown regions' — phraseology of which non-fictional writers were as guilty as the novelists — served to cement, rather than surmount, this gap in readers' minds.[15] The idea of colonial exploration was deliberately drawn upon by commentators later in the century, particularly Charles Booth in *In Darkest England and The Way Out* (1890). Whilst compassion and action were certainly stimulated, such phraseology did nothing to diminish the effects of, and acceptance of, hierarchies of power within English governmental and industrial administration. Indeed, by locking into a developing discourse of colonialism, one could argue that notions of class, almost of racial superiority, were implicitly being played upon, in a way v·hich, amplified by evolutionary theory, allowed later eugenicists to turn their attention to the desirability of curtailing breeding among slum dwellers in order to improve British stock. Additionally, the language serves as a reminder of the social distance between investigator and subject. The sense of exploration, of turning up unknown marvels, adds a taint of voyeurism to the task of observation and recording.

A minority of critics were antagonistic towards such enterprises of exploration and revelation: not on anti-humanitarian grounds, but because of the beliefs which they held about the proper nature of fiction. Thackeray, for example, reviewing Charles Lever's *St Patrick's Eve* in the *Morning Chronicle*, complained that:

> We like to hear sermons from his reverence at church; to get our notions of trade, crime, politics, and other national statistics, from the proper pages and figures; but when suddenly, out of the gilt pages of a pretty picture book, a comic moralist rushes forward, and takes occasion to tell us that society is diseased, the laws unjust, the rich ruthless, the poor martyrs, the world lop-sided, and *vice-versa*, persons who wish to lead an easy life are inclined to remonstrate against this literary ambuscadoe.[16]

Thackeray may have been writing very faintly tongue in cheek, but serious protests against didactic literary realism continued to be put forward: 'every season we are bored to death with a host of wretched and wearisome *pamphlets*, broken into chapters and interspersed with dialogues', protested the *North British Review*'s critic in November 1859, when discussing 'instructive novels', even though, admittedly, he was complaining that they did not live up to the characterisation and narrative excellence found in *Alton Locke*[17] The *Westminster Review*, slightly earlier, in 1857, maintained that the 'proper' vehicle for this type of protest already existed. 'Why relinquish the pamphlet, the ancient, approved, and honourable weapon of controversy, in order to overfreight fiction with a load that sinks it? Here is another novel of "purpose"', the critic went on, remonstrating against the prominence of workhouses and lunatic asylums in a novel entitled *Below the Surface*: 'well intended indeed, but failing in both ways — the fiction is burdened by the fact, and the fact rendered dubious and weak by the fiction'.[18] But by the time of these reviews, novels of social protest had, with a few exceptions, not only lost their immediate power to shock, but the literary, as well as topical success of the earlier fictions had encouraged subsequent imitators who depended considerably on newspaper reportage for their dryly presented protestations.

Yet it would be a mistake to think of even the earlier social problem fiction as work of radical protest or analysis. If statistics and case studies provided a means of gaining knowledge over that which was previously threatening through its very mysteriousness, fiction attempted a different mode of control: an appeal to the imagination through the careful manipulations of a plot. This plot, too, frequently functions as a check on potentially destructive energies. No mid-century novel ends on the defeatist notes of despair found later in the century, in, for example, George Gissing's *The Nether World* (1889) or Arthur Morrison's *A Child of the Jago* (1886). Yet no mid-century novelist flies in the face of contemporary evidence without the plot becoming patently absurd, as at the end of Frances Trollope's *Michael Armstrong: the Factory Boy* (1839-40), where the hero is the vehicle by which we are introduced first to the hell of the textile industry, then to a model factory run by a model employer, and then, in true rags-to-riches fashion, inherits a fortune, and spends two years developing his mind in a German university, before taking up a comfortable social position, sharing a castle on the banks of

the Rhine. Disraeli's *Sybil* (1845) is no less preposterous in its
cheatingly romantic plot. The aristocratic Egremont can hardly
conceal his amazement when he discovers that Sybil, with her
beauty, her 'fascinating simplicity', her manner of speaking 'with
such sweet seriousness of things of such vast import' is 'the
daughter of a workman at a manufactory', but the whole promise
inherent in the bringing together of the 'two nations — THE
RICH AND THE POOR' is completely undermined, not just by
the unrealistic, feudal characteristics of Disraeli's Young
Englandism, but by the crucial revelation that Sybil is of aristocratic birth after all.

Elizabeth Gaskell, despite the melodramatic episodes in *Mary
Barton* and *North and South*, is less conspicuously absurd in her
romanticism. Her firm Christian beliefs lead to a death-bed
reconciliation between master and workman in *Mary Barton*, in
an attempt to convince the reader that emotion can bridge the
class divide: 'Rich and poor, masters and men, were then
brothers in the deep suffering of the heart' (Chapter 35). But both
the demands of plot and Gaskell's own honesty prevent any
future within Manchester for the younger characters: an improb-
ably idyllic emigration is the only answer. The Yorkshire retreat
of Esther and Woodcourt, at the close of *Bleak House*, is a similar
evasion, on Dickens's part, of the problems they, and the fiction,
leave behind in London. Less escapist is the ending of *North and
South*, where Margaret, marrying Mr Thornton, enables them
both to return to Milton — a thinly-fictionalised version of
Manchester — where he can continue to explore new means of
running his factory. But he is realistic enough to admit that these
means are but 'experiments', and they are conducted without
much overall optimism:

> My utmost expectation only goes so far as this — that they
> may render strikes not the bitter, venomous sources of
> hatred they have hitherto been. A more hopeful man might
> imagine that a closer and more genial intercourse between
> classes might do away with strikes. But I am not a hopeful
> man. (Chapter 51)

Gaskell's message of Christian reconciliation is only practicable
on a small scale, it would seem. Yet in tempering her practicality,
she avoids falling into the Christian Socialist escapism of Charles
Kingsley, who, after drawing in graphic detail on Mayhew's

reports and on Blue Book evidence (nos 23, 24 and 25), rapidly retreats from the political implications of his evidence. Although his hero dies on his voyage of emigration, it is confidently suggested that he has thus been translated to the only country where true freedom, equality and brotherhood may be experienced: where the only worthwhile Chartism has nothing to do with the earthly franchise, but means fitness for another electorate: 'fit to be electors, senators, kings, and priests to God and to His Christ' (Chapter XL). Whilst Mayhew complained against Dickens's sentimentalising of seamstresses in *The Chimes*, calling his picture of lower-class life 'profound rubbish', in many ways, the bleakest mid-century ending is that of *Hard Times*, when the idealised representative of the working class, Stephen Blackpool, has been killed by falling down an unfenced mineshaft, and, even though Bounderby's fraudulency has been exposed, Gradgrind has learnt to bend 'his hitherto inflexible theories to appointed circumstances', and we have the depressingly worthy image of Rachael: 'a woman working, ever working, but content to do it, and preferring to do it as her natural lot' (Book the Third: Chapter 9), Louisa is left sombre and unfulfilled by the fireside. The onus for change is placed on author and reader: 'It rests with you and me, whether, in our two fields of action, similar things shall be or not', but Dickens is entirely and unhelpfully unspecific about what the reader's field of action may actually be.

The desire for a solution which underlies these fictional endings is plain, but it needs to be set against the overwhelming evidence that any wide-reaching improvements could not possibly be readily to hand. Fiction was certainly a means of exposing conditions against which some middle-class people still resolutely shut their eyes and noses. It was a means of reminding them, as, indeed, did many of the reports and articles, that hardship was something which affected individual lives, and must never be distanced through statistics. Moreover, it could have the effect of reinforcing not just the disquieting views of contemporary commentators, but also some of their ameliorative, whilst far from radical, suggestions for reform. This can be seen, for example, in the parallels between Elizabeth Gaskell's novels and the suggestions put forward by northern industrialists of the time (no. 10).

The purpose of this collection is three-fold. First, it provides some of the material which found its way directly into fiction, from Blue Books and other reports. Second, it amplifies the specific context in which novels would have been read at the time: it is improbable that a reader of *Hard Times* in *Household Words*, for example, would not also have been aware of the reporting of the Preston lock-out in that magazine's pages, or of the shocking reports, published simultaneously, about the accidents caused by unfenced machinery (nos 7, 8 and 12). And last, it reminds us that nineteenth-century readers and writers would have held in common a wide context in which to place the descriptions and the implications found within social problem fiction: a context not just of Blue Books, reports and surveys, but, especially, of a considerable amount of newspaper and periodical discussion. An awareness of this context enables us, however imperfectly, to bring to our reading of these texts some of the knowledge and opinions with which their original readers, too, would have approached them.

The evidence on pp. 254-5 has already been encountered earlier in extract 35: this indicates the degree of repetition in the documentation of the conditions in which the agricultural poor lived and worked.

Notes

1. Thomas Carlyle, *Past and Present*, 1843; Library Edition, London, 1897, p. [1].
2. B. Love, *The Handbook of Manchester*, Manchester, 1842, p. 97.
3. Unsigned article [Henry Morley], 'The Penny Saved; A Blue Book Catechism', *Household Words* 2, 19 October 1850, p. 81.
4. Charles Dickens to Charles Knight, 30 January 1855, *The Letters of Charles Dickens*, edited by Walter Dexter, London, 1938, II, p. 620.
5. Unsigned review article, 'Young Criminals', *Westminster Review* n.s. IV, 1853, p. 140.
6. Thomas Carlyle, *Chartism* 1840, in *Critical and Miscellaneous Essays*, Library Edition, London, 1899, vol. 4, p. 125.
7. See Martin Fido, 'The Treatment of Rural Distress in Disraeli's *Sybil*', *The Yearbook of English Studies* 5, 1975, pp. 153-63; Martin Fido, '"From His Own Observation": Sources of Working-class Passages in Disraeli's *Sybil*', *Modern Languages Review* 72, 1977, pp. 268-84; Anne Humphreys, *Travels into the Poor Man's Country: the Work of Henry Mayhew*, London, 1977; Sheila Smith, 'Willenhall and Wodgate: Disraeli's Use of Blue Book Evidence', *Review of English Studies* n.s.2, 1962, pp. 368-84; Sheila Smith, 'Blue Books and Victorian Novelists', *Review of English Studies* 21, 1970, pp. 23-40; Sheila Smith, *The Other Nation: The Poor in English Novels of the 1840s and 1850s*, Oxford, 1980.
8. See Martha Vicinus, *The Industrial Muse: A Study of Nineteenth-*

century British Working-class Literature, London, 1974.

9. Charles Dickens, speech to the Metropolitan Sanitary Association, 10 May 1851, *The Speeches of Charles Dickens*, edited by K.J. Fielding, Oxford, 1960.

10. Philip Collins, 'Dickens's Reading', *The Dickensian* LX, 1964, p. 168.

11. W.R.G. [W.R. Greg], 'Sybil', *Westminster Review* XLIV, 1842, p. 143.

12. Unsigned review article, 'Colliers and Collieries', *Quarterly Review* 70, 1842, p. 159.

13. Unsigned book notice, 'Children and Women in the Mines', *Spectator*, 14 May 1842, p. 462.

14. *Morning Chronicle*, 18 December 1849, p. 6.

15. Gertrude Himmelfarb, *The Idea of Poverty: England in the Early Industrial Age*, London, 1984, pp. 404-5.

16. William Makepeace Thackeray, 'Lever's St. Patrick's Eve — Comic Politics', *Morning Chronicle*, 3 April 1845, in *Contributions to the Morning Chronicle*, edited by Gordon N. Ray, Urbana, 1955.

17. Unsigned review article, 'Novels — Geoffrey Hamlyn and Stephan Langton', *North British Review* XXXI, 1859, p. 388.

18. Unsigned review article, 'Contemporary Literature', *Westminster Review* n.s. XII, 1857, p. 306.

Part One
The Industrial North and Midlands

1

In *Mary Barton*, Elizabeth Gaskell discriminates knowledgeably between various types of working-class housing. She demonstrates the difference made by prudent management, possible when at least one income is coming into the house, however difficult times may be, as is the case in the Barton household, and contrasts this with the conditions in which the workless Davenport family live, ill with the fever, their possessions all pawned. Some six or seven feet below street level, their cellar is only as wide as a man's outstretched arms; window panes are broken and stuffed with rags; a fetid smell is in the air, and there are 'three or four little children rolling on the damp, nay wet brick floor, through which the stagnant, filthy moisture of the street oozed up'. The family's fever 'was (as it usually is in Manchester) of a low, putrid, typhoid kind; brought on by miserable living, filthy neighbourhood, and general depression of mind and body. It is virulent, malignant, and highly infectious' (*Mary Barton*, Chapter 6).

Such a description may be compared with the picture of cellar housing given in Joseph Adshead's *Distress in Manchester*, 1842. Early in 1840, Adshead directed and superintended an investigation into the circumstances of some 12,000 Manchester families — about a third of the whole population — in order that nearly £4,000 worth of relief could be administered. He followed this by a further inquiry, and this work combines the results of the two. In his preface (p. viii) he states that he does not intend:

> to indulge in any declamatory appeals to the feelings of the reader on behalf of the suffering poor; but rather, to trust to the effect upon his cool judgment of a few simple statements ... in the hope that these will convince him that the existing distress is of a nature too settled and extensive to admit of mere temporary remedial measures; and that, therefore, the axe must be laid to the root of the evil.

Elizabeth Gaskell set *Mary Barton* back in 1839. This gave her the dramatic advantage of being able to use the events surrounding the presentation of the Chartist petition in that year. It also absolved her from being read as making an entirely direct charge against the conditions of contemporary Manchester. Appalling though these were, a local Borough Police Act of 1844 had led the city to order sanitary improvements to the houses of over 26,000 people between 1845 and 1847. Yet although in theory this affected many cellar dwellers, as Anthony Wohl points out in *Endangered Lives* (London, 1983, p. 298) 'these efforts in the 1840s were largely nullified by the enormous influx of immigrants into the city'.

See also A. Redford, *The History of Local Government in Manchester*, 3 vols, London, 1939.

Joseph Adshead, Distress in Manchester: Evidence (Tabular and Otherwise) of The State of the Labouring Classes in 1840-42, *London, 1842.*

(a) pp. 14-16
Adshead submits a table which 'will afford some idea of the extent to which cellar habitations are used in Manchester:

		FAMILIES LIVING IN CELLARS			
No	District	Families	Children under 12	Children above 12	Persons
1	Ancoats ...	555	950	395	2497
2	New Town ...	525	1024	377	2362
3	Deansgate ...	560	949	601	2520
4	Portland-st. ...	400	556	340	1800
		2040	3479	1713	9179

Although this proportion of the whole number included in the return (and relieved) — upwards of one-fifth — may not appear large when compared with that of other populous towns — (it is considerably less, we believe, than the relative number of cellar habitations in Liverpool) — it must be borne in mind that the cellars which are used as habitations by the poor have no other feature in common with the cellars attached to the middle class of dwelling-houses than that of their being below the level of the street. They are most of them neither drained nor soughed. They are consequently damp, — are always liable to be flooded, — and are almost entirely without the means of ventilation, having rarely but the outlets of door and window at the one side, and these almost hid below the level of the street.

But the above-ground habitations of the indigent poor are little better than the cellars, except in the matter of situation. Nothing in the shape of the meanest comforts of life are visible in them. Decent furniture there is none, — bricks, logs of wood, and other contrivances being frequently used as substitutes for tables and chairs, while the bag of shavings or litter of straw is laid in some corner, to be occupied nightly by its miserable tenants, with all its accumulation of impurities inevitably resulting from the condition and habits of the latter.

And not always are these abodes of squalor and poverty, whether cellars or ground-floor habitations, occupied by the members of one family alone. Frequently, different families occupy *opposite corners of the same room*, the sexes being no further separated than by the few feet of space which lie between their respective beds of straw. This state of things has come under my own observation repeatedly, in visiting the habitations of the poor. Six or eight persons have I witnessed inhabiting a damp cellar, males and females congregated together, with a line hung along the hovel for the use of the inmates, upon which were suspended, indiscriminately, their torn and dirty apparel; with other scenes of a nature too disgusting for recital.

In other instances, parents and children were found sleeping together in the same bed, without regard to age or sex. The following conversation took place between a member of the Relief Committee, and a poor widow who applied to the Committee for a bed: —

Examiner. — Have you a bed?

Widow. — I have one.

Examiner. — Is not one enough?

Widow. — No; I have a son.

Examiner. — What age is he?

Widow. — Nineteen years.

Examiner. — And where has *he* slept?

Widow. — With me; or he must have lain on the floor.

Of course a bed was given for the son.

It would be impossible to over-state the moral and social evils arising from this state of things. The domestic decencies must be utterly unknown where habits like these prevail; and every barrier against profligacy in its coarsest form must be broken down.

In a Parliamentary Report relative to the sanatory regulations of towns, it is observed that 'where there are children of both sexes, *mere decency* requires *four rooms*, — three for sleeping and one for daily use. These are the *least* that are sufficient to afford to an average family the house room necessary for decency.' Four rooms the 'least that is sufficient', while thousands of families in this town — and tens of thousands in the whole kingdom — have but one room, and that a hovel of the most wretched kind, for all the purposes of life!

(b) pp. 35-9
A feature of Distress in Manchester *are the reports which Adshead incorporates from missionaries working in various quarters of the city. This report is notable for the emphasis it places on the hardship of the respectable — as opposed to the 'intemperate' — working people.*

*This anonymous report was made in January 1842 by 'a gentleman whose attention was directed to the social and moral condition of the labouring classes, with a view to its improvement' (*Distress in Manchester, *p. 34).*

Dear Sir, — An engagement I had made to oblige a friend rendered it necessary that I should visit the inhabitants of several streets in Ancoats and in the neighbourhood of Oldham-road. As this district is not selected as the most destitute, I believe a few cases I shall state will give a very faithful illustration of the condition of tens of thousands of the manufacturing poor.

Upon the first day of our visitation I called at a house occupied by a poor man, a widower with one child, a boy between seven and eight; they were in a state of extreme poverty; the man is about thirty-five years of age, and professed himself able and most anxious to work, but had not been able to obtain any employment for many months; both were living upon what the child could obtain by begging. Upon quitting this house the man called our attention to an adjoining cellar, occupied by a woman who had been deserted by her husband. This cellar was both very dark and very damp, the roof not more than seven feet high, and the area of the floor not more than twelve square yards; its occupants were this woman and her child, a boy six years old, a widow, a lodger with three children, and a second widow with two children, sister of the woman who tenanted the cellar; these nine individuals are all crowded in a place so dark and contracted as to be unfit for the residence of any human being. It was in this abode of wretchedness that we witnessed a remarkable illustration of the sympathy and compassion of the poor for those who are still less favourably circumstanced. On the day previous to our visit one of these poor women had observed a poor houseless wanderer with two children, ready to sink with hunger and fatigue; this poor creature's husband had left her three months before to seek employment, which she was sure he had not been able to procure, or, as she said, he would soon have found her and let her know. Her poor hostess had no better accommodation to offer than a dark unpaved closet adjoining their cellar, and here, without bed or bedding beyond a handful of dirty shavings which she used as a pillow, the mother and her famishing children were thankful to take shelter: during the night the younger of the children, an infant eleven months old, died, doubtless from long exposure to cold and the want of that support which the breast of the poor, starved, and perishing mother had failed to supply. When we entered the cellar we saw this victim of want laid out upon a board suspended from the roof, and the other children (some of whom were so poorly provided with clothing as to be unfit to quit the cellar without indecent exposure) standing around; the poor mother had left her remaining child and gone out to beg assistance to inter her infant.

In the next house we entered we found two men, one twenty-seven, the other twenty-five, both weavers, and out of work; they both appeared in delicate health, one, however, much worse than the other; neither of them had been able to earn a shilling for several weeks. To our inquiry how they lived, they replied, 'We do indeed *exist*, we cannot say we live.' One of them produced a dish with potato peelings, which one of their wives had been successful in begging; this they assured us was the only food they had or expected to taste that day. These men were members of a temperance society, were both remarkably intelligent, and we inferred from the kind and patient manner in which they spoke of their poverty and its causes, which they appear perfectly to comprehend, that their minds were considerably under the influence of moral and religious principles. These men were not victims of intemperance, nor improvidence, nor idleness, nor disease, nor anything else which they could have foreseen or provided against; but, reduced and broken-hearted by the impossibility of obtaining work, they and their families are sinking in the midst of misery which they can neither remove nor flee from.

This is a spectacle more calculated than almost any other we can conceive to distress a rightly constituted mind. Men, with

21

physical strength, mental cultivation, and moral principle in active exercise, after having spent their time, and strength, and money, it may be, in learning a trade, starving in the largest manufacturing town in the world for the want of employment! And, why! ... Let the supporters of corn laws answer.

We were waited for at the door by a poor woman, who begged that we would visit her husband. We followed her to her home, which we found to be a small room nearly destitute of furniture, but well lighted and very clean. Her husband had been one of the kindest and hardest working men in the world, she said, but for the last two months he had never left the house; he had failed in all his efforts to get employment, and had at last given up the task as hopeless. He did not appear to observe our entrance; and when we spoke to him he appeared not to notice us; he had been for more than a week in a benumbed and helpless state, in which he had scarcely uttered a word; but he had given, in his wild unwonted stare and maniacal expression of countenance, fearful symptoms of mental derangement; his wife attributed his condition entirely to the want of food. Their only income was the wages of a boy who worked in a factory; these wages, at the present high price of provisions, would not supply the boy alone with sufficient food; his mother said that he more frequently returned to his work without tasting food than with a tolerable meal. Her husband had at first, when his own work entirely failed, refused to taste the food purchased with his son's wages, which he insisted should be reserved for him; but since his intellect had become deranged he seized and devoured with greediness whatever food came within his reach. The poor wife, whose lamentation it was distressing to hear, seemed sinking under an accumulation of sorrows. Our very hearts bled within us at the sight of the wretchedness we could not relieve; and we could not but think that if men who support corn laws were to witness such scenes, the fear, nay the very possibility, that they might, however remotely, be the cause, would be a sufficient reason for an immediate repeal. Should we not expect that they would make haste to wash their hands of the blood of the famishing poor?

Our next visit was to the dwelling of a widow with four daughters, all under fourteen years of age, and a female lodger. They had all been supported by factory labour, but since the destruction by fire of the mill at which they had worked, they had failed in procuring any other employment. The widow herself was in bad health, without the means of obtaining medical aid; in fact, it was her own opinion that it was unnecessary, for she said she was sure that if she had food to eat she should soon be well, but if relief was not speedily administered she would soon die. The lodger entered as we conversed with the widow; she was a young woman, twenty-two years of age; she acquainted us very particularly with the destitute circumstances of the family; they had not had more than one meal per day for many weeks, and nearly every article of furniture, clothing, and bedding had been parted with to obtain it. This young woman had been to purchase the meal for the day; she carried it covered in her gown. At my request she exposed it — a meal for six persons, and the only one for the day — a halfpennyworth of tea, a halfpennyworth of sugar, and two pennyworth of bread, and this she had purchased by pledging her only remaining petticoat!

We were surprised, on entering one house, the inmates of which were miserably poor, to observe what had once been a very elegant cabinet piano. The history of the instrument was this. The family had been in better circumstances. They had kept a provision shop, and in the time of their prosperity had devoted a portion of their gains to the education of their only daughter. The piano had been bought for her use; she had been carried off, in the bloom of her youth, by an insidious disease; and when trade began to fail, the customers were unable to pay, the poor man's property was lost, and the provision he had made for his child and his own declining years was absorbed in his profitless trade. But in the midst of all his poverty the piano was still retained as a memento of his beloved child.

Many were the families we visited who assured us they had not tasted food that day. Misery and want, hunger and nakedness, are not confined to particular localities: they are widely spread, and are spreading more widely. The number of the destitute is daily increasing. The universal testimony is, that there never was any distress equal to that which exists at present — that all other seasons of distress were trifling in comparison. The intemperate and the improvident, indeed, are the first to suffer in all seasons of distress; but it is long since distress has reached the sober, the industrious, the provident, and the respected among the labouring class.

We visited one house occupied by thirteen persons — father, mother, and eleven children. This house was without the least vestige of furniture; every article, even the lock from the door, had been sold to purchase bread. Three shillings per week was the amount of their regular income: this was the wages of one of the sons, who is employed as an errand boy. Four shillings and six-pence was all that they had to live upon for a whole week — three shillings brought by the boy, and one shilling and sixpence which had been obtained by the sale of the pan and table, which were the last articles of furniture they had to part with. This sum was expended by Wednesday; and for the next three days, till the Saturday evening, (the period of our visit,) the whole of the family, thirteen in number, had subsisted on 2¼d. worth of meal, which was prepared for use by mixing with cold water. The father of this family bears an excellent character; he had been for several years employed in chemical works, and had been very reluctantly discharged by his employers, when trade had become so very much depressed that the business could no longer be carried on without loss. This man's late employers had done all they could to serve him; they had even offered to guarantee his trustworthiness to any amount up to £400., but no employment could be obtained; and this poor, but truly respectable man, with all his knowledge of chemistry and his excellent character, is daily wandering through the streets of Manchester watching for coal carts, that he may follow them to their destination, and there plead as the greatest favour that can be done him, that he may be allowed to get them in for the sake of the few pence which such a service merits. Whatever he earns in this way is forthwith carried home to his famishing wife and family, among whom love for their parents and love for each other seem in a remarkable manner to have survived the circumstances of comfort in which they were formerly placed.

These cases (which might be increased to any number) will serve as an illustration of the general condition of the labouring poor of extensive districts in and around Manchester. I have pur-posely omitted any notice of the condition of the intemperate and the dissolute: in any state of trade they will be found in circum-stances very little more desirable that those in which they are at present found; but the thing most to be observed is this — that honesty, industry, and rigid economy avail not to avert from the suffering thousands the misery and the want by which they are fast sinking, without hope and without help. It is vain to think of private charity — it is spread far beyond the reach of the most extensive charity. If an amount equal to the subscription lately made in honour of the birth of the infant Prince of Wales were daily distributed, it would fall far short of the most pressing wants of the innumerable poor now deprived, by the operation of partial and cruel laws, of the opportunity of earning their bread by honest industry. The physical effects of the want and misery to which the poor are subjected are sufficiently obvious in the general ill health which prevails — slow fevers, depression of spirits, feebleness, and faintness, are the most common symptoms.

The education of the young is entirely out of the question, even if schooling were to be had without payment. The want of clothing is an insuperable obstacle to the attendance of the children of the poor in these districts.

For the same reason the Sunday Schools are not attended. Thousands of those who were and would be scholars in a more favourable state of trade, and many who have been usefully employed as teachers, have not the wherewith to cover their nakedness. It would be a matter of no surprise to those visiting these districts to hear, that while all kinds of manufactured goods were falling, *rags*, and rags *only*, have advanced to nearly double their former value.

As a necessary consequence, the moral condition of the unemployed poor is rapidly and fearfully deteriorating. It is vain, because contrary to all experience, to expect that moral qualities can for any considerable period co-exist with hunger and nakedness. That fretfulness and irritability of temper attendant upon the kind of physical suffering to which they are subjected, is more than sufficient to harden the most tender heart, blunt the keenest sensibility, and destroy the most amiable disposition.

2

Friedrich Engels (1820-95), the son of a prosperous German textile mill owner, spent from November 1842 to August 1844 in England. Based largely in Manchester, he was building up his knowledge of business in the cotton industry, spending his time in the mills and offices in which his father was a partner. Simultaneously, he was observing the conditions round him, his style informed by his journalistic experience, his interest stimulated through his growing concern with economic and social theory. The disturbances in England in 1842, particularly those in Lancashire, fed Engels's belief that the city represented the heart of the working-class movement, and, if potential for revolution existed anywhere in England, it could be found in Manchester. See Steven Marcus, *Engels, Manchester, and the Working Class*, New York, 1974.

Engels's study was published in Germany in 1845, but no English translation appeared until 1887. It could not, therefore, be said to be part of the immediate cultural context in which the work of Gaskell and others appeared, but nevertheless offers an outsider's interpretative view of the city and its problematic conditions. Albeit with an ultimately different political end, he shared in his humanism something of a starting point with Gaskell. Whilst her notion of Christian brotherhood informed the melodramatic death bed scene near the close of *Mary Barton*, with its consoling message 'Rich and poor, masters and men, were then brothers in the deep suffering of the heart' (*Mary Barton*, Chapter 35), Engels wrote in the belief that 'The hundreds of thousands of all classes and ranks crowding past each other, are they all not human beings with the same qualities and powers, and with the same interest in being happy?' (*Condition of the Working Class in England*, London, 1892, p. 24).

Friedrich Engels, The Condition of the Working Class in England in 1844, *with a Preface written in 1892, translated by Florence Kelley Wischnewetzky, 1892.*

(a) pp. 45-8
Engels begins his work with some considerations on the vastness of London, and then moves north, briefly looking at a couple of smaller manufacturing towns before turning to Manchester itself. The geographical features he describes, with the manufacturers' homes situated on the outskirts, is reflected in Mary Barton. *Jem Wilson, fetching an infirmary order for Davenport, 'had about two miles to walk before he reached Mr. Carson's house, which was almost in the country' (*Mary Barton, Chapter 6). In* Hard Times, *Gradgrind's Stone Lodge 'was situated on a moor within a mile or two of a great town' (*Hard Times, *I, Chapter 3). Apart from other considerations of space and health, atmospheric pollution was, of course, far less prevalent in the outskirts of cities.*

The whole assemblage of buildings is commonly called Manchester, and contains about four hundred thousand inhabitants, rather more than less. The town itself is peculiarly built, so that a person may live in it for years, and go in and out daily without coming into contact with a working-people's quarter or even with workers, that is, so long as he confines himself to his business or to pleasure walks. This arises chiefly from the fact, that by unconscious tacit agreement, as well as with outspoken conscious determination, the working-people's quarters are sharply separated from the sections of the city reserved for the middle-class; or, if this does not succeed, they are concealed with the cloak of charity. Manchester contains, at its heart, a rather extended commercial district, perhaps half a mile long and about as broad, and consisting almost wholly of offices and warehouses. Nearly the whole district is abandoned by dwellers, and is lonely and deserted at night; only watchmen and policemen traverse its narrow lanes with their dark lanterns. This district is cut through by certain main thoroughfares upon which the vast traffic concentrates, and in which the ground level is lined with brilliant shops. In these streets the upper floors are occupied, here and there, and there is a good deal of life upon them until late at night. With the exception of this commercial district, all Manchester proper, all Salford and Hulme, a great part of Pendleton and Chorlton, two-thirds of Ardwick, and single stretches of Cheetham Hill and Broughton are all unmixed working-people's quarters, stretching like a girdle, averaging a mile and a half in breadth, around the commercial district. Outside, beyond this girdle, lives the upper and middle bourgeoisie, the middle bourgeoisie in regularly laid out streets in the vicinity of the working quarters, especially in Chorlton and the lower lying portions of Cheetham Hill; the upper bourgeoisie in remoter villas with gardens in Chorlton and Ardwick, or on the breezy heights of Cheetham Hill, Broughton, and Pendleton, in free, wholesome country air, in fine, comfortable homes, passed once every half or quarter hour by omnibuses going into the city. And the finest part of the arrangement is this, that the members of this money aristocracy can take the shortest road through the middle of all the labouring districts to their places of business without ever seeing that they are in the midst of the grimy misery that lurks to the right and left. For the thoroughfares leading from the Exchange in all directions out of the city are lined, on both sides, with an almost unbroken series of shops, and are so kept in the hands of the middle and lower bourgeoisie, which, out of self-interest, cares for a decent and cleanly external appearance and *can* care for it. True, these shops bear some relation to

27

the districts which lie behind them, and are more elegant in the commercial and residential quarters than when they hide grimy working-men's dwellings; but they suffice to conceal from the eyes of the wealthy men and women of strong stomachs and weak nerves the misery and grime which form the complement of their wealth. So, for instance, Deansgate, which leads from the Old Church directly southward, is lined first with mills and warehouses, then with second-rate shops and alehouses; farther south, when it leaves the commercial district, with less inviting shops, which grow dirtier and more interrupted by beerhouses and gin-palaces the farther one goes, until at the southern end the appearance of the shops leave no doubt that workers and workers only are their customers. So Market Street running south-east from the Exchange; at first brilliant shops of the best sort, with counting-houses or warehouses above; in the continuation, Piccadilly, immense hotels and warehouses; in the farther continuation, London Road, in the neighbourhood of the Medlock, factories, beerhouses, shops for the humbler bourgeoisie and the working population; and from this point onward, large gardens and villas of the wealthier merchants and manufacturers. In this way any one who knows Manchester can infer the adjoining districts from the appearance of the thoroughfare, but one is seldom in a position to catch from the street a glimpse of the real labouring districts. I know very well that this hypocritical plan is more or less common to all great cities; I know, too, that the retail dealers are forced by the nature of their business to take possession of the great highways; I know that there are more good buildings than bad ones upon such streets everywhere, and that the value of land is greater near them than in remoter districts; but at the same time I have never seen so systematic a shutting out of the working-class from the thoroughfares, so tender a concealment of everything which might affront the eye and the nerves of the bourgeoisie, as in Manchester. And yet, in other respects, Manchester is less built according to a plan, after official regulations, is more an outgrowth of accident than any other city; and when I consider in this connection the eager assurances of the middle-class, that the working-class is doing famously, I cannot help feeling that the Liberal manufacturers, the 'Big Wigs' of Manchester, are not so innocent after all, in the matter of this sensitive method of construction.

(b) pp. 50-2; 53-5
Engels continues by describing the housing in the Old Town of Manchester, looking, it would seem, for the very worst examples of living conditions and insanitary streets.

Above Ducie Bridge, the left bank grows more flat and the right bank steeper, but the condition of the dwellings on both banks grows worse rather than better. He who turns to the left here from the main street, Long Millgate, is lost; he wanders from one court to another, turns countless corners, passes nothing but narrow, filthy nooks and alleys, until after a few minutes he has lost all clue, and knows not whither to turn. Everywhere half or wholly ruined buildings, some of them actually uninhabited, which means a great deal here; rarely a wooden or stone floor to be seen in the houses, almost uniformly broken, ill-fitting windows and doors, and a state of filth! Everywhere heaps of *débris*, refuse, and offal; standing pools for gutters, and a stench which alone would make it impossible for a human being in any degree civilised to live in such a district. The newly built extension of the Leeds railway, which crosses the Irk here, has swept away some of these courts and lanes, laying others completely open to view. Immediately under the railway bridge there stands a court, the filth and horrors of which surpass all the others by far, just because it was hitherto so shut off, so secluded that the way to it could not be found without a good deal of trouble. I should never have discovered it myself, without the breaks made by the railway, though I thought I knew this whole region thoroughly. Passing along a rough bank, among stakes and washing-lines, one penetrates into this chaos of small one-storied, one-roomed huts, in most of which there is no artificial floor; kitchen, living and sleeping-room all in one. In such a hole, scarcely five feet long by six broad, I found two beds — and such bedsteads and beds! — which, with a staircase and chimney-place, exactly filled the room. In several others I found absolutely nothing, while the door stood open, and the inhabitants leaned against it. Everywhere before the doors refuse and offal; that any sort of pavement lay underneath could not be seen but only felt, here and there, with the feet. This whole collection of cattle-sheds for human beings was surrounded on two sides by houses and a factory, and on the third by the river, and besides the narrow stair up the bank, a narrow doorway alone led out into another almost equally ill-built, ill-kept labyrinth of dwellings.

Enough! The whole side of the Irk is built in this way, a plan-less, knotted chaos of houses, more or less on the verge of unin-habitableness, whose unclean interiors fully correspond with their filthy external surroundings. And how could the people be clean with no proper opportunity for satisfying the most natural and ordinary wants? Privies are so rare here that they are either filled up every day, or are too remote for most of the inhabitants to use. How can people wash when they have only the dirty Irk water at hand, while pumps and water pipes can be found in decent parts of the city alone? In truth, it cannot be charged to the account of these helots of modern society if their dwellings are not more cleanly than the pig-sties which are here and there to be seen among them. The landlords are not ashamed to let dwell-ings like the six or seven cellars on the quay directly below Scotland Bridge, the floors of which stand at least two feet below the low-water level of the Irk that flows not six feet away from them; or like the upper floor of the corner-house on the opposite shore directly above the bridge, where the ground-floor, utterly uninhabitable, stands deprived of all fittings for doors and windows, a case by no means rare in this region, when this open ground-floor is used as a privy by the whole neighbourhood for want of other facilities! ...

Such is the Old Town of Manchester, and on re-reading my description, I am forced to admit that instead of being exagger-ated, it is far from black enough to convey a true impression of the filth, ruin, and uninhabitableness, the defiance of all con-siderations of cleanliness, ventilation, and health which char-acterise the construction of this single district, containing at least twenty to thirty thousand inhabitants. And such a district exists in the heart of the second city of England, the first manufacturing city of the world. If any one wishes to see in how little space a human being can move, how little air — and *such* air! — he can breathe, how little of civilisation he may share and yet live, it is only necessary to travel hither. True, this is the *Old* Town, and the people of Manchester emphasise the fact whenever any one mentions to them the frightful condition of this Hell upon Earth; but what does that prove? Everything which here arouses horror and indignation is of recent origin, belongs to the *industrial epoch*. The couple of hundred houses, which belong to old Manchester, have been long since abandoned by their original inhabitants; the industrial epoch alone has crammed into them the swarms of workers whom they now shelter; the industrial epoch alone has built up every spot between these old houses to win a covering for the masses whom it has conjured hither from the agricultural districts and from Ireland; the industrial epoch alone enables the owners of these cattlesheds to rent them for high prices to human beings, to plunder the poverty of the workers, to undermine the health of thousands, in order that they *alone*, the owners, may grow rich. In the industrial epoch alone has it become possible that the worker scarcely freed from feudal servitude could be used as mere material, a mere chattel; that he must let himself be crowded into a dwelling too bad for every other, which he for his hard-earned wages buys the right to let go utterly to ruin. This manufacture has achieved, which, without these workers, this poverty, this slavery could not have lived. True, the original construction of this quarter was bad, little good could have been made out of it; but, have the landowners, has the municipality done anything to improve it when rebuilding? On the contrary, wherever a nook or corner was free, a house has been run up; where a superfluous passage remained, it has been built up; the value of land rose with the blossoming out of manufacture, and the more it rose, the more madly was the work of building up carried on, without reference to the health or comfort of the inhabitants, with sole reference to the highest possible profit on the principle that *no hole is so bad but that some poor creature must take it who can pay for nothing better.* However, it is the Old Town, and with this reflection the bourgeoisie is comforted. Let us see, therefore, how much better it is in the *New Town*.

The *New Town*, known also as Irish Town, stretches up a hill of clay, beyond the Old Town, between the Irk and St. George's Road. Here all the features of a city are lost. Single rows of houses or groups of streets stand, here and there, like little villages on the naked, not even grass-grown clay soil; the houses, or rather cottages, are in bad order, never repaired, filthy, with damp, unclean, cellar dwellings; the lanes are neither paved nor supplied with sewers, but harbour numerous colonies of swine penned in small sties or yards, or wandering unrestrained through the neighbourhood. The mud in the streets is so deep that there is never a chance, except in the dryest weather, of walking without sinking into it ankle deep at every step. In the vicinity of St. George's Road, the separate groups of buildings approach each other more closely, ending in a continuation of lanes, blind alleys, back lanes and courts, which grow more and more crowded and irregular the nearer they approach the heart of the

31

town. True, they are here oftener paved or supplied with paved sidewalks and gutters; but the filth, the bad order of the houses, and especially of the cellars, remain the same.

(c) p. 63
Engels concludes:

If we briefly formulate the result of our wanderings, we must admit that 350,000 working-people of Manchester and its environs live, almost all of them, in wretched, damp, filthy cottages, that the streets which surround them are usually in the most miserable and filthy condition, laid out without the slightest reference to ventilation, with reference solely to the profit secured by the contractor. In a word, we must confess that in the working-men's dwellings of Manchester, no cleanliness, no convenience, and consequently no comfortable family life is possible; that in such dwellings only a physically degenerate race, robbed of all humanity, degraded, reduced morally and physically to bestiality, could feel comfortable and at home.

3

Without doubt, Elizabeth Gaskell knew human misery at first hand, from visits to the homes of her pupils at Lower Mosley Street Schools, and to those of the poor in her husband's congregation. William Gaskell had been appointed as a colleague to the Rev. John Gooch Robberds, minister at the Unitarian Cross Street Chapel in 1828, succeeding as senior minister in 1854. Cross Street Chapel was prosperous and fashionable at the time of the Gaskells, known locally as 'the carriage-way to heaven' (A.B. Hopkins, *Elizabeth Gaskell, Her Life and Work*, London, 1952, p. 45).

Monica Correa Frykstedt, in '*Mary Barton* and the *Reports of the Ministry to the Poor*: A New Source', *Studia Neophilologica*, LII, 1980, pp. 333-6, has shown that, in addition to direct knowledge, Gaskell had an occasional verbal dependence on the Reports of the Unitarian Domestic Mission Society, founded at Cross Street Chapel in 1833 for the purpose of visiting the poor, distributing food, bedding, clothes and soup tickets, and spreading the word of the Gospel. William Gaskell was on its committee from 1833 to his death in 1884, acting as Secretary from 1841 onwards. In particular, Elizabeth Gaskell referred to the first report of John Layhe, covering the period April 1841 to April 1842. The passages which follow are reproduced almost verbatim in Chapter 8 of *Mary Barton*. As Frykstedt comments (p. 335): 'In view of the criticism Gaskell incurred on the publication of *Mary Barton* for having drawn an exaggerated picture of the problems harassing industrial Manchester, her anxiety to give a truthful account is noteworthy. Equally significant, of course, is the fact that Elizabeth Gaskell chose to draw on official Unitarian documents rather than some other factual source.'

Unitarian Domestic Mission Society: Reports of the Mission to the Poor, in Manchester, 1842.

Report, 1842, p. 19

At the present, however, I have reason to think, that the indigence and sufferings of the operatives of Manchester, with other concurring cases, have induced a suspicion in the minds of many persons, that their legislators, their magistrates, their employers, and even the ministers of religion, are, in general, their oppressors and enemies, and are in league for their prostration and enthralment.

Report, 1842, pp. 34-5

And when I hear, as I have heard, of the sufferings and privations of the poor — of provision shops where ha'porths of tea, butter, and even flour, are sold to accommodate the indigent — of parents sitting in their clothes by the fireside during the whole night, for seven weeks together, in order that their only bed, and bedding might be reserved for the use of their large family — of others sleeping upon the cold hearth-stone for weeks, in succession, without adequate means of providing themselves with sustenance and warmth — of others being compelled to fast for days together, unsustained by any probability of the speedy approach of better fortune — living, moreover, or rather starving in a crowded garret, or damp cellar, as they sometimes do, and gradually sinking under the combined influence of want, despondency, and corroding anxiety into a premature grave — and when I see, that whatever exaggerations or faults there may be in this, sufficient evidence of the destitution and misery of their condition still remains in their care-worn looks, and excited feelings, and desolate homes — while in most cases, some humane and virtuous emotions co-exist with all their wretchedness, I cannot wonder, though I much regret, that many of them should be induced to speak and act with unreasonable precipitation.

4

In *Mary Barton*, Gaskell expresses strong reservations about the power and activity of trades' unions. She saw them as products of class division and oppression, but believed that they merely served to reproduce and perpetuate these characteristics. For her, they were dangerous in their power to play on understandably volatile emotions. In Chapter 15, she condemns them for their violence and inhumanity, attacking the 'foot-sore, way-worn, half-starved looking' power-loom workers who came into Manchester during the turn-out, looking for work. 'Combination is an awful power. It is like the equally mighty agency of steam; capable of almost unlimited good or evil. But to obtain a blessing on its labours, it must work under the direction of a high and intelligent will; incapable of being misled by passion, or excitement. The will of the operatives had not been guided to the calmness of wisdom.'

In her apprehension of trades unionism, Gaskell was adopting an attitude which had become established among the Lancashire middle classes. It can be paralleled in much contemporary comment. Peter Gaskell, in *The Manufacturing Population of England*, 1833, was one of the earliest writers on factory condditions, deeply concerned with the effects of factory work upon health. In Chapter XI of this work, he considers the issue of Combinations.

Peter Gaskell: The Manufacturing Population of England, its Moral, Social, and Physical Conditions, and the Changes which have arisen from the Use of Steam Machinery, with an Examination of Infant Labour, *London, 1833.*

(a) pp. 296-303

The total want of confidence which at present marks the relations of the master-manufacturer and his hands, and the feelings of deep hatred which are too prevalent amongst them, have been brought about chiefly by unadvised combinations on both sides.

It may be truly stated, that they are in organized opposition, in banded societies, for the purpose of injuring the interests of each other, from a mistaken and groundless hope that such injury would benefit themselves. It could do no such thing: and they only heighten the unavoidable misfortunes incident upon their separate states, by a course of proceeding at variance with every thing just and charitable, and which, by its demoralizing agency, is rapidly unfitting them from ever regaining a position, with reference to each other, which is alone compatible with their best interests.

Combination is justifiable only when a disposition is plainly shewn to take certain advantages which may be more or less injurious to either party. On the one hand, the master may wish and endeavour to exact more work from his hands without increasing their wages, and thus add to his profits at the expense of their labour. Here he may find himself thwarted in his purpose. His men scatter themselves amongst his neighbours, or refuse to work, knowing that he cannot afford to let his machinery and stock in trade remain idle. Under these circumstances, if his neighbours do not embrace his cause, he is compelled to take back his hands upon their own terms, having possibly to make certain sacrifices, as to mill regulations, as a propitiation. The passive combination of the men here gains them their object; and, in this particular instance, perhaps the conduct of the individual master might be wrong. But this triumph by no means leaves them in the same relative situation which they held before. Their natural order is to some extent reversed, and the men have learnt a dangerous power. Farther still, the character of the master is lowered in their estimation; they have no faith in him, and are eternally jangling and disputing upon points of discipline. On the other hand, this power having once been acknowledged, the men, in their turn, become more unreasonable, and during a run of trade, or seizing upon some other favourable juncture, demand either a lessening of the period of labour, or an increased rate of payment for that which they already go through. The master demurs; his hands strike, and he finds himself on the very verge of ruin in consequence. He holds out if he can; and the men, having their own sufferings to contend with, in the end return at their old prices, or an increase so small, as to be a straw in the balance compared to what they have lost during their wilful idleness.

It is quite obvious that occurrences of this nature, so detrimental to the interests of the men on the one hand, and the masters on the other, must lead to the adoption of some measures having for their intention the equalization or protection of both against the caprice, avariciousness, and unreasonable and untimely demands. Unfortunately, each party made their own arrangements. The men under the belief that they were all powerful, and the masters in self-defence, with the farther understanding that they would assist each other. On both sides funds were collected, delegates and secretaries appointed, and labour and monied capital came into direct collision.

A history of the privations borne by the workmen in some of these insane contests, would present an awful picture of human suffering, and a picture not the less awful of rapid demoralization. So far have these gone sometimes, as to threaten the ruin of an entire and flourishing town or district, and have involved in it not only the interests of the two conflicting parties, but the race of shop-keepers and others dependent upon them for their support. The most extensive emigrations have taken place, poor-rates have been doubled, and society disorganised.

These struggles have uniformly been most disastrous to the men, and must ever be so. It is in vain that in their rage worked up into madness by heartless demagogues, by hunger, by the sight of their famishing children, they have taken the law into their own hands, and dreadful proofs have they given how unfit were they to wield it for their own benefit. Incendiarism, machine breaking, assassination,[1] vitriol throwing,[2] acts of diabolical outrage, all have been perpetrated for intimidation or revenge; but in all cases with the like result, or when partial success has attended them, it has been but temporary.

The extent to which combinations exist amongst workmen is only fully shewn when a general strike in a particular branch of trade takes place. Then they are seen ramifying in every direction, embracing all trades alike, each having their separate rules and code of laws, but all uniting in one point, to support the operative, when he either voluntarily abstracts himself from employ, or is driven out by some new demand on the part of his master. Each trade has a sort of corporate board for the management of its funds, the protection so called of its particular interests, and this board is paid for its services out of a specific allowance made by every workman who is a member of the union or combination. The sums thus abstracted from the pockets of the deluded artizan, have been all very considerable, the regulations being compulsory in the extreme.

No workman is allowed to act according to the dictates of his own feelings — he is compelled to become a member, or subject himself to a course of annoyances and injuries which have repeatedly ended in death. This arbitrary and tyrannical assumption of power, is one of the greatest evils attending upon the system of combinations amongst the operatives. However well-disposed the industrious and economical workman may be, he is placed upon a level with the most profligate and idle, who are in general the stirrers up of these strikes; he is condemned against his own judgment to abstain from working at a price, low perhaps, and barely sufficient but still enough for his wants; to be satisfied with two or four shillings per week from the union fund for the support of his family, in the place of earning amongst them twenty or twenty-five shillings; to remain in idleness for weeks in succession, to the utter ruin of his habits — and is deprived of all stimulus to be a good and industrious citizen, by the certainty that he is liable to be turned out of employment from causes over which he has no controul, and which not unfrequently he cannot comprehend.

When it is borne in mind how great a proportion of the labourers employed in factories consists of females and children, the evil presents itself in a still more striking point of view. In nineteen cases out of twenty these can have nothing to do with the originating the turn out [sic], which is equally, however, operative upon them, a regular compliment and series of hands being necessary for the working of a mill. They are thus subjected to starvation and idleness, both exercising a most powerful influence upon their moral and social character — an influence of the most debasing quality.

The operations of manufacturing yarn from the raw material, it is true, is distinct from the manufacturing it into cloth — so far the spinner and the weaver are completely separated; they are, however often carried on simultaneously in the same mill, the same steam-engine serving for both purposes. Occasions have occurred when the spinners have turned out leaving the weavers in employ, and vice versa the weavers have turned out leaving the spinners in employ, each supposing itself to have separate causes for complaint or satisfaction. The great turn outs have, however, involved both, or when they have been partial, the injury, though less, has still been felt by the whole — the members of the same family or household being indiscriminately composed of spinners, weavers, and their dependants.

It has repeatedly happened that the disputes which have ended in a general turn-out have had reference only to a very small portion of the hands — spinners of a particular class for example, such as coarse or fine yarns in the demand for which some change has come on, which may have necessitated the master to reduce the wages paid for its manufacture, but so complete and determinate has been the organization amongst the whole union, that thousands have deserted their occupation and submitted to every sort of suffering incident to the deepest poverty.

(b) pp. 311-13

Gaskell continues to enumerate the undesirable effects of combinations: workmen organising among themselves are necessarily removed from talking confidentially to their masters; someone who takes part in a long turn-out is in danger of financially crippling themselves and their family even after they have begun work again, and, above all, union activities tend 'to the destruction of social order, and the security of life and property' (p. 306).

The moral influence of combinations upon the character of the manufacturing population, has been exceedingly pernicious. It has placed a barrier between the master and the hands which can never be removed, but with the utmost difficulty; for neither dare trust the other. Suspicion has usurped the place of confidence; an utter alienation of all friendly feelings — mutual fear — hatred, and a system of espionage totally subversive of every thing honourable in their intercourse.

Nothing can more strongly mark the demoralization brought about by the agency of turn-outs, the result of combination, than the acts which have been committed by the men, and openly boasted of. Cutting away cloth from the looms of those better disposed individuals who preferred working for the support of their families, to starving in obedience to a fiat to strike — a system of inquisitorial visitation ruinous to neighbourly kindness — the darker crime of vitriol-throwing — more cowardly and treacherous than the stab of the Italian bravo — the waylaying and abusing obnoxious individuals — and the stain which must ever rest upon them, indelibly marked, and branding them with infamy — that of murder.

The demonstrations of vengeance, carried into effect in some instances have at times forced the masters to arm themselves — to garrison their houses and mills, and have placed a whole district in a state of siege, with all the disorganization of social ties incident to civil warfare. No man was safe — no family secure from midnight disturbance; shots were fired into the rooms where it was believed the master had his resting place. By day he had to use every precaution to avoid falling into the hands of an infuriated mob — his family reviled — loaded with the most opprobrious epithets — hooted and hissed wherever opportunity offered; no wonder that feelings of bitterness were roused against those who thus wantonly violated all the forms of decency and justice.

(c) p. 319

It is morally impossible that the condition of the great bulk of the labouring community can be ever permanently benefited so long as they permit themselves to be led away by designing and factious individuals, who live upon their passions and ignorance. Till a restoration of confidence between them and their employers they will be liable to this misleading. Whenever any question having reference to the interests of either party is under discussion, these agitators immediately stir themselves to effect a breach between the employers and the employed, and it very frequently happens, that the first intimation that a master receives of his men interesting themselves on any subject, is the sight of a petition containing the signatures of all of them. This display of want of confidence on the part of the men, and the secrecy and sometimes little understood way in which they receive information, renders the masters jealous and suspicious, and spite of their prudence, they shew their feelings pretty plainly. Hence it is that so little progress is as yet made towards a proper understanding between them, whilst the actions of each are scrutinized closely; when, on the one hand, it should be ready obedience, and, on the other, confidence and affability.

(d) pp. 323-6

Peter Gaskell's solution to the problem of industrial discontent is ultimately the same as Elizabeth Gaskell's: the establishment of greater understanding between master and men, the former 'taking a personal and positive interest in the welfare of those immediately under them ... shewing them that they are sincerely anxious to assist' (p. 321); the latter coming to understand something of the economic operations of the cotton trade.

If the workmen could be brought to understand some of these truths, a better chance would be given for a union taking place between them and the masters, and both would succeed in keeping up a remunerating price for their separate capitals; whereas the men, on the one hand, by injuring the property of their masters, compel them to reduce their wages as a compensation, or to demand such excellence of work, and to cut off so much for fines, that it amounts to the same thing as reduction; whilst on the other hand the master, finding his hands thus turbulent and unruly, turns all his energies to improvements in his machinery, and endeavours, by throwing off an increased quantity of work, to make amends for the incertitude in his labourers. This often produces gluts, which injure, again, both masters and men. Another advantage would be gained by a mutual understanding: during turn-outs great numbers of new hands come into the town or district where it exists, generally hand-loom weavers, or operatives from other classes of manufacturers, or individuals from the mining districts; and, rather than have their mills remaining totally idle, the masters engage these, spite of the violence and resistance of the old hands: but then they are ignorant of the details of spinning or weaving; much has to be taught them; a great deal of work is spoiled, and much loss sustained for a time. The men finding their places partially occupied, and their obstinacy and turbulence yielding before continued privations, gladly return at the old prices: many of necessity cannot be taken in, as it would be a manifest injustice to discharge the hands they have, even though inferior in capability for producing good work. Thus they are compelled to seek work somewhere else, or lower their wages, and have been instrumental in introducing a greater number of hands than can find present employ, and hence the foundation for another reduction of wages before any very long period.

The most important benefit which the men would derive from coalescing with their masters, and agreeing to some certain standard rules for their mutual regulation, is that both would very soon think each other trustworthy, and those feelings of hostility and bitterness which now exist between them, and which are kept up by combinations — delegates — secretaries — would be done away with. It will be in vain for the men to expect to do this, so long as they submit to the dictates of parties interested in keeping up mischief between them and their masters. The moral revolution which this would at once produce, would be an excellent basis for rearing a superstructure of social arrangements, which might snatch the men and their families from their present degradation. One thing is quite certain, that if they do not adopt some plan of this nature, they will miss the opportunity, and will condemn themselves to a life of servitude to an iron master, who is already more than threatening them. Let them remember that already the steam-engine, though applied to the same purposes as human labour for so very few years, performs as much work, in simple power, as two millions and a half of human beings! Let them farther remember, that each steam-loom is nearly four times as effective as the hand-loom, and that improvements are hourly taking place in its applicability — giving it endowments — approximating it with the most delicate operations of the human hand; and let them remember, also, that it never tires; that to it eight, ten, twelve, fourteen, or twenty hours are alike! To endeavour to arrest its progress would be madness: they cannot turn back the stream of events — the onward current of the age — their efforts would be equally impotent and ruinous. They may, however, compete with it on more equal ground if they choose, and may prevent the accelerations of its career by working steadily, orderly, and systematically. Every effort which they have made to retard or destroy the progress of machinery, has only hurried on the march of improvement; and if they persevere in such a course of proceedings, they will become its victims, bound hand and foot, and resembling, in their condition, the serfs — the *glebæ adscripti* of a former period. Their attempts to break up the social confederacy by violence and outrage, and thus bring on such internal disorder as would deprive the nation of its manufacturing pre-eminence, must and will be suppressed by the strong arm of the law.

The urgent note on which Peter Gaskell ends this chapter has its coun-
terpart in the fears of working-class violence which runs through mid-
century fiction:

Much should be done — and done vigorously and resolutely.
Like other great revolutions in the social arrangement of
kingdoms, it is to be feared that the explosion will be permitted to
take place, undirected by the guiding hand of any patriotic and
sagacious spirit, and its fragments be again huddled together in
hurry and confusion; and finally to undergo a series of painful
gradations, from which the imagination turns with sickening
terror (p. 341).

1. The deliberate assassination of Thomas Ashton, son of Mr. S.
Ashton, one of the principal cotton manufacturers in the neighbourhood
of Manchester, during the strike in 1831-2, was an act of the most atro-
cious villainy. Returning from the mill early in the evening through a
bye-road, he was shot through the chest within a very few yards both of
the mill and his father's house — a victim less deserving his untimely fate
it would have been difficult to have selected — for he was distinguished
by his general kindness to the men, and endeared by his amiable qualities to his friends. The crime would seem to have been perpetrated by
three people in company, who had been seen lurking about during the
early part of the evening. Large rewards were offered both by government
and his connexions, but have hitherto had no result, and it seems probable that its perpetrators will escape the punishment so richly deserved
by their act — save the hell of their own consciences — or that the strange
retributive justice, which has marked similar atrocities, will in course of
time bring them to light.

2. The crime of vitriol throwing is a novel feature in the annals of the
country. It consists of putting into a wide necked bottle a quantity of sul-
phuric acid — oil of vitriol as it is commonly called — and throwing this
upon the person of the obnoxious individual, being either directed to the
face or dress merely, or of throwing a quantity upon any work offensive to
the party. The caustic nature of this fluid renders it a formidable weapon
when it is applied to any exposed part of the body, and in several
instances loss of sight has resulted from it, and in a vast number of others
very great suffering has resulted from its application. It is immediately
destructive to the texture of cloth from its corrosive qualities. This
demoniacal proceeding was exceedingly prevalent during the turn out of
1830-1, many of the masters not daring to stir out during the evening.

5

Similar sentiments to Peter Gaskell's are found in B. Love's *The Handbook of Manchester*, 1842, a second and enlarged edition of *Manchester as it Is*, 1839. Engels consulted the earlier version when writing *The Condition of the Working Class*.

B. *Love*, The Handbook of Manchester, *Manchester, 1842.*

(a) p. 97

... experience does not seem to teach operatives the wisdom of allowing trade to be open, and masters and men to be unrestricted in their operations. Perhaps nothing has contributed more to exalt the inventive genius of our mechanical men and engineers, than the unsufferable annoyances to which they have been subjected by trades' unions. The folly of working men, — to reduce the talented and unskilful, the idle and the industrious, artizan, to one common level; and to insist that the veriest dolt, that ever stumbled through his apprenticeship, shall rank with the intelligent and diligent, — is of an extreme character, and unworthy this age of the *'diffusion of knowledge'*.

(b) pp. 143-4
In the last eight years

... the morals of the lower classes in Manchester have suffered considerable damage by the influence of Socialism. That dia-bolical system has spread itself widely here. Its advocates have erected a large building, in which their disciples assemble, and in which are delivered lectures suited to the tastes of the *sect*. These are frequently given on Sunday evenings, and are attended with music and other circumstances that tend to destroy, especially in the minds of young people, all respect for the sanctity of the Sabbath. The undisturbed promulgation of Socialism has given a sort of latitudinarianism to immorality. Hence blasphemous pla-cards have been posted on the walls of the town with impunity, and blasphemous publications sold to a great extent.

6

The melodramatic central incident in *Mary Barton*, the shooting of Henry Carson by John Barton, has been variously received. Raymond Williams, for example, maintains that it is a highly unrepresentative act within a novel where the primary focus is representational: he believes it to be a dramatisation of the fear of violence prevalent among Manchester's upper middle class in the late 1840s (*Culture and Society 1780-1950*, London, 1958, p. 90). John Lucas goes further than this, claiming that the murder represents a structural form of sublimation: 'by means of it she can *simplify* a complexity which has become too terrific for her to accept consciously'. The inclusion of a murder is a neat way to impose order on the muddle, so that 'a neat pattern can realise itself: class antagonism producing a violence from which springs reconciliation' (John Lucas, *The Literature of Change*, Sussex, 1977, p. 173).

Gaskell herself made a claim for the incorporation of the assassination in terms which suggest imaginative projection rather than typicality. She denied that she had been influenced by any specific incident, but the parallels with one particular attack are nevertheless close. In *The Manufacturing Population of England*, Peter Gaskell had reminded his readers of the murder of Thomas Ashton on the night of 3 January 1831. On 16 August 1852, Elizabeth Gaskell replied to Sir John Potter, brother-in-law of the deceased man, who had claimed that she was drawing on this event, and had caused distress to his family:

> Of course I had heard of young Mr Ashton's murder at the time when it took place; but I knew none of the details, nothing about the family, never read the trial (if trial there were, which I do not to this day know;) and [that] if the circumstance were present to my mind at the time of my writing Mary Barton it was so unconsciously; although it's occurence, and that of one or two similar cases at Glasgow at the time of a strike, were, I have no doubt, suggestive of the plot, as having shown me to what lengths the animosity of irritated workmen would go.
> (*The Letters of Mrs Gaskell*, edited by J.A.V. Chapple and Arthur Pollard, Manchester, 1966, p. 196.) Contemporary

accounts of the Ashton murder show precisely why it fuelled contemporary fears about the operations of trades unions.

Using Henry Carson's death as a narrative tool to aid her theme of reconciliation through the pain of bereavement, the acknowledgement that master and employee could be brothers in the suffering of the heart, Gaskell shied away from making the wider connections drawn by Engels in *The Condition of the Working Class*:

When society places hundreds of proletarians in such a position that they inevitably meet a too early and unnatural death, one which is quite as much a death by violence as that by the sword or bullet; when it deprives thousands of the necessaries of life, places them under conditions in which they *cannot* live — forces them through the strong arm of the law, to remain in such conditions until that death ensues which is the inevitable consequence — knows that these thousands of victims must perish, and yet permits these conditions to remain, its deed is murder just as surely as the deed of the single individual; disguised, malicious murder, which does not seem what it is, because no man sees the murderer, because the death of the victim seems a natural one, since the offence is of omission rather than commission. But murder it remains (Friedrich Engels, *The Condition of the Working Class in England*, pp. 95-6).

Thomas Middleton: Annals of Hyde and District, *London, 1899*

(a) pp. 85-7

The *Stockport Advertiser*, of the 7th of January, 1831, contains the following report of this occurrence: —

HORRID MURDER

On Monday last one of the most cruel and sanguinary murders which ever disgraced a civilised people was perpetrated on the body of Mr. Thomas Ashton, eldest son of Samuel Ashton, Esq., of Pole Bank, Werneth, in this parish, so early as seven o'clock in the evening. The victim of this cold-blooded and diabolical act of assassination, who was in his 24th year, and remarkable for his kind and conciliating disposition and manners, had the management of a new mill belonging to his father at Woodley, from whence he had just returned and was on his way to the other mill at Apethorn to superintend for his younger brother, James, who had just left home to spend the evening with a family near Stockport. The father and mother were in the house at the time waiting the return of the carriage to join the brother and the other part of the family who had gone with him, and the effect of so distressing a communication may more easily be imagined than described. It appeared on the examination of the witnesses before the coroner that the unfortunate gentleman had not proceeded on the public highway, after quitting the private road, which leads from Pole Bank to Apethorn Mills, more than 30 yards before he was shot; and it would appear on examination of the premises about the fatal spot that the assassins had awaited his approach, sitting behind a hedge bank on the road side, which situation gave them the best opportunity of seeing or hearing the approach of their victim from his father's house down the private pathway. The breast was perforated at the edge of the bone by two bullets from a horse pistol or blunderbuss which passed out at the left shoulder blade, having taken an oblique direction upwards. His death must have been instantaneous, for when found the right hand was in his great coat pocket — a manner of placing it quite usual with him when walking. He was lying in a shallow ditch on the contrary side of the road to the one generally taken by the family after going to the mill, and this is accounted for by the supposition that he must have retreated to the other side when approached by the assassin in order to avoid him. The muzzle of the weapon appears to have been placed close to his breast, as the wadding had perforated his garments, and part of it (some coarse blue paper) had entered his body, and was concealed in the sternum. Other parts of it (some white adhesive plaister) which had covered the balls, having been folded four times, had not entered the body, but was removed with the clothes; and the use of this extraordinary material will, in all probability, lead to the detection of the villain.

It is perhaps necessary to supplement this report by the few following particulars. The Ashtons, even at that time, were one of the largest and best known manufacturing families in the North of England. Thomas Ashton, the victim of the murder, was the eldest son of Samuel Ashton, of Pole Bank, who owned two mills, one at Woodley and one at Apethorn. Thomas managed the

Woodley mill, and James Ashton, a younger brother, was the manager at Apethorn. It was the custom of the brothers to visit their respective mills each evening, but on the 3rd January, 1831, James, who had received an invitation to a Ball at Highfield House, near Stockport, requested his elder brother to visit the Apethorn mill in his stead. Whilst proceeding to carry out this request, Mr. Thomas Ashton was, as already stated, shot dead in Apethorn Lane about seven o'clock in the evening. A third and younger brother was the late Mr. Benjamin Ashton, J.P., whom popular rumour erroneously assigns as the intended victim of the murder.

The inquest, which was held on Wednesday, January 5th, 1831, at the Boy and Barrel Inn, Gee Cross, substantiated the items given in the newspaper account. One of the witnesses, a servant at Pole Bank, said 'Mr. Ashton left the house a little after seven to officiate for his brother, having just before that time arrived thither from the mill at Woodley. In a quarter of an hour after his departure, information was brought to the family of the melancholy event. The messenger who brought the intelligence first asked for Mr. Thomas, and on being told that he had gone out, said he believed he was down in the lane badly hurt. In ten minutes afterwards he was brought in dead.' Another witness, who discovered Mr. Ashton, said that 'he stumbled over him as he lay in the road, and thinking it was somebody drunk, went to Swindells' farm, adjoining the spot, and procuring a lanthorn was able to identify him. The body was carried to Pole Bank in an arm-chair and laid out on the kitchen dresser.' Several witnesses swore to 'having seen three suspicious men, armed with a gun, parading the lane close to the spot of the murder shortly before the report of fire-arms was heard', and it was stated that 'the people of the farm just below the scene of the murder, who were milking at the time the shot was fired, were immediately afterwards startled by three men rushing through the farmyard and jumping over a gate into the meadow'. Ultimately the jury returned a verdict of 'Wilful Murder against three persons unknown'.

Notwithstanding a reward of £1,500, and a promise of pardon from the king to any one of the three suspected persons who would give evidence, unless such a person was the one who actually fired the shot, the crime remained a mystery for several years.

(b) pp. 88-9; 90-2

In April, 1834 ... the excitement was rekindled, when it became known that a man in Derby gaol had made statements likely to throw considerable light upon the matter. The statements referred to led to the arrest of two men in Marple, who were, in the course of the ensuing week, privately examined by Captain Clark and remanded. A final examination took place on May 5th, 1834, and after eighteen witnesses had been called the men were committed for trial, and removed in irons to Chester.

Before the day of trial arrived it was generally known throughout the district that William Mosley, one of the three prisoners, had turned King's evidence, and was to be brought as a witness against his companions. The trial took place in the Crown Court of Chester Castle, before Baron Parke, on the 6th August, 1834, and the greatest interest was taken in the proceedings. The prosecution was conducted by the Attorney-General, and the hearing lasted the whole of the day, until exactly eleven o'clock at night ...

The greatest interest, of course, was centred in the evidence of William Mosley, the informer. Having stated that he was brother to the prisoner Mosley, witness deposed to meeting the two prisoners at the Stag's Head, Marple, on the Wednesday before the murder. One of them asked him if he was out of work, and on being told that he was — but was going to Macclesfield the next day to procure employment — Garside said he had better stop a few days as they could secure him a better job than any he could find. On the following Sunday, according to agreement, the three met on Marple Bridge between twelve and one o'clock. From thence they went to Compstall Brow, at the top of which they met two men. Mosley, at the request of his brother, stood aside, and the men talked with the prisoners. He could not hear all what was said, but he heard something about the Union. To quote the witness's own words —

'They remained talking about an hour, and when they went I joined my brother and Garside, and I asked them what they were going to do, and they both said they had agreed with those men to shoot one of the Mr. Ashtons. I asked what it was for, and they said it was on account of the Union — the turnout. I asked what they must have for it, and they said £10. They said I must meet them on Werneth Low, at Wright's Tower, on the 3rd of January, about four or five o'clock at night. On the Monday I set out from

Romiley, to go to Wright's Tower, at about four o'clock. I could
not see them there. I then went on to the Gravel Pits, and I met
with them standing there. On leaving the Gravel Pits we went by
the footpath to the turnpike road, and then we went to the end of
the lane leading down to the canal ... When we got to the lane
Garside and me changed shoes. I had a pair of well-nailed shoes.
Garside put one on, and I kept the other. I took his hat and gave
him my cap. No other exchange was made. When we were about
twenty or thirty yards down the lane we met a man, and next a
little girl met us. A little further on we met a boy with a lantern,
and then a man opposite the clap gate leading to Mr. Ashton's.
My brother went across the road to look at him. He bent down to
look in his face. He passed on. Garside asked Joseph whether he
knew him, and he said no. We all then went over the hedge into
the field, and stopped in the footpath leading up to Mr. Ashton's.
I was on the higher ground and could see him. They were sat on
the ditch bank with their heads down, one a little higher than the
other. A short space afterwards there came a man down the footpath toward the clap gate. Garside got up, came and met him in
the field before he got through the gate, and pointed the piece at
him. He gave way. Garside fired the piece. When Mr. Ashton
gave way he only went a little out of the way. Garside met him
and he went back. He had got through the clap gate when the
shot was fired, and he was going along the road towards the mill.
The man who was shot fell across the road, with his head towards
the right hand side, opposite to where I was. The last man who
passed us could not have got out of hearing when the shot was
fired. We immediately ran away, and I made the best of my way
across the fields to the second canal bridge. We were to meet at
the first bridge, and I retreated back to the first bridge, and they
were standing on the bridge. Garside had the piece in his hand,
and I asked him had he shot him. He said "Yes, dead enough.
He never stirred at after." ... I asked which of the Messrs. Ashton
they had shot, and they said *it didn't matter which it was, it was one
of them.* We parted at Hatherlow. I saw them again on the following Wednesday on the road leading to Marple Bridge. When I
saw them the man Schofield, or Stansfield, was with them. He
pulled out three sovereigns and said he had settled with them
two, and would settle with me. I received two of them. He pulled
out a book for us all to sign, to say we had had the money. We all
went down on our knees then, and made a confession to God;
declaring to God that we would never tell, and praying to God to

strike us dead if we told. We did it one after another. We every-
one held a knife in turn over the other while we said so.'

It is unnecessary to go further into the evidence. The judge's
charge to the jury was two hours and eight minutes in length.
Without leaving the box the jury returned a verdict of 'guilty'
against James Garside and Joseph Mosley. Both prisoners fainted
when the verdict was given, and fell to the floor. They were raised
and supported by the officers to hear the passing of the sentence,
at the conclusion of which they sank back into the arms of the
officers, and in that state were removed from sight.

7

The Preston lock-out of 1853-4 has long been recognised as lying
behind the scenes of industrial unrest in *Hard Times* and *North and
South*. 'Locked out', by James Lowe, gives the outlines of this dispute. It appeared in *Household Words* a few months before the
serialisation of *Hard Times* began, in the same magazine, on 1
April 1854.

Preston had, in the early 1840s, become conspicuous both for
its prosperity, and for the growth of its working population, something which necessarily had an adverse effect on living conditions.
Its death rate in the 1840s was allegedly the highest in the United
Kingdom. Despite the depression in the Lancashire cotton trade
in 1846-8, the industry experienced a boom in the next few years.
However, the manufacturers refused to restore the wage reductions which they had made during the depression. Throughout
Lancashire — indeed, throughout Britain — workers in a variety
of industries campaigned for a 10 per cent rise in wages, and were
prepared to strike in order to achieve it. In August, cotton
manufacturers in Stockport (6 August) and Blackburn (18
August) gave in: pressure was on other employers in North-east
Lancashire to follow suit. Preston had never previously been
known for industrial militancy, one reason why unionists were so
keen to give support to the struggle here, since if the operatives
could not or would not succeed in obtaining the 10 per cent, it
was feared that it would be taken back in other towns. Gradually,
the workers in the town came out on strike. By September, politi-

cal meetings were an almost daily occurrence. On 15 October, the masters in Preston and surrounding areas began to lock out the workers. No wages at all in local circulation meant that no subscriptions could be paid to the operatives' organisations which were aiding the struggle, though support continued to be sent from all over the country. More importantly, the employees were, in effect, being starved back to work: work on the employers' terms, not their own. Unfortunately, they had chosen a time to strike when there was little danger of hurting trade, especially as the internal rebellion in China in 1853 had led to a dramatic reduction in exports to that country. As the *Liverpool Journal* of 5 November 1853 commented: '... the men have made one of the greatest mistakes it was possible for them to make. Their warehouses are glutted. They have 20 weeks' stock on hand. The China market is closed. There are goods enough in the Indian seas without purchasers, to supply the market, when the trade is opened, for months. They [the masters] say that they were never in a better position for fighting the question than now.'

In 'Locked Out', Cowler can almost certainly be identified with George Cowell, a local man, a weaver and Methodist, and a calm and logical speaker. Together with Mortimer Grimshaw, he was a prominent leader of the turn-outs and an indefatigable traveller and speech-maker on behalf of the Preston workers. Grimshaw may lie behind the portrayal of Swindle: see no. 8 for further comments on this fiery orator.

The standard work on the Preston strike is H.I. Dutton and J.E. King, *'Ten Per Cent and No Surrender': The Preston Strike, 1853-1854*, Cambridge, 1981.

Unsigned article [James Lowe], 'Locked Out', Household Words, vol. VIII, 10 December 1853, pp. 345-8

PRESTON — situated upon the banks of the Ribble, some fifteen miles from the mouth of that river — is a good, honest, work-a-day looking town, built upon a magnificent site, surrounded by beautiful country; and, for a manufacturing town, wears a very handsome and creditable face. Preston concentrates within itself all the factories of the district; so that, with one or two insignificant exceptions, it may be said that there are no factories within many miles of Preston not within the town itself. This seems an unimportant fact at first, but it exercises a powerful influence over the state of the labour market. The feeling of isolation is so strong in the town, that people from a short distance are spoken of as 'foreigners'.

As we glide into the station-yard, our first exclamation is, 'What a dirty place!' Well, it is a dirty place that station-yard of Preston, and it doesn't do justice to the town. How her Majesty contrives to eat her luncheon within its precincts, when she passes through from her Highland home, we cannot imagine. The only pleasant sight within its boundaries, is the fresh face and golden ringlets of the little newsvendor, known to every traveller in this part of the kingdom, whose loyal practice it is, upon the occasions of Queen Victoria's passages through the town, to present her Majesty with copies of the morning papers on a silver salver.

We pass out of the station, astonished to perceive that the atmosphere, instead of being thick and smoky, is as clear here as the air upon Hampstead Heath. An intelligent Prestonian explains that now, there are fifty tall chimneys cold and smokeless, and that ought to make a difference. Forty-one firms have 'locked out' their hands, and twenty-one thousand workpeople are obliged to be at play. Preston in full work is, we learn, different from many other manufacturing towns. It is surrounded by agriculture — a smoky island in the middle of an expansive corn-field. The consequence is, that it enjoys a great supply of labour, and has less competition than at other places.

By this time we find ourselves on a level plain of marshy ground, upon the banks of the Ribble, and below the town of Preston. This is called THE MARSH, and it is at once the Agora and the Academe of the place. Here, if report speaks truly, do the industrial Chloes of Preston listen to the amorous pleadings of their swains; here modern Arachnes (far excelling Minerva in their spinning, whatever may be said of their wisdom), cast skilful webs about the hearts of their devoted admirers; here, too, do the mob-orators appear in times of trouble and contention, to excite, with their highly spiced eloquence, the thoughtless crowd; over whom they exercise such pernicious sway. When we arrive, the place is covered with an immense multitude of children at play.

Children, indeed: the extreme youth of the majority is remarkable. Mere lads in barragon jackets, and lasses considerably under twenty, pattering about in their little clogs (a distinguishing mark of the factory lass), form an overpowering proportion of the operative population. At least two-thirds of the hands employed upon a factory are under age; the parents either stay at home and mind the house, while their sons and daughters are working; or perhaps the mother takes in washing, whilst the father follows some handicraft trade out of doors. To marry a widow with five or six grown-up daughters, instead of being regarded as a misfortune, is here looked upon as a slice of good luck; whilst, on the better side of the picture, it is no uncommon thing to ask a young girl what her father is doing, and to receive for reply: — 'Oh! he joost stops at home. There's foive on us to keep un atween us.' This strange revolution in the natural order of things has been effected by the mighty power of steam. It has its bright side, but it also has its dark side. When you enter one of these vast workshops, you see a world of complex machinery alive and busy; every wheel illustrating the dominion of the human intellect; yet it is a mournful subject of reflection, but it is nevertheless an undoubted fact, that nine-tenths of the human beings tending and controlling the wondrous creature, are so ignorant they cannot read and write, while more than one half are destitute of either accomplishment. Indeed, it is no uncommon thing to find an overlooker, a man in authority, and exercising proportionate influence over his fellow work-men, who can neither read a newspaper, nor sign his own name. The Sunday schools teach some of them to read, but writing is not looked upon as a Christian accomplishment, and the 'unco'righteous' set their faces against writing on Sunday. To appreciate the fearful significance of this fact, we must recollect the preponderating influence necessarily possessed by those who can read and write, and when we come to reflect upon the way in which authority works upon an uncultivated mind, we shall not wonder at the testimony of one of the clearest-headed masters in Preston, when he says that he has invariably found that the cleverest workman (that is to say, clever in every respect, his work, his reading, and his writing) is always the greatest agitator. Comparative ability and shrewdness on the one side, ignorance, youth and ambition on the other: what must not be the inevitable result?

Play is going on upon the Marsh with a vengeance; 'Kiss in the ring' is being briskly carried on; the sterner sort of lads are engaged in leap-frog or football. There are few symptoms of care and contention here, and for all we can see the lads and lasses might have turned out for an hour's recreation, only to return with a sharpened appetite for labour. On one part of the marsh an old punt has stranded, and its deck forms a convenient rostrum for the hypæthral or open-air orators of Preston. A meeting is about to take place, over which John Gruntle is to preside, and at which Cowler, Swindle, and O'Brigger are expected to address the people. Presently, a small knot of persons get upon the deck of the punt, the crowd thickens around them, 'kiss in the ring' is suspended, the foot-ball is at rest, a few reporters make their appearance on the punt, note-books in hand; Gruntle is voted into the chair, and one of those meetings which thirty years ago would have been a criminal offence is formally opened.

Gruntle is not very prolix — he is an old stager, and used to these things. In a few words he states the object of the meeting, and announces to the audience that their friend Cowler will address them. At this name a shout rends the air. Cowler is evidently the chosen of the people; rightly or wrongly, they hold him in great regard. His appearance is very much in his favour, for he wears the look of a straightforward honest man; a smile plays around his mouth as he steps forward with the air of a man sure of his audience; but the feverish and anxious expression of the eyes tells of sleepless nights and of constant agitation. 'Respected friends', he begins; and, in a trice, he has plunged into the middle of the question. He has been accused, he says, of fostering agitation, and gaining advantage from the strike. Why, how can they say that, when his constant cry has been for the masters to open their mills, and give the operatives their just rights? Let them only do that, and he'll soon show them how glad he'll be to give over agitating. It's not such very pleasant work, either, is agitating. For example, he himself hasn't been to bed for these two nights. Last night they got the money that their good friends in the neighbouring towns had sent them, so he sat up to take care of it, for fear some one should come and borrow it from them. (Laughter.) The editor of the London *Thunderer*[1] had been abusing him. Well! here was a thing! Twenty years ago such a thing was never thought of as that a working man should be noticed by a London paper. But the editor had not been very courteous; he had called him 'a fool', because he said that it was a shame for the wives of the cotton lords to wear silks and satins, whilst the factory lasses were forced to be contented with plain cotton. Was he a fool for that? ('Noa! Noa!' Great excitement among the lasses, and exclamations of 'Eh! Lord!')

To Cowler succeeds Swindle, a lean and hungry Cassius, the very example of an agitator; a man who has lived by literary garbage, without fattening upon the unwholesome stuff. He seems half tipsy; his eyes roll, and his gesticulations are vehement. One more glass of whisky and he would be prepared to head an insurrection. He rants and raves for a quarter of an hour, and we are pleased to observe that his audience are too sensible to care much about him.

Then comes O'Brigger, oily-tongued, and with a brogue. He complains that it has been charged against 'um that he is an Irishman. So he is, faith! and he's moighty proud av it. The manufacturers are all av them toirants. However, this toime they will learrn that the people av England are not to be opprissed; for they will get such a flogging as never they had in the coorse av their lives. He is appy to inform his koind friends that their funds are upon the increase intirely. As the pockets av the masters becomes moore and moore empty, so will the pockets av the operatives grow fuller and fuller. Thus O'Brigger continues to pour into the ears of these poor people the delusive strains of hope, and leads them to believe that in the dire struggle between Capital and Hunger, the latter will prove victorious; and as he proceeds, each fallacious picture is welcomed with an exclamation of 'Wo'ont that be noice?'

When O'Brigger has concluded, it is the turn of a crowd of the delegates to have their say. There is the delegate from this town, and the delegate from that factory; all with marvellous stories about the tyranny of the masters, the woes of the operatives, and the determination of each particular district to stand by Preston to the last. They all end by fiercely denouncing the manufacturers, whom they term 'the miserable shoddyocracy', a term derived from 'shoddy', the refuse of cotton stuff, and 'κρατέω' to govern; being, in fact, the result of uniting the Pindaric and Tim Bobbin dialects.

We walk sadly from 'the Marsh', and reach a locked-up and smokeless factory, at the gates of which a knot of young girls are singing and offering for sale some of the Ten Per Cent. Songs, taking their name from the origin of the strike. In eighteen hundred and forty-seven, when trade was very bad, the masters told their workpeople that they could no longer afford to pay the wages that they had been paying, and that they must take off ten per cent.; upon the understanding, as the workpeople allege, that when times got better they would give them the ten per cent. back again. Whether such a promise was, or was not, actually given, we cannot presume to determine, for the masters emphatically deny it; but it is quite certain that, at the beginning of the previous year, the Stockport operatives combined successfully to force the ten per cent from *their* masters, and the Preston operatives aided them with funds. They acted upon Napoleon's principle of combining forces upon single points in succession, and so reducing the enemy is [*sic*] detail. Then it was that the Preston masters, fearing that similar tactics would be turned against themselves, combined to oppose the attempt, and eventually 'locked out' their operatives. The songs are not remarkable for much elegance and polish, but they possess some earnestness and fire, and are undoubtedly composed by the operatives themselves. We step forward, tender a penny to one of the singers, and receive the following song, composed by an operative at Bamber Bridge: —

TEN PER CENT!
A New Song, on the Preston Strike.

COME all you men of freedom,
    Wherever you may be,
I pray you give attention,
    And listen unto me.
It's of this strike in Preston town,
    Their courage being good,
I do believe they will stand firm
    Whilst they have life and blood.
Chorus — So now, my boys, don't daunted be,
    But stand out to the fray;
We ne'er shall yield, nor quit the field,
    Until we've won the day.

In eighteen forty-seven, my boys,
    I am sorry for to say,
They took from us the ten per cent.,
    Without so much delay;
And now we want it back again,
    Our masters, in a pout,
Said they would not grant it us,
    So we're every one locked out.
Chorus — So now, &c.

There's Blackburn and there's Stockport, too,
    As I have heard them say,
Are ready to support us now,
    And cheer us on our way.
So all unite into one band,
    And never do consent
To go into your mills again,
    Without the ten per cent.
Chorus — So now, &c.

In Preston town I do believe,
    The masters are our foes,
But some of them, before it's long,
    Will wear some ragged clothes.
But we'll unite both one and all,
    And never will lament,
When this great war is ceased,
    About the ten per cent.
Chorus — So now, &c.

The winter it is coming on,
    It will be very cold,
But we'll stand out for our demand,
    Like warriors so bold.
But if the masters don't give way,
    And firmly give consent,
We'll stand out till their mills do fall,
    All for the ten per cent.
Chorus — So now, &c.

Now to conclude and make an end
    Of this my simple song,
I hope the masters will give in,
    And that before it's long.
Before the masters' tyranny
    Shall rule our rights and laws,
We'll have another strike, my boys,
    If ever we have cause.
Chorus — So now, &c.

These ballads vary constantly to meet the exigencies of passing events. A disgraceful riot at Blackburn, in which some inoffensive persons were attacked for cotton-spinners, is celebrated by the Prestonian operatives in the following epic strain: —

The Preston manufacturers,
    To Blackburn they did go,
To the Black Bull in Darwen Street,
    Their tyranny to show.
The gallant troops of Blackburn
    Full soon did find it out,
They sent broken bones to Preston,
    And the rest run up the spout.
      Hurrah! my boys, hurrah!
        I'd have them be aware,
      Or the cotton lords of Preston
        Will be drove into a snare.

The tyrants of proud Preston
  Have returned home with shame,
Beat out by bold Blackburn,
  Who have won the laurel's fame.
To subdue the foes of Preston,
  Their minds are firmly bent,
To throw off the yoke of bondage,
  And restore the ten per cent.
    Hurrah! my boys, &c.

Tyrtæus[2] wakened not more enthusiasm in the breast of his auditors, than these simple doggrels do among the rude but earnest crowds which throng to hearken to them. In one of the committee rooms, the work of distributing the funds volunteered by the operatives of the neighbouring towns towards the support of their brethren is going on. These funds are collected by six committees, and are distributed for the relief of a little more than fourteen thousand of the hands. Since the commencement of the strike upwards of twenty-four thousand pounds have been contributed by the poor for the support of the poor. Each committee relieves its own hands. The Power-loom Weavers' Committee cares for the interests of the weavers, the winders, the warpers, the twisters, the dressers, the helpers, and the reachers; the Spinners' and Self-actors' Committee sees to the spinners, the miners, the piecers, and the bobbiners; the card-room hands have their committee, and the throstle-spinners, the tape machine sizers, and the power-loom overlookers theirs; each collects and distributes its funds without in any way interfering with the others. The proceedings in the room we peep into are quiet, orderly, and business-like.

Again we sally out into the dingy streets, and find that the evening is closing in over them. More knots of 'lads and lasses' idling about the corners, more bands of singers, solitary famine-striken faces, too, plead mutely for bread, and even worse expedients are evidently resorted to for the purpose of keeping body and soul together: in Preston, as elsewhere, the facilities for crime are too abundant, and we repeat to ourselves those lines of Coleridge: —

Oh I could weep to think, that there should be
Cold-bosomed lewd ones, who endure to place
Foul offerings on the shrine of misery,
And force from Famine the caress of Love.[3]

58

Ignorance of the most deplorable kind is at the root of all this sort of strife and demoralizing misery. Every employer of labour should write up over his mill door, that Brains in the Operative's Head is Money in the Master's Pocket.

1. *The Times.*
2. Poet of the seventh century B.C., who encouraged the Spartans by his war songs.
3. Samuel Taylor Coleridge, *The Outcast*, 1796, 11. pp.9-12.

8

Dickens visited Preston himself in January 1854. He wrote to Forster, in rather disappointed tones: '... I am afraid I shall not be able to get much here. Except the crowds at the street-corners reading the placards pro and con; and the cold absence of smoke from the mill-chimneys; there is very little in the streets to make the town remarkable. I am told that the people "sit at home and mope". The delegates with the money from the neighbouring places come in to-day to report the amounts they bring; and tomorrow the people are paid. When I have seen both these ceremonies, I shall return. It is a nasty place (I thought it was a model town) ...' 29 January 1854: *The Letters of Charles Dickens*, edited by Walter Dexter, 1937, II, p. 538.

The differences in emphasis between 'On Strike' and Dickens's treatment of the issues in *Hard Times*, have been well discussed. See, in particular, Geoffrey Carnall, 'Dickens, Mrs Gaskell, and the Preston Strike', *Victorian Studies*, VIII, 1964, pp. 31-48. There is a similarity in tone between Dickens's article and most of the press comment on the Preston strike: a belief that it was mistaken, yet an insistence that the virtues of the working people were clearly visible in their conduct. In *Hard Times*, on the other hand, those who are most conspicuous in their 'remarkable gentleness ... an untiring readiness to help and pity one another' (I, Chapter 6) are not the operatives — with the exception of Stephen and Rachael — but the circus people. Even more noticeably, Dickens shifts his ground when describing the union meeting, in *Hard Times* II, Chapter 4. The quiet, persuasive personality and words of Cowell are there in the *Household Words* reporting, but obliterated from the novel. Whereas in the earlier piece, Gruffshaw — or Grimshaw — is treated as an obvious firebrand, contrasting with the general calm orderliness which characterised the dispute, the fiction gives him pride of place, allowing the fist-clenching, teeth-setting, arm-pounding, cunning agitator to function as a prototype for the trade unionists at their most iniquitous and unsympathetic.

Unsigned article [Charles Dickens], 'On Strike', Household Words, vol. VIII, 11 February 1854, pp. 553-9.

Travelling down to Preston a week from this date, I chanced to sit opposite to a very acute, very determined, very emphatic personage, with a stout railway rug so drawn over his chest that he looked as if he were sitting up in bed with his great coat, hat, and gloves on, severely contemplating your humble servant from behind a large blue and grey checked counterpane. In calling him emphatic, I do not mean that he was warm; he was coldly and bitingly emphatic as a frosty wind is.

'You are going through to Preston, sir?' says he, as soon as we were clear of the Primrose Hill tunnel.

The receipt of his question was like the receipt of a jerk of the nose; he was so short and sharp.

'Yes.'

'This Preston strike is a nice piece of business!' said the gentleman. 'A pretty piece of business!'

'It is very much to be deplored', said I, 'on all accounts.'

'They want to be ground. That's what they want, to bring 'em to their senses', said the gentleman; whom I had already began to call in my own mind Mr. Snapper, and whom I may as well call by that name here as by any other.

I deferentially enquired, who wanted to be ground?

'The hands', said Mr. Snapper. 'The hands on strike, and the hands who help 'em.'

I remarked that if that was all they wanted, they must be a very unreasonable people, for surely they had had a little grinding, one way and another, already. Mr. Snapper eyed me with sternness, and after opening and shutting his leathern-gloved hands several times outside his counterpane, asked me abruptly, 'Was I a delegate?'

I set Mr. Snapper right on that point, and told him I was no delegate.

'I am glad to hear it,' said Mr. Snapper. 'But a friend to the Strike, I believe?'

'Not at all,' said I.

'A friend to the Lock-out?' pursued Mr. Snapper.

'Not in the least,' said I.

Mr. Snapper's rising opinion of me fell again, and he gave me to understand that a man *must* either be a friend to the Masters or a friend to the Hands.

'He may be a friend to both,' said I.

Mr. Snapper didn't see that; there was no medium in the Political Economy of the subject. I retorted on Mr. Snapper, that Political Economy was a great and useful science in its own way and its own place; but that I did not transplant my definition of it from the Common Prayer Book, and make it a great king above all gods. Mr. Snapper tucked himself up as if to keep me off, folded his arms on the top of his counterpane, leaned back, and looked out of window.

'Pray what would you have, sir,' enquired Mr. Snapper, suddenly withdrawing his eyes from the prospect to me, 'in the relations between Capital and Labor, *but* Political Economy?'

I always avoid the stereotyped terms in these discussions as much as I can, for I have observed, in my little way, that they often supply the place of sense and moderation. I therefore took my gentleman up with the words employers and employed, in preference to Capital and Labor.

'I believe,' said I, 'that into the relations between employers and employed, as into all the relations of this life, there must enter something of feeling and sentiment; something of mutual explanation, forbearance, and consideration; something which is not to be found in Mr. McCulloch's dictionary, and is not exactly stateable in figures; otherwise those relations are wrong and rotten at the core and will never bear sound fruit.'

Mr. Snapper laughed at me. As I thought I had just as good reason to laugh at Mr. Snapper, I did so, and we were both contented.

'Ah!' said Mr. Snapper, patting his counterpane with a hard touch. 'You know very little of the improvident and unreasoning habits of the common people, *I* see.'

'Yet I know something of those people, too,' was my reply. 'In fact, Mr. ——,' I had so nearly called him Snapper! 'in fact, sir, I doubt the existence at this present time of many faults that are merely class faults. In the main, I am disposed to think that whatever faults you may find to exist, in your own neighbourhood for instance, among the hands, you will find tolerably equal in amount among the masters also, and even among the classes above the masters. They will be modified by circumstances, and they will be the less excusable among the better-educated, but they will be pretty fairly distributed. I have a strong expectation that we shall live to see the conventional adjectives now apparently inseparable from the phrases working people and lower orders, gradually fall into complete disuse for this reason.'

'Well, but we began with strikes,' Mr. Snapper observed impatiently. 'The masters have never had any share in strikes.'

'Yet I have heard of strikes once upon a time in that same country of Lancashire,' said I, 'which were not disagreeable to some masters when they wanted a pretext for raising prices.'

'Do you mean to say those masters had any hand in getting up those strikes?' asked Mr. Snapper.

'You will perhaps obtain better information among persons engaged in some Manchester branch trades, who have good memories,' said I.

Mr. Snapper had no doubt, after this, that I thought the hands had a right to combine?

'Surely,' said I. 'A perfect right to combine in any lawful manner. The fact of their being able to combine and accustomed to combine may, I can easily conceive, be a protection to them. The blame even of this business is not all on one side. I think the associated Lock-out was a grave error. And when you Preston masters — '

'*I* am not a Preston master,' interrupted Mr. Snapper.

'When the respectable combined body of Preston masters,' said I, 'in the beginning of this unhappy difference, laid down the principle that no man should be employed henceforth who belonged to any combination — such as their own — they attempted to carry with a high hand a partial and unfair impossibility, and were obliged to abandon it. This was an unwise proceeding, and the first defeat.'

Mr. Snapper had known, all along, that I was no friend to the masters.

'Pardon me,' said I, 'I am unfeignedly a friend to the masters, and have many friends among them.'

'Yet you think these hands in the right?' quoth Mr. Snapper.

'By no means,' said I; 'I fear they are at present engaged in an unreasonable struggle, wherein they began ill and cannot end well.'

Mr. Snapper, evidently regarding me as neither fish, flesh, nor fowl, begged to know after a pause if he might enquire whether I was going to Preston on business?

Indeed I was going there, in my unbusinesslike manner, I confessed, to look at the strike.

'To look at the strike!' echoed Mr. Snapper, fixing his hat on firmly with both hands. 'To look at it! Might I ask you now, with what object you are going to look at it?'

'Certainly,' said I. 'I read, even in liberal pages, the hardest Political Economy — of an extraordinary description too sometimes, and certainly not to be found in the books — as the only touchstone of this strike. I see, this very day, in a to-morrow's liberal paper, some astonishing novelties in the politico-economical way, showing how profits and wages have no connexion whatever; coupled with such references to these hands as might be made by a very irascible General to rebels and brigands in arms. Now, if it be the case that some of the highest virtues of the working people still shine through them brighter than ever in their conduct of this mistake of theirs, perhaps the fact may reasonably suggest to me — and to others besides me — that there is some little thing wanting in the relations between them and their employers, which neither political economy nor Drumhead proclamation writing will altogether supply, and which we cannot too soon or too temperately unite in trying to find out.'

Mr. Snapper, after again opening and shutting his gloved hands several times, drew the counterpane higher over his chest, and went to bed in disgust. He got up at Rugby, took himself and counterpane into another carriage, and left me to pursue my journey alone.

When I got to Preston, it was four o'clock in the afternoon. The day being Saturday and market-day, a foreigner might have expected, from among so many idle and not over-fed people as the town contained, to find a turbulent, ill-conditioned crowd in the streets. But, except for the cold smokeless factory chimneys, the placards at the street corners, and the groups of working people attentively reading them, nor foreigner nor Englishman could have had the least suspicion that there existed any interruption to the usual labours of the place. The placards thus perused were not remarkable for their logic certainly, and did not make the case particularly clear; but, considering that they emanated from, and were addressed to people who had been out of employment for three-and-twenty consecutive weeks, at least they had little passion in them, though they had not much reason. Take the worst I could find:

'FRIENDS AND FELLOW OPERATIVES,

'Accept the grateful thanks of twenty thousand struggling Operatives, for the help you have showered upon Preston since the present contest commenced.

'Your kindness and generosity, your patience and long-continued support deserve every praise, and are only equalled by the heroic and determined perseverance of the outraged and insulted factory workers of Preston, who have been struggling for some months, and are, at this inclement season of the year, bravely battling for the rights of themselves and the whole toiling community.

'For many years before the strike took place at Preston, the Operatives were the down trodden and insulted serfs of their Employers, who in times of good trade and general prosperity, wrung from their labour a California of gold, which is now being used to crush those who created it, still lower and lower in the scale of civilization. This has been the result of our commercial prosperity! — *more wealth for the rich and more poverty for the Poor!* Because the workpeople of Preston protested against this state of things, — because they combined in a fair and legitimate way for the purpose of getting a reasonable share of the reward of their own labour, the *fair dealing* Employers of Preston, to their eternal shame and disgrace, *locked up* their Mills, and at one fell swoop deprived, as they thought, from twenty to thirty thousand human beings of the means of existence. Cruelty and tyranny always defeat their own object; it was so in this case, and to the honour and credit of the working classes of this country, we have to record, that, those whom the rich and wealthy sought to destroy, the poor and industrious have protected from harm. This love of justice and hatred of wrong, is a noble feature in the character and disposition of the working man, and gives us hope that in the future, this world will become what its great architect intended, not a place of sorrow, toil, oppression and wrong, but the dwelling place and the abode of peace, plenty, happiness and love, where avarice and all the evil passions engendered by the present system of fraud and injustice shall not have a place.

'The earth was not made for the misery of its people; intellect

64

was not given to man to make himself and fellow creatures unhappy. No, the fruitfulness of the soil and the wonderful inventions — the result of mind — all proclaim that these things were bestowed upon us for our happiness and well-being, and not for the misery and degradation of the human race.

'It may serve the manufacturers and all who run away with the lion's share of labour's produce, to say that the *impartial* God intended that there should be a *partial* distribution of his blessings. But we know that it is against nature to believe, that those who plant and reap all the grain, should not have enough to make a mess of porridge; and we know that those who weave all the cloth should not want a yard to cover their persons, whilst those who never wove an inch have more calico, silks and satins, than would serve the reasonable wants of a dozen working men and their families.

'This system of giving everything to the few, and nothing to the many, has lasted long enough, and we call upon the working people of this country to be determined to establish a new and improved system — a system that shall give to all who labour, a fair share of those blessings and comforts which their toil produce; in short, we wish to see that divine precept enforced, which says, "Those who will not work, shall not eat."

'The task is before you, working men; if you think the good which would result from its accomplishment, is worth struggling for, set to work and cease not, until you have obtained the *good time coming*, not only for the Preston Operatives, but for yourselves as well.

By Order of the Committee.

'*Murphy's Temperance Hotel, Chapel Walks, Preston, January 24th, 1854.*'

It is a melancholy thing that it should not occur to the Committee to consider what would become of themselves, their friends, and fellow operatives, if those calicoes, silks, and satins, were *not* worn in very large quantities; but I shall not enter into that question. As I had told my friend Snapper, what I wanted to see with my own eyes, was, how these people acted under a mistaken impression, and what qualities they showed, even at that disadvantage which ought to be the strength and peace — not the weakness and trouble — of the community. I found, even from this literature, however, that all masters were not indiscriminately unpopular. Witness the following verses from the New Song of the Preston Strike:

'There's Henry Hornby, of Blackburn, he is a jolly brick,
He fits the Preston masters nobly, and is very bad to trick;
He pays his hands a good price, and I hope he will never sever,
So we'll sing success to Hornby and Blackburn for ever.

'There is another gentleman, I'm sure you'll all lament,
In Blackburn for him they're raising a monument,
You know his name, 'tis of great fame, it was late Eccles of honour,
May Hopwood, and Sparrow, and Hornby live for ever.

'So now it is time to finish and end my rhyme,
We warn these Preston Cotton Lords to mind for future time.
With peace and order too I hope we shall be clever,
We sing success to Stockport and Blackburn for ever.
          'Now, lads, give your minds to it.'

The balance sheet of the receipts and expenditure for the twenty-third week of the strike was extensively posted. The income for that week was two thousand one hundred and forty pounds odd. Some of the contributors were poetical. As,

'Love to all and peace to the dead,
May the poor now in need never want bread.

three-and-sixpence.'
The following poetical remonstrance was appended to the list of contributions from the Gorton district:

Within three walls the lasses fair
Refuse to contribute their share,
Careless of duty — blind to fame,
For shame, ye lasses, oh! for shame!
Come, pay up, lasses, think what's right,
Defend your trade with all your might;
Fer if you don't the world will blame,
And cry, ye lasses, oh, for shame!
Let's hope in future all will pay,
That Preston folks may shortly say —
That by your aid they have obtain'd
The greatest victory ever gained.

Some of the subscribers veiled their names under encouraging sentiments, as Not tired yet, All in a mind, Win the day, Fraternity, and the like. Some took jocose appellations, as A stunning friend, Two to one Preston wins, Nibbling Joe, and The Donkey Driver. Some expressed themselves through their trades, as Cobbler Dick, sixpence, The tailor true, sixpence, Shoemaker, a shilling, The chirping blacksmith, sixpence, and A few of Maskery's most feeling coachmakers, three and threepence. An old balance sheet for the fourteenth week of the Strike was headed with this quotation from MR. CARLYLE. 'Adversity is sometimes hard upon a man; but for one man who can stand prosperity, there are a hundred that will stand adversity.' The Elton district prefaced its report with these lines:

Oh! ye who start a noble scheme,
     For general good designed;
Ye workers in a cause that tends
     To benefit your kind!
Mark out the path ye fain would tread,
     The game ye mean to play;
And if it be an honest one,
     Keep stedfast in your way!

Although you may not gain at once
     The points ye most desire;
Be patient — time can wonders work;
     Plod on, and do not tire:
Obstructions, too, may crowd your path,
     In threatening, stern array;
Yet flinch not! fear not! they may prove
     Mere shadows in your way.

Then, while there's work for you to do,
     Stand not despairing by,
Let 'forward' be the move ye make,
     Let 'onward' be your cry;
And when success has crowned your plans,
     'Twill all your pains repay,
To see the good your labour's done —
     Then droop not on your way.

In this list, 'Bear ye one another's burthens', sent one Pound fifteen. 'We'll stand to our text, see that ye love one another' sent nineteen shillings. 'Christopher Hardman's men again, they say they can always spare one shilling out of ten', sent two and sixpence. The following masked threats were the worst feature in any bill I saw:

> If that fiddler at Uncle Tom's Cabin blowing room does not pay Punch will set his legs straight.
> If that drawer at card side and those two slubbers do not pay, Punch will say something about their bustles.
> If that winder at last shift does not pay next week, Punch will tell about her actions.

But, on looking at this bill again, I found that it came from Bury and related to Bury, and had nothing to do with Preston. The Masters' placards were not torn down or disfigured, but were being read quite as attentively as those on the opposite side.

That evening, the Delegates from the surrounding districts were coming in, according to custom, with their subscription lists for the week just closed. These delegates meet on Sunday as their only day of leisure; when they have made their reports, they go back to their homes and their Monday's work. On Sunday morning, I repaired to the Delegates' meeting.

These assemblages take place in a cockpit, which, in the better times of our fallen land, belonged to the late Lord Derby for the purposes of the intellectual recreation implied in its name. I was directed to the cockpit up a narrow lane, tolerably crowded by the lower sort of working people. Personally, I was quite unknown in the town, but every one made way for me to pass, with great civility, and perfect good humour. Arrived at the cockpit door, and expressing my desire to see and hear, I was handed through the crowd, down into the pit, and up again, until I found myself seated on the topmost circular bench, within one of the secretary's table, and within three of the chairman. Behind the chairman was a great crown on the top of a pole, made of particoloured calico, and strongly suggestive of May-day. There was no other symbol or ornament in the place.

It was hotter than any mill or factory I have ever been in; but there was a stove down in the sanded pit, and delegates were seated close to it, and one particular delegate often warmed his hands at it, as if he were chilly. The air was so intensely close and hot, that at first I had but a confused perception of the delegates down in the pit, and the dense crowd of eagerly listening men and women (but not very many of the latter) filling all the benches and choking such narrow standing-room as there was. When the atmosphere cleared a little on better acquaintance, I found the question under discussion to be, Whether the Manchester Delegates in attendance from the Labor Parliament, should be heard?

If the Assembly, in respect of quietness and order, were put in comparison with the House of Commons, the Right Honorable the Speaker himself would decide for Preston. The chairman was a Preston weaver, two or three and fifty years of age, perhaps; a man with a capacious head, rather long dark hair growing at the sides and back, a placid attentive face, keen eyes, a particularly composed manner, a quiet voice, and a persuasive action of his right arm. Now look'ee heer my friends. See what t' question is. T' question is, sholl these heer men be heerd. Then 't cooms to this, what ha' these men got t' tell us? Do they bring mooney? If they bring mooney t'ords t' expences o' this strike, they're welcome. For, Brass, my friends, is what we want, and what we must ha' (hear hear hear!). Do they coom to us wi' any suggestion for the conduct of this strike? If they do, they're welcome. Let 'em give us their advice and we will hearken to 't. But, if these men coom heer, to tell us what t' Labor Parliament is, or what Ernest Jones's opinions is, or t' bring in politics and differences amoong us when what we want is 'armony, brotherly love, and con-cord; then I say t' you, decide for yoursel' carefully, whether these men ote to be heerd in this place. (Hear hear hear! and No no no!) Chairman sits down, earnestly regarding delegates, and holding both arms of his chair. Looks extremely sensible; his plain coarse working man's shirt collar easily turned down over his loose Belcher neckerchief. Delegate who has moved that Manchester delegates be heard, presses motion — Mr. Chairman, will that delegate tell us, as a man, that these men have anything to say concerning this present strike and lock-out, for we have a deal of business to do, and what concerns this present strike and lock-out is our business and nothing else is. (Hear hear hear!) — Delegate in question will not compromise the fact; these men want to defend the Labour Parliament from certain charges made against them. — Very well, Mr. Chairman, Then I move as an amendment that you do not hear these men now, and that you proceed wi' business — and if you don't I'll look after you, I tell you that. (Cheers and laughter) — Coom lads, prove't then! — Two or three hands for the delegates; all the rest for the business. Motion lost, amendment carried, Manchester deputation not to be heard.

But now, starts up the delegate from Throstletown, in a dreadful state of mind. Mr. Chairman, I hold in my hand a bill; a bill that requires and demands explanation from you, sir; an offensive bill; a bill posted in my town of Throstletown without my knowledge, without the knowledge of my fellow delegates who are here beside me; a bill purporting to be posted by the authority of the massed committee sir, and of which my fellow delegates and myself were kept in ignorance. Why are we to be slighted? Why are we to be insulted? Why are we to be meanly stabbed in the dark? Why is this assassin-like course of conduct to be pursued towards us? Why is Throstletown, which has nobly assisted you, the operatives of Preston, in this great struggle, and which has brought its contributions up to the full sevenpence a loom, to be thus degraded, thus aspersed, thus traduced, thus despised, thus outraged in its feelings by un-English and unmanly conduct? Sir, I hand you up that bill, and I require of you, sir, to give me a satisfactory explanation of that bill. And I have that confidence in your known integrity, sir, as to sure that you will make reparation to Throstletown for this scandalous treatment. Then, in hot blood, up starts Gruffshaw (professional speaker) who is somehow responsible for this bill. O my friends, but explanation is required here! O my friends, but it is fit and right that you should have the dark ways of the real traducers and apostates, and the real un-English stabbers, laid bare before you. My friends when this dark conspiracy first began — But here the persuasive right hand of the chairman falls gently on Gruffshaw's shoulder. Gruffshaw stops in full boil. My friends, these are hard words of my friend Gruffshaw, and this is not the business — No more it is, and once again, sir, I, the delegate who said I would look after you, do move that you proceed to business! — Preston has not the strong relish for personal altercation that Westminster hath. Motion seconded and carried, business passed to, Gruffshaw dumb.

Perhaps the world could not afford a more remarkable contrast than between the deliberate collected manner of these men proceeding with their business, and the clash and hurry of the engines among which their lives are passed. Their astonishing fortitude and perseverance; their high sense of honor among themselves; the extent to which they are impressed with the responsibility that is upon them of setting a careful example, and keeping their order out of any harm and loss of reputation; the noble readiness in them to help one another, of which most medical practitioners and working clergymen can give so many affecting examples; could scarcely ever be plainer to an ordinary observer of human nature than in this cockpit. To hold, for a minute, that the great mass of them were not sincerely actuated by the belief that all these qualities were bound up in what they were doing, and that they were doing right, seemed to me little short of an impossibility. As the different delegates (some in the very dress in which they had left the mill last night) reported the amounts sent from the various places they represented, this strong faith on their parts seemed expressed in every tone and every look that was capable of expressing it. One man was raised to enthusiasm by his pride in bringing so much; another man was ashamed and depressed because he brought so little; this man triumphantly made it known that he could give you, from the store in hand, a hundred pounds in addition next week, if you should want it; and that man pleaded that he hoped his district would do better before long; but I could as soon have doubted the existence of the walls that enclosed us, as the earnestness with which they spoke (many of them referring to the children who were to be born to labor after them) of 'this great, this noble, gallant, godlike struggle'. Some designing and turbulent spirits among them, no doubt there are; but I left the place with a profound conviction that their mistake is generally an honest one, and that it is sustained by the good that is in them, and not by the evil.

Neither by night nor by day was there any interruption to the peace of the streets. Nor was this an accidental state of things, for the police records of the town are eloquent to the same effect. I traversed the streets very much, and was, as a stranger, the subject of a little curiosity among the idlers; but I met with no rudeness or ill-temper. More than once, when I was looking at the printed balance-sheets to which I have referred, and could not quite comprehend the setting forth of the figures, a bystander of the working class interposed with his explanatory forefinger and helped me out. Although the pressure in the cockpit on Sunday was excessive, and the heat of the room obliged me to make my way out as I best could before the close of the proceedings, none of the people whom I put to inconvenience showed the least impatience; all helped me, and all cheerfully acknowledged my word of apology as I passed. It is very probable, notwithstanding, that they may have supposed from my being there at all — I and my companion were the only persons present, not of their own order — that I was there to carry what I heard and saw to the opposite side; indeed one speaker seemed to intimate as much.

On the Monday at noon, I returned to this cockpit, to see the people paid. It was then about half filled, principally with girls and women. They were all seated, waiting, with nothing to occupy their attention; and were just in that state when the

71

unexpected appearance of a stranger differently dressed from themselves, and with his own individual peculiarities of course, might, without offence, have had something droll in it even to more polite assemblies. But I stood there, looking on, as free from remark as if I had come to be paid with the rest. In the place which the secretary had occupied yesterday, stood a dirty little common table, covered with five-penny piles of halfpence. Before the paying began, I wondered who was going to receive these very small sums; but when it did begin, the mystery was soon cleared up. Each of these piles was the change for sixpence, deducting a penny. All who were paid, in filing round the building to prevent confusion, had to pass this table on the way out; and the greater part of the unmarried girls stopped here, to change, each a six-pence, and subscribe her weekly penny in aid of the people on strike who had families. A very large majority of these girls and women were comfortably dressed in all respects, clean, whole-some and pleasant-looking. There was a prevalent neatness and cheerfulness, and an almost ludicrous absence of anything like sullen discontent.

Exactly the same appearances were observable on the same day, at a not numerously attended, open air meeting in 'Chadwick's Orchard' — which blossoms in nothing but red bricks. Here, the chairman of yesterday presided in a cart, from which speeches were delivered. The proceedings commenced with the following sufficiently general and discursive hymn, given out by a workman from Burnley, and sung in long metre by the whole audience:

Assembled beneath thy broad blue sky,
To thee, O God, thy children cry.
Thy needy creatures on Thee call,
For thou art great and good to all.

Thy bounty smiles on every side,
And no good thing hast thou denied;
But men of wealth and men of power,
Like locusts, all our gifts devour.

Awake, ye sons of toil! nor sleep
While millions starve, while millions weep,
Demand your rights; let tyrants see
You are resolved that you'll be free.

Mr Hollins's Sovereign Mill was open all this time. It is a very beautiful mill, containing a large amount of valuable machinery, to which some recent ingenious improvements have been added. Four hundred people could find employment in it; there were eighty-five at work, of whom five had 'come in' that morning. They looked, among the vast array of motionless power-looms, like a few remaining leaves in a wintry forest. They were protected by the police (very prudently not obtruded on the scenes I have described), and were stared at every day when they came out, by a crowd which had never been large in reference to the numbers on strike, and had diminished to a score or two. One policeman at the door sufficed to keep order then. These eighty-five were people of exceedingly decent appearance, chiefly women, and were evidently not in the least uneasy for themselves. I heard of one girl among them, and only one, who had been hustled and struck in a dark street.

In any aspect in which it can be viewed, this strike and lock-out is a deplorable calamity. In its waste of time, in its waste of a great people's energy, in its waste of wages, in its waste of wealth that seeks to be employed, in its encroachment on the means of many thousands who are laboring from day to day, in the gulf of separation it hourly deepens between those whose interests must be understood to be identical or must be destroyed, it is a great national affliction. But, at this pass, anger is of no use, starving out is of no use — for what will that do, five years hence, but overshadow all the mills in England with the growth of a bitter remembrance? — political economy is a mere skeleton unless it has a little human covering and filling out, a little human bloom upon it, and a little human warmth in it. Gentlemen are found, in great manufacturing towns, ready enough to extol imbecile mediation with dangerous madmen abroad; can none of them be brought to think of authorised mediation and explanation at home? I do not suppose that such a knotted difficulty as this, is to be at all untangled by a morning-party in the Adelphi; but I would entreat both sides now so miserably opposed, to consider whether there are no men in England, above suspicion, to whom they might refer the matters in dispute, with a perfect confidence above all things in the desire of those men to act justly, and in their sincere attachment to their countrymen of every rank and to their country. Masters right, or men right; masters wrong, or men wrong; both right, or both wrong; there is certain ruin to both in the continuance or frequent revival of this breach. And from the ever-widening circle of their decay, what drop in the social ocean shall be free!

9

John Goodair, although no supporter of trades unions, remained outside the Masters' Association which organised the Preston lock-out. His pamphlet *Strikes Prevented*, which appeared in the latter part of 1854, illustrates a current of feeling present in certain manufacturing circles: a belief that industrial conflict could be avoided if only employers and employees treated each other with mutual respect, worked for each other, and came to understand each others' problems and points of view. Such comprehensive paternalism on behalf of the masters was advocated by, among others, Hugh Tremenheere, Edwin Chadwick and Sir J.P. Kay-Shuttleworth, friend of Elizabeth Gaskell. Mr Carson, in *Mary Barton*, is her first attempt to fictionalise such an ideal, but his reforms are suggested through rather insubstantial remarks: those in his confidence were well aware that his dearest wish was that:

a perfect understanding, and complete confidence and love, might exist between masters and men; that the truth might be recognised that the interests of one were the interests of all; and as such, required the consideration and deliberation of all; that hence it was most desirable to have educated workers, capable of judging, not mere machines of ignorant men; and to have them bound to their employers by the ties of respect and affection, not by mere money bargains alone; in short, to acknowledge the Spirit of Christ as the regulating law between both parties (Chapter 37).

But this was not enough for some critics of the novel, who insisted that Gaskell had favoured the working man, in the person of John Barton, at the expense of fully understanding the masters' case (see especially W.R. Greg's article in the *Edinburgh Review*, LXXXIX, 1849, pp. 402-35). As she approached the writing of *North and South*, she admitted to Lady Kay-Shuttleworth that perhaps she had, indeed, been one-sided, since she felt more strongly on the side of the workers: 'I know, and have always owned, that I have represented *but one* side of the question, and no one would welcome more than I should, a true and earnest representation of the other side.' She is prepared to believe that there *are* good mill-owners, but maintains that much is yet to be discovered about 'the right position and mutual duties of employer, and employed'. To illustrate the problematic workings of theory and practice, she cites the case of Samuel Greg, brother of the critic, who, in attempting to put his benevolent schemes into practice, has seen his profits tumble (letter to Lady Kay-Shuttleworth, 16 July [? 1850], *Letters*, ed. Chapple and Pollard, pp. 119-20). None the less, in *North and South*, she tries, in her portrayal of Mr Thornton, to represent a mill-owner who is aware not just of a need for philanthropy, but of achieving some kind of understanding between master and men which lies beyond the mere 'cash nexus'. Through Thornton's mouth, she covers her own uncertainties about the ultimate success of such attempts by having him admit that they are but 'experiments' (Chapters 50 and 51). Goodair, as Section (d) in particular shows, is, however, far more rigorous than Gaskell in his belief that a 'natural' class hierarchy should be maintained. Not for him the sentiments of Christian brotherhood, which Gaskell suggests spring up between Thornton and the mill-worker, Higgins: 'Once brought face to face, man to man, with an individual of the masses around him, and (take notice) *out* of the character of master and workman, in the first instance, they had each begun to recognise that "we have all of us one human heart"' (Chapter 50). Through the melodramatic circumstances of her plot, Gaskell hints, nevertheless, that the conditions which led to such a reconciliation were highly unusual ones.

Strikes Prevented *by A Preston Manufacturer [John Goodair], London and Manchester, 1854.*

(a) pp. 6-7

I can bear testimony to the great advantage which I have often derived in carrying out the different operations of my business, from the suggestions of intelligent workmen; and I have no doubt that many other employers can do so likewise. I confess, too, that at a time when, having the control of a large establishment, I cultivated a habit of meeting and discussing questions with my workmen, both questions affecting the public concernment, and questions relating to our business; — I confess that I derived quite as much benefit from these discussions as they did, — and how much that was may be inferred from the fact that, after the institution of that habit, I never had a dispute with my operatives. And I will here say that, at those meetings, I have heard an amount of sound and various information, expressed with native strength and eloquence, such as would have surprised any one not conversant with the Lancashire population. It was from those meetings that I derived the settled conviction which I now entertain, that the operatives do not lack the power, but only the means, of forming sound and independent opinions.

(b) pp. 8-9

... altogether I believe that there is a sufficient educational machinery in the manufacturing districts to teach reading, writing, and cyphering, and a knowledge of common things to every child that needs to be taught. But what is really wanted is the education of the adult intellect. We bestow upon children the rudiments of knowledge, preparing their mind for the reception of ideas (whether good or evil), and then we cast them adrift upon the world to be educated by experience, and to absorb all the notions, and all the prejudices, and all the fallacies, with which chance may surround them; and then we commit the absurdity of wondering that they go wrong. What *must* be their inevitable fate under such a system as this, we have lately witnessed in the deplorable condition of Preston. A dispute arises, there is no sympathy shown to the operatives by the employers, but much real or pretended sympathy is shewn by the delegates, who tell them fine-spun theories about the results of Trades' Unions, who talk to them in an inflated manner about their rights and their wrongs (exaggerating these and inflaming those), who tell them that a strike is the only means of setting them right, and who never yet have interfered without widening the breach in which they attempt to gain a footing. Thus it is that Strikes are the order of the day, that there is an utter absence of sympathy between the employers and the employed, and that both parties, instead of uniting for mutual good, think of nothing so much as to how they may injure and bring down each other — forgetful that in wounding their opponents they are aiming at their own life.

The feeling which ought first of all to be cultivated in a mill, as the groundwork of all future plans for the amelioration of the operatives, is one of perfect confidence between them and their employer; without this, all attempts at innovation will not only be in vain, but will be viewed with suspicion and alarm. I believe that many employers, desiring to do well by their operatives, have been deterred at the very outset of their endeavours by finding that they were received in any way but a friendly spirit by those whom they designed to benefit; but this fact, instead of disheartening, should only have excited them to persevere, by affording an additional proof of the necessity for establishing a friendly bond of union. Surely there can be no more affecting proof of the necessity for a change of treatment, when we find that the first motions of kindness are received with apprehension and distrust! Until perfect confidence is established nothing can be done, because the operatives themselves will do nothing; and, much as the employer may do, his labour will be in vain, unless the employed meet him half way and give him their willing and hearty assistance in carrying out his plans.

(c) pp. 13-15

Having now put within the reach of the operatives the means of acquiring sound information upon public and general subjects, the next step should be to organise a plan for enabling them to meet periodically, for the purpose of interchanging their ideas, and stimulating each other, by competition, to a still greater acquisition of useful knowledge. I have already referred to my own experience in promoting discussions among the operatives in my employ, and it is to that practice I mainly attribute the perfect understanding and good feeling which subsisted between us. In these discussions (which may be held upon some selected evening every week) the men only should be suffered to take part; the political and public topics of the day, the opinions of the press, the state of trade, discoveries in practical science and in mechanics (especially such as bear upon the cotton trade), and, lastly, the conduct and discipline of their own mill, will always furnish useful and fruitful subjects for discussion. From the last division of subjects (namely, those relating to the conduct of the mill), I have derived very great advantage. It will very often happen that the men may fancy themselves to be suffering under a grievance which does not really exist, and which a very little explanation will at once remove: sometimes, too, a real grievance may be in existence, which the employer needs only to be informed of to remedy. In some mills, such is the fear of the consequence of being thought to be a grumbler, that the men will often draw lots to determine who will be the bearer of a complaint which may have been long seeking expression; so fearful are they of being marked out for the displeasure of the manager or overlooker. But, with the privilege of bringing forward all points connected with the mill to open discussion, this fear can have no foundation. The complaint is made openly in the face of the whole mill; it is confuted or redressed, as the necessities of the case may seem to require, and every man in the mill will be a jealous watch that he who urges the complaint is not prejudiced by his boldness. To make these discussions efficient it necessarily follows that the employer himself should take every possible opportunity of being present; not only to hear these complaints, but also to assist, by his superior knowledge and experience, the progress of the discussion; and when he is unavoidably absent he should be represented by his manager, who ought to be a person capable of acting as his substitute.

After the mill itself, the general laws which govern trade, the manner in which foreign competition acts upon the English manufacturer, and the causes which influence the fluctuations of the market, will form very valuable subjects of discussion. There is no point upon which the working classes are more at sea than the profits of their employers. They know nothing of the state of markets, nothing of foreign competition, and, because they see the manufacturer living in a better style than themselves, they imagine that his profits are enormous, and that he is robbing them of their just earnings, in order to support himself and his family in luxury. If these things were properly ventilated and discussed, they would at once understand that to conduct a large mill requires a very large capital, the mere interest upon which ought in itself to be a considerable income, and the possession of which entitles the manufacturer to live in a better state than they, who have no capital at all. Their eyes would be opened to those risks and chances of commerce of which they appear to be altogether ignorant; they would hear of the losses as well as the gains, of the bankruptcies as well as the large fortunes which fall to the lot of the employing class, and they would understand that, so long as good trade supplies them with constant employment, and gives them the means of supporting their families in comfort and respectability, they have no reason to envy a position for which the great majority of them are not only unprovided but unfitted to fulfil. These, and similar questions, so indispensable to a right understanding of their true position, would force themselves upon their attention during such discussions as those which I recommend.

(d) pp. 17-18

In conclusion, I would impress upon the operatives that they also have their duties to perform, and that without their zealous co-operation the most philanthropic endeavours to benefit them will be in vain. Nothing can be done for the man who obstinately refuses to put his own shoulder to the wheel. We cannot compel people to receive a benefit, and, unless they meet us some part of the way (so far, at least, as good feeling is concerned), our most strenuous endeavours will be but labour in vain. They must learn to know that there *must* be masters and that there *must* be men; they must strive to understand and to appreciate the difficulties and uncertainty which beset the path of their employers, and, when they have at last risen from ignorance into a clear under-standing of their true rights and duties, they will learn the lesson of contentment, and know how to appreciate the benefits of a combination *with* instead of *against* their employers. They will learn that union is an admirable institution when formed for sensible and advantageous ends; but that, when it has for its object the dictation of an arbitrary value to labour, it becomes a dangerous weapon of evil, whether wielded by masters or by men.

10

The *Friendly Letters on the Recent Strikes*, by Samuel Robinson, a Wilmslow manufacturer, were another product of the 'long and unhappy contest at Preston' (p. 1). Robinson allows the defeat of the operatives on this occasion to act as an example of how turn-outs in general are likely to fail. He advises labourers to try to obtain higher wages when they think they are entitled to do so, but to take care both that their claim is a just one, and that the methods which they use to enforce it are just. Again, he places his trust in the achievement of mutual understanding, and in Samuel Smiles's popular principle of self-help. As in the case of Goodair, however, the emphasis on co-operation goes hand-in-hand with comfortable assumptions about the *status quo* which are much more conservative than the general drift of the views held by Gaskell, if not, perhaps, by the other best-known writers of social problem fiction. Yet the behaviour of Higgins and his workmate in *North and South,* stopping over hours to finish a piece of work in an anonymous act of goodwill to both overlooker and master (Chapter 50) shows precisely the sense of disinterested duty demanded in (d).

[Samuel Robinson], Friendly Letters on the Recent Strikes *from a Manufacturer to his own Workpeople, London, 1854.*

(a) p. 26 Robinson questions those who are

disposed to grudge the wealthy manufacturer his large fortune? Remember, how often that large fortune is only the well-merited reward of long years of toil, of steady perseverance, of constant saving, and much self-denial; of great knowledge of business, and unflinching attention to it.

(b) pp. 27-8

You would, indeed, have a just title to complain, if the road to fortune were not left as open to you as to others. But it is not so. Thousands of these very capitalists at whom there is so much railing have risen out of your own ranks. Thousands are so rising every day, and winning competence and wealth. None of you are withholden from trying for the same prizes. But to win them you will have to practise the same virtues by which others have won them: industry, frugality, temperance, activity, prudence, and self-denial — the disposition, I mean, to refuse yourself *some present pleasure* in order to secure some *distant* but *much greater* good. These are the conditions of your success, AND THERE ARE NO OTHERS.

(c) p. 31 Robinson firmly believes

... that more intimate and friendly communication between masters and men upon such subjects is not only desirable but absolutely needful. It is high time, that these struggles of physical strength and brute force should give way to reason and more kindly feeling. They are not honourable to either party. But the necessary condition of this better state of things must be more mutual confidence. And to secure this, you will have to do your part as well as your masters.

(d) p.33

... sympathy, properly speaking, is the feeling which two or more people have for one another, or for the same thing. We have not much right to *ask* for sympathy, if we are not ready to *give* it. I am quite willing to admit, that masters are not always so alive to their great responsibilities as might be desirable. Occupied with the proper management of their business, and feeling — and justly feeling — that this is, and ought to be, whether they regard themselves or those they employ, their first great object, it is not very unlikely that they may be at times less thoughtful than they perhaps ought to be about the comforts, feelings, and interests of the men. On the other hand, may I not ask, — Are the men usually very thoughtful about the interests of their master? Are they not very ready to believe that he may safely be left to take care, and does take care of himself? Do they watch over his property as if it were their own? and use the materials and other things which pass through their hands with all the economy and carefulness which they might? Can they be relied upon — I speak of them now of course as a body, not as individuals — can they be relied upon in general for the steady and conscientious performance of their duties; the same when their master is absent as when his eye is upon them? In putting these questions I by no means would be understood to mean, that neglect of duty on the one side excuses it on the other. All that I mean to say is, that all the fault is not *on one side only*, and that we should each of us amend our own ways before we can censure too severely those of others.

11

W. Cooke Taylor's *Handbook of Silk, Cotton, and Woollen Manufacturers* (1843) provides a comprehensive history of the spinning and weaving industries in the north of England. His appeal is to members of the middle and upper classes through shared cultural references. Thus these trades are traced back in time, with many appeals to classical and biblical texts, in order to stress their respectability as occupations. Taylor notes the strikingly rapid accumulation of the population in manufacturing areas, and the ensuing fear which is engendered. In describing the power of the crowd in apprehensive images of natural savagery, Taylor holds his apprehension in common with contemporary novelists. Margaret Hale, in *North and South,* is aware of an 'unusual heaving' among the mass of humans around her as she goes to visit Thornton's mother. From every narrow lane which opens out onto Marlborough Street comes a 'low distant roar'. As she rings the bell to Thornton's house, Margaret not only hears 'the ominous gathering roar, deep-clamouring' but looks round 'and heard the first long far-off roll of the tempest; saw the first slow-surging wave of the dark crowd come, with its threatening crest, tumble over, and retreat' (Chapter 21). As the crowds come closer, the roaring is no longer invested with the awe-inspiring force of the elements, but is among the characteristics which degrade the demonstrators into animals.

W. *Cooke Taylor:* The Handbook of Silk, Cotton, and Woollen Manufacturers, *London, 1843.*

p. 201

It would be absurd to speak of factories as mere abstractions, and consider them apart from the manufacturing population. That population is a stern reality, and cannot be neglected with impunity. As a stranger passes through the masses of human beings which have been accumulated round the mills and print-works in Manchester and the neighbouring towns, he cannot contemplate these 'crowded lives' without feelings of anxiety and apprehension almost amounting to dismay. The population, like the system to which it belongs, is NEW; but it is hourly increasing in breadth and strength. It is an aggregate of masses, our conceptions of which clothe themselves in terms that express something portentous and fearful. We speak not of them indeed as of sudden convulsions, tempestuous seas, or furious hurricanes, but as of the slow rising and gradual swelling of an ocean which must, at some future and no distant time, bear all the elements of society aloft upon its bosom, and float them — Heaven knows whither. There are mighty energies slumbering in those masses. Had our ancestors witnessed the assemblage of such a multitude as is poured forth every evening from the mills of Union-street, magistrates would have assembled, special constables would have been sworn, the riot act read, the military called out, and most probably some fatal collision would have taken place. The crowd now scarcely attracts the notice of a passing policeman, but it is, nevertheless, a crowd, and therefore susceptible of the passions which may animate a multitude.

12

The proofs of *Hard Times* indicate that Dickens changed his mind about showing the degree to which masters laid themselves open to criticism on one particular and controversial issue, that of industrial safety. For in the printed version Dickens deleted his heartfelt intervention on the topic. Perhaps this was to avoid antagonising the manufacturing profession, and the class interests with which they were identified, or, since he was in fact habitually fearless in including such criticism in *Household Words*, his revision may have been a move to deter the label of 'industrial novel' from being attached to a work which, after all, was as much, if not more, concerned with attacking Utilitarianism and promoting the values of the imagination and direct human feeling.

In Part II, Chapter 13, Stephen thanks Rachael gently for all that she does for him: 'Thou changest me from bad to good. Thou mak'st me humbly wishfo' to be more like thee, and fearfo' to lose thee when this life is ower, an a' the muddle cleared awa'.' At this point, Dickens had inserted a set speech about the dangers of unfenced machinery:

'Thou'st spokken o' thy little sister. There agen! Wi' her child arm tore off afore thy face.' She turned her head aside, and put her hand up. 'Where dost thou ever hear or read o' *us* — the like o' *us* — as being otherwise than onreasonable and cause o' trouble? Yet think o' that. Government gentleman comes and make's report. Fend off the dangerous machinery, box it off, save life and limb; don't rend and tear human creeturs to bits in a Chris'en country! What follers? Owners sets up their throats, cries out, "Onreasonable! Inconvenient! Troublesome!" Gets to

Secretaries o' States wi' our deputations, and nothing's done. When do *we* get there wi' our deputations, God help us! We are too much int'rested and nat'rally too far wrong t'have a right judgment. Happly we are; but what are they then? I' th' name o' th' muddle in which we are born and live and die, what are they then?' 'Let such things be, Stephen. They only lead to hurt, let them be!' 'I will, since thou tell'st me so, I will. I pass my promise.'

After the words 'nothing's done', Dickens inserted a footnote on the corrected proofs, the inclusion of which, if it had remained, would have represented a complete departure from his habitual practice: 'See Household Words vol. IX page 224, article entitled GROUND IN THE MILL.' This article had appeared in the same issue as Chapters 7 and 8 of *Hard Times*, and hence acts as an example of how reading a text in the immediate context of its original publication can serve to amplify the social messages carried by the fiction itself. A reader of 1854 would have been able to add, even without the projected footnote of Dickens, the knowledge of factory conditions with which *Household Words* had furnished them to the rather less explicit descriptions contained in the novel, since the source to which Dickens directed them was not an isolated article on the need to protect the workforce from dangerous machinery, but part of a small campaign conducted by *Household Words*. It was followed by 'Fencing with Humanity', *Household Words*, vol. XI, 14 April 1855, pp. 241-4, which in addition to recording the fact that the Home Secretary had ordered that the law be enforced to the utmost gives further horrific examples of accidents. It also contains the following passage, very much in the spirit of *North and South*, which had appeared in twenty-two serial parts in *Household Words* between 2 September 1854-27 January 1855:

... let it not be supposed that we attack this grave and general shortcoming in any spirit of unkind feeling against mill-owners as a body. The very same report that tells us of these base things, tells also of noble enterprises nobly ventured, and of a fine spirit shown by other chieftains of the cotton class. Sir John Kincaid writes of 'the praiseworthy liberality of some mill-owners, which was gradually extending itself, in providing comfortable accommodation for their workers during meal hours, and before commencing work in the morning.' The Messrs. Scott of Dumfries, have established at their works, a kitchen and refreshment room. For a penny they supply a quart of porridge and milk, a pint of tea or coffee, with milk and sugar, or a quart of broth with meat, adding potatoes for another halfpenny. The Quality of each article supplied was reported by the sub-inspector to be substantial and good. The Messrs. Scott have also lately added a reading-room, lighted with gas at their own expense, for the benefit of their workers. At the cotton mills, near Lanark, an apartment has also been fitted up at the expense of the company, for the accommodation of their workers during meal hours, and provided with a comfortable fire in cold weather.

He concludes by warmly commending the new town being built for his manufacturers by Mr Titus Salt, at Saltaire, near Bradford (p. 243).

'Death's Cyphering-Book', *Household Words*, vol. XI, 11 May 1855, pp. 337-41, vigorously attacks the National Association of Manufacturers which was being formed to resist the law requiring the fencing-off of dangerous machinery. It complains that both their meeting, and the Manchester press in general, had accused *Household Words* of hounding the manufacturers. In 'More Grist to the Mill', *Household Words*, vol. XI, 11 July 1855, pp. 605-6, a couple of other horrible accidents are recounted, and the antagonism towards unco-operative mill-owners renewed. Raising money among themselves, they were attempting to procure a repeal of the inspector's power of examining operatives privately, and of instructing the injured how they could proceed for damages against their employers:

Who, after this, can share the indignation of the cotton owners when poor operatives strike, — when they subscribe money to sustain each other in a combination against what they believe — though not always rightly — to be grievous wrong. The operatives strike against hunger, against what he thinks hard dealing on the part of his employers. The employer strikes against humanity, and shows how hardly *he* can deal, by subscribing to help and be helped in a struggle against the necessity of furnishing protection to the lives of his workpeople (p. 606).

Henry Morley, author of *Ground in the Mill*, started his career as a practising doctor. His first publications were a 'Tract upon Health for Cottage Circulation' and 'Interrupted Health and

Sick-room duties', both of 1847. He was one of the members of
the medical profession who, during the late 1840s, took an
increasingly serious view of the question of hygiene, and decided
to devote his life, from 1848, to attempting to advance sanitary
reform, through publications and practical intervention. His first
job was teaching in Manchester: 'What I wished to do was made
known, friends were soon found, none more cordial and helpful
than Mr. and Mrs. Gaskell' (Henry Morley, *Early Papers and Some
Memories*, London, 1891, p. 28). Soon afterwards, when living and
working in Liverpool, he placed some articles on 'How to make
Home Unhealthy' in John Forster's *Examiner*, and graduated to
writing leaders for the publication. After various approaches had
been made to him, Morley agreed to move to London and work
full time, and salaried, for *Household Words*, writing and re-writing
his own and others' articles.

*Unsigned article [Henry Morley], 'Ground in the Mill', Household
Words, vol. IX, 22 April 1854, pp. 224-7.*

'It is good when it happens', say the children, — 'that we die
before our time.' Poetry may be right or wrong in making little
operatives who are ignorant of cowslips say anything like that.
We mean here to speak prose. There are many ways of dying.
Perhaps it is not good when a factory girl, who has not the whole
spirit of play spun out of her for want of meadows, gambols upon
bags of wool, a little too near the exposed machinery that is to
work it up, and is immediately seized, and punished by the
merciless machine that digs its shaft into her pinafore and hoists
her up, tears out her left arm at the shoulder joint, breaks her
right arm, and beats her on the head. No, that is not good; but it
is not a case in point, the girl lives and may be one of those who
think that it would have been good for her if she had died before
her time.

She had her chance of dying, and she lost it. Possibly it was
better for the boy whom his stern master, the machine, caught as
he stood on a stool wickedly looking out of window at the sun-
light and the flying clouds. These were no business of his, and he
was fully punished when the machine he served caught him by
one arm and whirled him round and round till he was thrown
down dead. There is no lack of such warnings to idle boys and
girls. What right has a gamesome youth to display levity before
the supreme engine. 'Watch me do a trick!' cried such a youth to

his fellow, and put his arm familiarly within the arm of the great iron-hearted chief. '*I'll* show you a trick', gnashed the pitiless monster. A coil of strap fastened his arm to the shaft, and round he went. His leg was cut off, and fell into the room, his arm was broken in three or four places, his ankle was broken, his head was battered; he was not released alive.

Why do we talk about such horrible things? Because they exist, and their existence should be clearly known. Because there have occurred during the last three years, more than a hundred such deaths, and more than ten thousand (indeed, nearly twelve thousand) such accidents in our factories, and they are all, or nearly all, preventible.

These few thousands of catastrophes are the results of the administrative kindness so abundant in this country. They are all the fruits of mercy. A man was limewashing the ceiling of an engine-room: he was seized by a horizontal shaft and killed immediately. A boy was brushing the dust from such a ceiling, before whitewashing: he had a cloth over his head to keep the dirt from falling on him; by that cloth the engine seized and held him to administer a chastisement with rods of iron. A youth while talking thoughtlessly took hold of a strap that hung over the shaft: his hand was wrenched off at the wrist. A man climbed to the top of his machine to put the strap on the drum: he wore a smock which the shaft caught; both of his arms were then torn out of the shoulder-joints, both legs were broken, and his head was severely bruised: in the end, of course, he died. What he suffered was all suffered in mercy. He was rent assunder, not perhaps for his own good; but, as a sacrifice to the commercial prosperity of Great Britain. There are few amongst us — even among the masters who share most largely in that prosperity — who are willing, we will hope and believe, to pay such a price as all this blood for any good or any gain that can accrue to them.

These accidents have arisen in the manner following. By the Factory Act, passed in the seventh year of Her Majesty's reign, it was enacted, among other things, that all parts of the mill-gearing in a factory should be securely fenced. There were no buts and ifs in the Act itself; these were allowed to step in and limit its powers of preventing accidents out of a merciful respect, not for the blood of the operatives, but for the gold of the mill-owners. It was strongly represented that to fence those parts of machinery that were higher than the heads of workmen — more than seven feet above the ground — would be to incur an expense wholly unnecessary. Kind-hearted interpreters of the law, therefore, agreed with mill-owners that seven feet of fencing should be held sufficient. The result of this accommodation — taking only the accounts of the last three years — has been to credit mercy with some pounds and shillings in the books of English manufacturers; we cannot say how many, but we hope they are enough to balance the account against mercy made out on behalf of the English factory workers thus: — Mercy debtor to justice, of poor men, women, and children, one hundred and six lives, one hundred and forty-two hands or arms, one thousand two hundred and eighty-seven (or, in bulk, how many bushels of) fingers, for the breaking of one thousand three hundred and forty bones, for five hundred and fifty-nine damaged heads, and for eight thousand two hundred and eighty-two miscellaneous injuries. It remains to be settled how much cash saved to the purses of the manufacturers is a satisfactory and proper off-set to this expenditure of life and limb and this crushing of bone in the persons of their workpeople.

For, be it strictly observed, this expenditure of life is the direct result of that goodnatured determination not to carry out the full provision of the Factory Act, but to consider enough done if the boxing-off of machinery be made compulsory in each room to the height of seven feet from the floor. Neglect as to the rest, of which we have given the sum of a three-years' account, could lead, it was said, only to a few accidents that would not matter — that would really not be worth much cost of prevention. As kings do no wrong, so machines never stop; and what great harm is done, if A, putting a strap on a driving pulley, is caught by the legs and whirled round at the rate of ninety revolutions in a minute? — what if B, adjusting gear, gets one arm and two thighs broken, an elbow dislocated and a temple cracked? — what if C, picking some cotton from the lathe strips, should become entangled, have an arm torn off, and be dashed up and down, now against the floor, and now against the ceiling? — what if D, sowing a belt, should be dragged up by the neckerchief and bruised by steam-power as if he were oats? — what if the boy E, holding a belt which the master had been sewing, be suddenly snapped up by it, whirled round a hundred and twenty times in a minute, and at each revolution knocked against the ceiling till his bones are almost reduced to powder? — what if F, oiling a shaft, be caught first by the neckerchief, then by the clothes, and have his lungs broken, his arm crushed, and his body torn? — what if G, pack-

ing yarn into a cart, and stretching out his hand for a corner of
the cart-cover blown across a horizontal shaft, be caught up,
partly dismembered, and thrown down a corpse? — what if H,
caught by a strap, should die with a broken back-bone, and I die
crushed against a beam in the ceiling, and little K, carrying waste
tow from one part to another, be caught up by it and have his
throat cut, and L die after one arm had been torn off and his two
feet crushed, and M die of a fractured skull, and N die with his
left leg and right arm wrenched from their sockets, and O, not
killed, have the hair of his head torn away, and P be scalped and
slain, and Q be beaten to death against a joist of the ceiling, and
R, coming down a ladder, be caught by his wrapper, and
bruised, broken, and torn till he is dead, and S have his bones all
broken against a wall, and all the rest of the alphabet be killed by
boiler explosions or destroyed in ways as horrible, and many
more men be killed than there are letters in the alphabet to call
them by? *Every case here instanced has happened, and so have many
others, in the last three years.* Granted, but what can all this matter,
in the face of the succeeding facts? — that to enclose all horizontal shafts in mills would put the mill-owners to great expense;
that little danger is to be apprehended from such shafts to prudent persons, and that mill-owners have a most anxious desire to
protect the lives and limbs of their work people. These are the
facts urged by a deputation of manufacturers that has been
deprecating any attempt to make this anxiety more lively than it
has hitherto been.

They found such deprecation necessary. When it became very
evident that, in addition to a large list of most serious accidents,
there were but forty lives offered up annually to save mill-owners
a little trouble and expense, a circular was issued by the factory-
inspectors on the last day of January in the present year, expressing their determination to enforce the whole Factory Act to the
utmost after the first of June next, and so to compel every shaft of
machinery, at whatever cost and of whatever kind, to be fenced
off. Thereupon London beheld a deputation, asking mercy from
the Government for the aggrieved and threatened manufacturers.
We have, more than once, in discussing other topics of this kind,
dwelt upon the necessity of the most strict repression of all mis-
placed tenderness like that for which this committee seems to
have petitioned. Preventible accidents must be sternly prevented.

Let Justice wake, and Rigour take her time,

For, lo! our mercy is become our crime.

The result of the deputation is not wholly satisfactory. There follows so much interference by the Home Office in favour of the mill-owners, as to absolve them from the necessity of absolutely boxing-up all their machines, and to require only that they use any precautions that occur to them for the prevention of the accidents now so deplorably frequent. Machinery might, for example, be adjusted when the shafts are not in motion; ceilings whitewashed only when all the machinery is standing still; men working near shafts should wear closely-fitting dresses, and so forth. Manufacturers are to do as they please, and cut down in their own way the matter furnished for their annual of horrors. Only of this they are warned, that they must reduce it; and that, hereafter, the friends of injured operatives will be encouraged to sue for compensation upon death or loss of limb, and Government will sometimes act as prosecutor. What do we find now in the reports? For severe injury to a young person caused by gross and cognisable neglect to fence or shaft, the punishment awarded to a wealthy firm is a fine of ten pounds twelve shillings costs. For killing a woman by the same act of indifference to life and limb, another large firm is fined ten pounds, and has to pay one guinea costs. A fine of a thousand pounds and twelve months at the treadmill would, in the last case, have been an award much nearer the mark of honesty, and have indicated something like a civilised sense of the sacredness of human life. If the same firm had, by an illegal act of negligence, caused the death of a neighbour's horse, they would have had forty, fifty, sixty pounds to pay for it. Ten pounds was the expense of picking a man's wife, a child's mother, limb from limb.

We have not spoken too strongly on this subject. We are indignant against no class, but discuss only one section of a topic that concerns, in some form, almost every division of society. Since, however, we now find ourselves speaking about factories, and turning over leaves of the reports of Factory Inspectors, we may as well have our grumble out, or, at any rate, so far prolong it as to make room for one more subject of dissatisfaction. It is important that Factory management should be watched by the public; in a friendly spirit indeed — for it is no small part of our whole English mind and body — but with the strictness which every man who means well should exercise in judgment on himself, in scrutiny of his own actions. We are told that in one Inspector's

district — only in one district — mills and engines have so multiplied, during the last three years, in number and power, that
additional work has, in that period, been created for the employment of another forty thousand hands. Every reporter has the
same kind of tale to tell. During the last year, in our manufacturing districts, additions to the steam power found employment for an additional army of operatives, nearly thirty thousand
strong. The Factory system, therefore, is developing itself most
rapidly. It grows too fast, perhaps; at present the mills are, for a
short time, in excess of the work required, and in many cases lie
idle for two days in the week, or for one or two hours in the day.
The succession of strikes, too, in Preston, Wigan, Hindley,
Burnley, Padiham, and Bacup and the other places, have left a
large number of men out of employ, and caused, for a long time,
a total sacrifice of wages, to the extent of some twenty thousand
pounds a week. These, however, are all temporary difficulties: the
great extension of the Factory system is a permanent fact, and it
must be made to bring good with it, not evil.

The law wisely requires that mill-owners, who employ children, shall also teach them, and a minimum, as to time, of
schooling is assigned. Before this regulation was compulsory,
there were some good schools kept as show-places by certain persons; but, when the maintenance of them became a necessity,
and schools were no longer exceptional curiosities, these show-
places often fell into complete neglect; they were no longer goods
that would attract the public. In Scotland this part of the Factory
Law seems to be well worked; and, for its own sake, as a beneficial requirement. That does not, however, seem to be the case in
England. All the Inspectors tell us of the lamentable state of the
factory schools in this country; allowance being, of course, made
for a few worthy exceptions. It is doubtful whether much good
will come out of them, unless they be themselves organised by
men determined that they shall fulfil their purpose. English
Factory children have yet to be really taught.

> Let them prove their inward souls against the notion
>   That they live in you, or under you, O wheels!
> Still, all day, the iron wheels go onward,
>   Grinding life down from its mark;
> And the children's souls, which God is calling sunward,
>   Spin on blindly in the dark.

Here they are left spinning in the dark. Let Mr. Redgrave's

account of a factory school visited by him, near Leeds, suffice to show: —

> It was held in a large room, and the Inspector visiting it at twenty minutes before twelve, found the children at play in the yard, and the master at work in the school-room, sawing up the black board to make fittings of a house to which he proposed transferring his business. The children being summoned, came in carelessly, their disorderly habits evidently not repressed by their master, but checked slightly by the appearance of a strange gentleman. Two girls lolling in the porch were summoned in, and the teacher then triumphantly drew out of his pocket a whistle, whereupon to blow the order for attention. It was the only whole thing that he had to teach with. There were the twenty children ranged along the wall of the room able to contain seven times the number; there were the bits of black board, the master's arms, with a hand-saw, and a hammer for apparatus, and there were the books, namely, six dilapidated Bibles, some copy books, one slate, and half-a-dozen ragged and odd leaves of a 'Reading made Easy.' To such a school factory children were being sent to get the hours of education which the law makes necessary. Doubtless, that sample is a very bad one, but too many resemble it.

'They know the grief of man but not the wisdom', these poor childish hearts. They are now rescued from day-long ache and toil; we have given them some leisure for learning, though, as yet but little more than the old lesson to learn.

13

Earlier evidence for the horrors of industrial accidents can be found in the *Narrative of the Experience and Sufferings of William Dodd, Factory Cripple*, 1841. Dodd's evidence, however, may not be entirely reliable, since he was a man who wrote with an understandable axe to grind. Disraeli certainly used Dodd's *The Factory System Illustrated in a Series of Letters to Lord Ashley*, London, 1842, when composing *Sybil.* Its influence is seen especially in Book II, Chapters 9 and 10. (See Martin Fido, '"From His Own Observation": Sources of Working-class Passages in Disraeli's *Sybil'*, *Modern Languages Review*, 72, 1977, pp. 268-84.) But Fido argues that Disraeli had to make a restrained use of his source, since it was the work of an exposed scoundrel. Ashley had engaged Dodd's service to carry out investigations into abuses in northern factories. In 1844, as the campaign to impose the Ten-Hour Bill on the manufacturers gained strength, Ashley was challenged over his employment of Dodd by questioners in the House of Commons who revealed that Dodd had threatened to report adversely to Ashley on certain industrialists unless they paid his blackmail demands.

William Dodd, Narrative of the Experience and Sufferings of William Dodd, Factory Cripple, *London, 1841.*

(a) pp. 15-18

One great cause of ill health to the operatives in factories, is the dust and lime which is continually flying about. A large quantity of skin-wool and cow's hair are used in the manufacture of coarse rugs, carpets, &c. This is obtained from the skins of the animals after they get killed, by means of a strong solution of lime-water. This lime thus gets intermixed with the wool and hair, and in this state it is sold to the manufacturer; it is then put through the teaser, in order to shake out the lime and dust; and, as the teaser goes at an immense speed, the work-people, the machine, and all around, are covered with the lime; and consequently, every inspiration of air in such an atmosphere, must carry with it and lodge upon the lungs a portion of these pernicious ingredients: the result is, difficulty of breathing, asthma, &c.

On finding myself settled for life in the factories, as it was then pretty evident I should not be able to do anything else, I began to think of getting a step higher in the works. It will be necessary to observe, that hitherto I had only been a piecer; so I put myself forward as well as I was able, and master soon noticed me, and gave me a higher place, where the labour was not so very distressing, but the care and responsibility was greater: and although I was the work of an exposed scoundrel. Ashley had engaged able.

A great many are made cripples by over-exertion. Among

those who have been brought up from infancy with me in the factories, and whom death has spared, few have escaped without some injury. My brother-in-law and myself have been crippled by this cause, but in different ways; my sister partly by over-exertion and partly by machinery. On going home to breakfast one morning, I was much surprised at seeing several of the neighbours and two doctors in our house. On inquiring the cause, I found that my second sister had nearly lost her hand in the machinery. She had been working all night, and, fatigued and sleepy, had not been so watchful as she otherwise would have been; and consequently, her right hand became entangled in the machine which she was attending. Four iron teeth of a wheel, three-quarters of an inch broad, and one-quarter of an inch thick, had been forced through her hand, from the back part, among the leaders, &c.; and the fifth iron tooth fell upon the thumb, and crushed it to atoms. It was thought, for some time, that she would lose her hand. But it was saved; and, as you may be sure, it is stiff and contracted, and is but a very feeble apology for a hand. This accident might have been prevented, if the wheels above referred to had been boxed off, which they might have been for a couple of shillings; and the very next week after this accident, a man had two fingers taken off his hand, by the very same wheels — and still they are not boxed off!

The gentlemen she was working for at the time had immense wealth, most of which, I have reason to believe, was got by the factories. They paid the doctor, and gave her ten shillings! — which was about three farthings per day for the time she was off work. To this sum was added seven shillings more, subscribed by the work-people! I need not say, that she has been a cripple ever since, and can do very little towards getting a living.

After the wool has been oiled, as before described, it is then put through the first teaser, from which it is carried to the second teaser, where it is prepared for the carding-engine. I had once a very narrow escape from death by this machine, when about 16 years of age, in the following manner: —

After finishing one sort of wool, it is usual to clean all the loose wool from the top and sides of the machine, previous to begin-ning another sort. This I was doing in the usual way, with a broom, and, as use begets habits of carelessness in boys, I had not used that degree of care requisite in such places. The conse-quence was, that the cylinder of the machine caught hold of the broom, and, if I had not had the presence of mind to let go my hold, I must have been dragged in with it. The broom was torn in a thousand pieces — a great number of the iron teeth were broken out and scattered in all directions — and, by the care of a kind Providence, I came off with a few slight wounds, from these teeth having stuck into me in several places.

The wool is then handed forward from the second teaser to the carding-engine, where it is prepared for the piecer; it was in this sort of engine my sister had her right hand so dreadfully lacerated.

(b) pp. 25-7

In 1834, the present law for the regulation of factories was about being put in force. I, being appointed time-keeper for the works, had to take the children before the doctor to be examined, as certificates were required from him, that they were of proper age to be admitted into the factory. I cannot describe my feelings as I went on those occasions, accompanied by about a score of little stunted figures, some of whom had been working in the factories for years, and whose parents had been in vain trying to get them something else to do; but I well remember, that I had great difficulty in convincing the doctor of their being of the age required, although I had no doubt of it myself, as I was well acquainted with their parents at the time of the children's birth; but their appearance was so much against them, that I fancied on some occasions, from certain expressions that the doctor made use of, that he thought I was deceiving him. Had he known my inmost thoughts, he would not for a moment have suspected me.

One of the most trying circumstances that occurred to me in all my factory experience, happened in the winter of 1834-5. I had then a youth, of about 17 years of age, placed under me, for the purpose of learning some of the higher branches of the business. I had been giving him directions what to do one day, and had gone up into the room above, for the purpose of superintending some other part of the works, when suddenly one branch of the machinery stopped, and, on turning round to inquire the cause, I was met by several persons, nearly out of breath, who said to me, 'Tom has got into the gig, and is killed.' I ran down in haste, but it was too true: he was strangled. A great many bones were broken, and several ghastly wounds were inflicted on various parts of his person!

After his mangled body was extracted from the machinery, by

unscrewing and taking the machine in pieces, it was laid in a recess on the ground-floor, the same in which the accident occurred, to await a coroner's inquest, the works being all stopped, and the hands dismissed. One by one they gradually went home, and left me alone for some time. The reader may more easily imagine, than I can describe my feelings on this occasion, as I paced, with folded arms, the flags of this dreary place. It was a cold, wet night. I had a flickering light burning beside me, just sufficient to cast a sombre and gloomy appearance over the three water-wheels and the heavy machinery by which I was surrounded. Not a sound broke upon my ear, except the wind and rain without, and the water trickling through the wheels within, with the mangled remains of that youth, whom I had carefully instructed in his business, and looked upon almost like a son, laying bleeding beside me.

This boy's death occurred partly through his own carelessness, as he had no business at the place; but the same thing might have happened to people who had business there; and consequently, it shows the necessity of boxing up all parts of machines, and the gearing by which such machines are propelled, where there is the least appearance of danger. Had this precaution been adopted in every mill, such calamities could not have happened; and, in many thousands of cases, limbs and lives which have been lost would have been preserved.

If anything was wanted to make me disgusted with the system, this and other circumstances would have supplied the deficiency; for while I and hundreds of work-people were toiling and sweating day after day for the bare necessaries of life — struggling, as it were, against wind and tide, and still hoping that some favourable turn would afford a resting-place for our wearied and emaciated frames — the manufacturers were amassing immense wealth, and thus converting what ought to have been a national blessing into a national curse — 'adding field to field, and house to house', and rolling about in their carriages, surrounded by every luxury that this world can give, and looking upon us poor factory slaves as if we had been a different race of beings, created only to be worked to death for their gain.

14

Dodd's description of atmospheric pollution in the mills has its fictional counterpart in the complaint of Bessy Higgins in *North and South*:

I began to work in a carding-room ... and the fluff got into my lungs and poisoned me ... Little bits, as fly off fro' the cotton, when they're carding it, and fill the air till it looks all fine white dust. They say it winds round the lungs, and tightens them up. Anyhow, there's many a one as works in a carding-room, that falls into a waste, coughing and spitting blood, because they're just poisoned by the fluff (Chapter 13).

Dickens makes a satiric dig at those who fall into the mistake of under-rating the physiological implications of this fluffy waste when, in *Hard Times*, he has the fastidious Harthouse recount how he asked directions to Bounderby's residence from 'one of the working people; who appeared to have been taking a shower-bath of something fluffy, which I assume to be the raw material' (Book II, Chapter 1). But contemporaries could still speak of the industrial processes in tones of innocent aesthetic wonderment, a legacy of eighteenth-century responses. See Erasmus Darwin, *The Botanic Garden*, quoted p. 121, and, more generally, Francis L. Klingender, *Art and the Industrial Revolution*, London, 1947.

W. Cooke Taylor: The Handbook of Silk, Cotton, and Woollen Manufacturers, *London, 1843, p. 119.*
  The carding machine is being described.

Its wooden covering is a series of narrow panels; and, if one of these be lifted, it will be seen that each of them is a card, and that a cylinder covered with cards occupies the interior of the box, between which and the more moveable cards forming the cover of the box the wool is drawn into straight fibres, after which its fleeces are wound spirally round the second cylinder, which is called a *doffer*, so as to remove the carded cotton in a continuous filmy sheet. The cotton is slipped from the doffer by the action of a slip of metal, finely toothed like a comb, which, being worked against the cylinder by means of a crank, beats or brushes off the cotton in a fine filmy fleece. The cloud-like appearance of the carded cotton, as it is brushed from the doffer or finishing cylinder by the crank and comb, is singularly beautiful; a breath seemed to disturb the delicacy of its texture, and to the touch it is all but impalpable.

15

'"Sybil" is ... a political treatise, a warming-up of speech materials, a transcript of blue-book incident and adventure ... with all his feeling for the people, Mr. Disraeli appears to have studied them in the pages of the parliamentary or statistical Reports referred to, rather than to have "eaten with them, drank with them, or prayed with them," as Shylock says' (unsigned review, *Athenaeum*, 17 May 1845, p. 477). Disraeli's contemporaries were quick to recognise his dependence on the official evidence of the Blue Books, both through specific references which he made and through the tone of his writing. His use of sources has attracted considerable critical attention: see Louis Cazamian, *The Social Novel in England 1830-1850* (first published as *Le Roman social en Angleterre*, Paris, 1903), translated by Martin Fido, London, 1973; Martin Fido, 'The Treatment of Rural Distress in Disraeli's *Sybil*', *The Yearbook of English Studies*, 5, 1975, pp. 153-63; Fido, '"From His Own Observation": Sources of Working-Class Passages in Disraeli's *Sybil*', *Modern Languages Review*, 72, 1977, pp. 268-84; Sheila Smith, 'Willenhall and Wodgate: Disraeli's Use of Blue Book Evidence', *Review of English Studies*, n.s. 2, 1962, pp. 368-84, and *The Other Nation* (Oxford, 1980).

Between them, they find evidence of a wide number of borrowed, adapted and cobbled-together sources, among them the two *Reports of the Children's Employment Commission* (1843); Edwin Chadwick's *Report on the Sanitary Condition of the Labouring Population of Great Britain* (1843); the 1843 *Reports on Agriculture*; the *Report from the Select Committee on the Payment of Wages* (1842); the *First Report of the Midland Mining Commission (South Staffordshire)* (1843) and Dodd's *The Factory System Illustrated*.

The description of Wodgate (Book III, Chapter 4) owes much

to the description of Willenhall, near Wolverhampton, which R.H. Horne incorporated into his Appendix to the Second Report of the Children's Employment Commission (Trades and Manufactures). Details from the portrayal of Wolverhampton (such as the name of Hell-house Yard) and Sedgley are used also, to a far lesser extent. As Smith points out (*The Other Nation*, p. 71), not only does Disraeli take one of the very worst areas of the Black Country to make his point about the self-seeking sector of the upper classes, but he damns the place still further by depriving it of both church and chapel, even though Horne gathered depositions through the Sunday Schools attached to the Church of England, the Wesleyans, the Baptists and the Primitive Methodists. Disraeli also ignores Horne's observation that in the midst of all the filth and degradation, real efforts are often made to keep homes themselves clean.

Richard Hengist Horne (1802-84) had approached Thomas Talfourd in November 1839, asking that, as an MP, he should put forward Horne's name as a candidate for sub-commissioner on the new Royal Commission to investigate the physical and mental conditions of children in mines and factories. A writer of independent means, his interest had been aroused by his friends, among them the sanitary reformer Thomas Southwood Smith, a principal founder of the Health of Towns Association (1839) and the Metropolitan Association for the Improvement of the Dwellings of the Industrial Classes (1842). Smith was already a Commissioner at the time Horne wished his own name to be put forward. In March 1841, Horne visited the Wolverhampton area as a sub-commissioner, interviewing children in schools, Sunday Schools and factories. His descriptions are among the most graphically written in the whole report, and were denounced by some of the more squeamish MPs as 'offensive'. See Ann Blainey: *The Farthing Poet: A Biography of Richard Hengist Horne 1802-1884*, London, 1968.

[R.H. Horne], Children's Employment Commission: Appendix to the Second Report of the Commissioners: Trades and Manufactures, *Parliamentary Papers 1843, vol. XV, p. 599.*
Horne describes Willenhall, near Wolverhampton:

382. There are but few good houses in the town. By the term good, I do not mean large and commodious, but use the word in the English sense of comfortable. The majority of the houses are

very indifferent, and nearly all those inhabited by the working classes are of a squalid description, often presenting the last state of want and wretchedness.

383. There are many narrow passages, as in Wolverhampton, averaging from 2½ feet to 3½ feet wide. They lead into little courts and yards, where dwellings and workshops are always found.

384. Some of the houses in the main street have an interval of about 2 feet between them, the whole length of which is used as a sewer for all manner of filth, but without any grating or means for it to be carried off.

385. There are many straggling lanes, leading up hill and down hill, with hovels and workshops at irregular intervals. Here and there you pass through a tortuous lane, — which should rather be called a gut, being only 2 or 3 feet wide, — enclosed between broken walls, rising over mounds of half-hardened dirt and refuse, sinking towards declivities of mud and slush, and leading to other dwellings and workshops, some on the declivities and some on the small level, these latter having puddles and pools of stagnant water and filth accumulated in front of their doors and windows.

386. There are no other means for the admission of air into these abodes but from the doors and windows in front, as they have none at the back.

387. There is no under-ground drainage to any of these places; and very seldom, indeed, have they any privies.

388. Many of these dwellings and workshops 'look out' upon a general dust and dung hill, where everything offensive is deposited. These proximate prospects are considered an advantage by the owners of the dwellings, because it establishes their right of use in an unquestionable manner. Those families who are living at a certain distance from these accumulations, or at such an interval as may render their claim doubtful on either side, are driven from one 'forbidden ground' to another, under circumstances which cannot be mentioned, but in which the rage of all the special pleaders, and the discomfiture of one, would be indescribably ludicrous, were not the whole proceeding indescribably revolting.

389. I am compelled to allude to this degrading fact because almost every quarrel which takes place among the inhabitants of these guts or lanes originates entirely in the attempt of some individual who dares to encroach upon the domestic dirt-heap of

other parties, the proximity or 'look-out' of whose doors and windows manifests their right to the exclusive accommodation.

390. Windows are sometimes within 6 feet of these dirt-heaps, but commonly within from 9 to 15 feet.

391. There are two redeeming circumstances to the above condition of things. The first is, that there is generally a pump on the higher ground of these straggling guts, lanes, yards, or alleys. A stream of water, therefore, after many wanderings and various deposits by the way, eventually reaches some hole or bed, or else runs down and disperses itself in the street.

392. The other redeeming circumstance is the extraordinary fact, that amidst all this degradation and filth, and amidst all the squalor of bare and dilapidated abodes and general destitution, it very frequently happens that the inside of the poorest houses is perfectly clean. If the clothing of the women be mere rags, they keep them clean. It is frequently the same with regard to their children at home who are too young to work; they, also, are as clean as children could be kept in such circumstances. I do not include the men and boys who work; they are nearly all dirty, independently of the smut of the forge.

393. I have entered the houses and hovels of journeymen locksmiths and key-makers, indiscriminately and unexpectedly, and seen the utmost destitution; no furniture in the room below but a broken board for a table, and a piece of a plank laid across bricks for a seat, with the wife hungry, — almost crying with hunger, — and in rags, yet the floor was perfectly clean. I have gone up stairs, and seen a bed on the floor of a room 7 feet long by 6 high at one side, but slanting down to nothing, like a wedge, where a husband, his wife, and three children slept, and with no other article in the room of any kind whatever except the bed; and I have seen a broken old bedstead, with an old bag laid upon the sacking in place of bedclothes, with no other article of any kind in the room, and the same want of food in the family; yet the clothes on the bed in the former instance were perfectly clean; so was the floor, in both instances; so were the stairs; they were not merely clean, they were really white, and more resembled the boards of a dairy in a large farmhouse than anything that could have been anticipated of the little wretched hovel of a poor locksmith of Willenhall.

394. Besides the numerous dirt-heaps, small pools, and doorway slushes fronting or adjoining the dwellings and workshops, there are in the town of Willenhall two vast masses of stagnant

filth and putrescence, sufficient to breed a plague throughout the whole of England.

395. Mr. Biddle, surgeon, who has resided 20 or 30 years in the town, conducted me to one of these enormous accumulations, which runs — or rather creeps — along a field, partly under a hedge, at the bottom of the churchyard. At my particular request Mr. Biddle made a special examination of this and the other mass of filth, and communicated the result to me in writing, to which I beg to call your attention.

> Sir,   *Willenhall, near Wolverhampton, April 12th, 1841.*
>
> I HAVE looked over the filthy accumulations of mud which you and I talked about: the one place you saw with me, you know is very bad; it extends at least from 200 to 300 yards, and contains *many scores of tons of putrid filth.* This runs all along the southern side of the town, and indeed we may say in the very heart of the town. On the western and north-western side there is as much, or more, filthy stagnant accumulations of the same kind, amounting, I have no doubt, to some hundred tons. We may well have typhus, &c., which we have now, and have had for a long time, more or less.
>
> I remain, &c.
> (Signed) J. BIDDLE, *Surgeon.*

396. What must be the condition of these masses in the hot weather, and what effect they may then have upon the senses, I cannot pretend to say; but on my visit, during a cool day in April (the 4th), to the one at the bottom of the churchyard, the stench was most revolting. The appearance it presented to the eye, in some places, was that of a livid, tawney putrescence. As I looked at it I could not help thinking I saw it crawl. But its general appearance was that of a dead settlement of a dark spotty hue, — not a scum, but evidently a deep substance. It seemed a reservoir of leprosy and plague. Mr. Biddle subsequently told me that 'in summer it was quite intolerable to pass the place. There were enough marsh exhalations from it to fill a whole country with fever.'

16

One friend and correspondent of R.H. Horne was Elizabeth Barrett Browning. She wrote to him on 7 August 1843, letting him know of her sentimentalised protest poem, which had been inspired by his reports: 'If you ever look into Blackwood, condescend this month to look at *me*. Because my "Cry of the Children" owes its utterance to your exciting causations.' *Letters of Elizabeth Barrett Browning Addressed to Richard Hengist Horne, With Comments on Contemporaries*, edited by S.R. Townshend Mayer, vol. I, 1887, p. 80. Barrett Browning concentrates less on concrete, painful details than on emotional response:

'For oh,' say the children, 'we are many,
   And we cannot run or leap;
If we cared for any meadows, it were merely
   To drop down in them and sleep.
Our knees tremble sorely in the stooping,
   We fall upon our faces, trying to go;
And, underneath our heavy eyelids drooping,
   The reddest flower would look as pale as snow;
For, all day, we drag our burden tiring
   Through the coal-dark, underground —
Or, all day, we drive the wheels of iron
   In the factories, round and round.

'For, all day, the wheels are droning, turning, —
   Their wind comes in our faces, —
Till our hearts turn, — our head, with pulses burning,
   And the walls turn in their places:
Turns the sky in the high window blank and reeling,
   Turns the long light that drops adown the wall,
Turn the black flies that crawl along the ceiling,
   All are turning, all the day, and we with all,
And all day, the iron wheels are droning,
   And sometimes we could pray,
"Oh ye wheels" (breaking out in a mad moaning),
   Stop! be silent for to-day!"'

Elizabeth Barrett Browning, 'The Cry of the Children', 1843, stanzas VI and VII.

Reports by R.H. Horne, Esq., on the Employment of Children and Young Persons in the Iron Trades and other Manufactures of South Staffordshire,

*and the neighbouring parts of Worcestershire and Shropshire; and on the
actual State, Condition, and Treatment of such Children and young persons:* Children's Employment Commission: Appendix to the
Second Report of the Commissioners: Trades and Manufactures,
Parliamentary Papers 1843, vol. XV, pp. 688-9.

Depositions taken at the Wesleyan Methodist Sunday School.
No. 149. April 4. *Joseph Patrick,* aged 15 nearly:
Works at knob-locks, has worked at it nearly three years; is a
parish apprentice in the house; his master never beats him;
behaves well; he has plenty to eat, and a good bed; nothing at all
to complain of; can read not write; was never at a day-school;
always goes to the Methodist Sunday-school; has attended it
nearly two years.

Cleanly and well clothed; very poor in size and stature for his
age. He could not reply to any scriptural questions of the simplest
kind.

No. 150. April 4. * * * * * * (spells it * * *), aged 14 nearly:
Works at dead-locks; is an in-door apprentice; his master does
not beat him much, only sometimes with a stick or some thick
ropes, and sometimes with the handle of the hammer, and then
he feels it for two or three days. Has enough to eat; works from 6
in the morning till 10 at night, with half an hour for breakfast, an
hour for dinner, and half an hour for tea; can read, not write;
don't learn him to write at school; knows the names of St. Peter,
and Moses, in books, but does not know who they were; never
learnt that; they never questions him.

Stunted in stature, cleanly, healthy, and well clothed. Could
not reply to any scriptural questions of the simplest kind. His
master's name is ———. The boy came from Coventry. The
premium given was 3*l.*

No. 151. April 4. *William Hubbard,* aged 12:
Works at Dutch-locks; is pretty well treated; is only beaten sometimes by his master with his hand, or a stick, or the hammer-heft;
has enough to eat; is pretty well satisfied.

A sickly-looking boy, and weak; cleanly; pretty well clothed.

No. 152. April 4. *Walter Brindly,* aged 17:
Works at padlocks; has worked at it nearly five years; his master
treats him well; does not beat him; never has, to signify; has a
brother who was cruelly beaten sometimes by his master; has

enough to eat, and a good bed; was never at a day-school; has attended the Sunday-schools of different kinds about seven years; can read, only in the thin books, easy words of one syllable; has heard of the Apostles; does not know if St. Peter was one, nor if St. John was one, unless it was St. John Wesley; does not know anything about Job; never heard of Samson; twice 30 are 50; twice 25 are 90; ten farthings are 2½d.; 30 pence is 2s. 4d.; knows about Jack Sheppard; saw him acted at Hudson's craft — a show at Willenhall Wake; Jack Sheppard danced Jim Crow, and pleased 'em all very much.

Very cleanly and well clothed; good health, and comparatively well grown.

No. 153. April 4. *Stephen Hort*, aged 17:
Works at rim-locks and dead'uns; has worked at it five years; his master treats him pretty well, nothing to speak of, nor nothing to complain of; cannot read; knows his letters; never heard of the Twelve Apostles; never heard of Solomon, nor Job, nor Samson; has heard of Pontius Pilate; thinks he was one of the Twelve Apostles; thinks he has heard that read at the free school; twice 20 are 40; twenty farthings are 5d.; twenty pence are 2s. all but 4d. — a shilling and eightpence; never learnt to count only by his own head; twice 200 doesn't know; but there are ten hundred to a thousand.

Very cleanly and well clothed; healthy, and comparatively well grown.

No. 154. April 4. * * * * * *, aged 14:
Works at brass padlocks; is an inn-door apprentice; has enough to eat, and a clean bed; his master sometimes beats him with his hand, or a cane, or the hammer-handle — gives him a crack on the head with it; his master hit him yesterday on the head with the stale [handle] of the hammer; the bumps on his head were much bigger than now; they are gone down; he also hit him on the back too; can show the mark; it aches when it's touched; he was struck for not doing something as his master wished, but he was doing it as well as he could, and which he thought the quickest way, and the best way; it was only packing up the locks. Cannot read or write; can read some of his letters.

Poorly grown; very badly clothed; very clean. His head and back (which I examined) bore the marks of the blows. His master's name is ———. The boy is a native of Willenhall.

No. 155. April 4. * * * * * *, aged 11:

Cannot spell his name; work at keys; is an inn-door apprentice; has not enough to eat; sometimes goes without his breakfast, because he has too much work to do before breakfast, and he can't do it; often goes without his dinner for the same reason; his master often beats him with a cane on his hand; does not feel it all day — about half an hour; works from 6 in the morning till 9 at night in the summer, and from 7 in the morning till 10 at night in the winter. Never heard of the Books of Job, or the Psalms of David; never heard of Jonah; never heard of King George; does not know the Queen's name; does not know how much money ten farthings are, nor five farthings; knows about Jack Sheppard; saw him acted in a show, Mr. Lowe's show at Willenhall Wake.

Very little for his age; healthy, cleanly, and well clothed.

No. 156. April 4. * * * * * *, aged 12:

Cannot spell his name; works at latches; has not enough to eat — very often not enough; has a good bed; is not often beaten, but his master is a-cursing at him every day of his life; once knocked him down with his fist; catched him a blow across the face, and kicked him when he was down; knocked his head against the wooden stump, so that he didn't know where he was for a few minutes; when he came to himself his master began to curse at him, and swore at him, damn his eyes and limbs, and all manner of that; it was all because he did not square the latches properly, and he couldn't with a bad file; it was a very bad file he had, an old one; his master knowed that well enough. Does not know what religion he is; does not know what I mean; never heard of Jonah; does not understand me; has heard of Jesus Christ; knows who he was; he was everywhere.

Poorly grown, healthy, cleanly; pretty well clothed; naturally quick and intelligent, but utterly neglected. His master's name is ———. The boy came from Atherstone. Premium doubtful.

17

In '"From His Own Observation": Sources of Working Class Passages in Disraeli's *Sybil*', Martin Fido maintains that

Disraeli's essential presentation of the miners' grievances derives from the *First Report from the Midland Mining Commissioners (South Staffordshire)*, 1843, rather than from the *Children's Employment Commissioners' Report (Mines)*, as had been suggested by earlier commentators. This is not to say, however, that details from this latter report, lodged in the memories of Disraeli's readers, may not have indirectly informed their reading of the novel. In particular, the description of the tommy-shop in Book III, Chapter 3 leans heavily on the evidence collected by Thomas Tancred, the commissioner interviewing the miners in an attempt to find evidence to explain the causes for the dissatisfaction which had led to the Plug Plot, or general strike, of 1842.

(a) First Report from the Midland Mining Commissioners (South Staffordshire), *British Sessional Papers, 13 (588), London, 1843, p. xciii.*
    The evidence is that of an anonymous Bilston woman:

The women will be fighting and tearing to get in.

About a month or six weeks ago, one Thursday, I went home at 11 o'clock in the day; I was there certainly before 12, having only called at my mother-in-law's on the way, and it was 8 o'clock at night before I got home, having only called to leave some tommy on the road, and was not delayed five minutes ...

There was a great crowd to get flour ... When at last I got into the shop my bonnet was off, and my apron was all torn, with the women all trying who should get in first.

There were two women carried off who had fainted, and I helped them come to themselves, and that got me out of my turn and made me wait longer. And there was a little boy who wanted a loaf for his mother, and having no dinner, he was quite smothered, and I thought he was dead, and the sweat poured off him. Ah, it's cruel work in the tommy-shop.

Banks's shop has got much worse of late since young Mr. Charles Banks came to the shop; he swears at the women when the women are trying to crush in with children crying in their arms. He is a shocking little dog.

At this shop, —

Flour is 2s. 2d. a peck.

Bacon 8d. per pound, fat, and 9d. the lean.

Butter (only fresh sold) 1s. 2d. We weighed it twice, and it was one pound and a new penny piece over, not an old one. (Butter is

107

said to be sold by a pound of 20 ounces) ...

Yellow soap 7*d.* per pound ...

All the best bits of meat are to go to the butties, and the pieces with bones in are chopped up for the colliers wives.'

As Fido comments (p. 281), 'It is notable that in dramatising this incident Disraeli makes one of his rare gestures in the direction of intensifying the evils reported in an official report.' According to the Bilston woman, it was the other women themselves who were responsible for the chaos in the shop, fighting in their eagerness to jump the queue, but Disraeli puts the blame on the violently unappealing character of the man serving.

18

The introduction to Book III, Chapter 1 of *Sybil*, where Disraeli gives a generalised description of the mining region, is more notable for its formal rhetoric of horror than for the specificity of its detail. It lacks the immediacy of the Commissioners' Reports, and completely plays down the descriptions of promiscuous sexuality which formed a particularly shocking part in the depositions.

Evidence collected by J.C. Symons Esq., Children's Employment Commission: Appendix to First Report of Commissioners: Mines, *1842, Part I: Reports and Evidence from Sub-Commissioners: Yorkshire Coal-field, pp. 252-4.*

No. 113. *Ann Eggley*, hurrier in Messrs. Thorpe's colliery. Examined March 22. 18 years old: —

I'm sure I don't know how to spell my name. We go at four in the morning, and sometimes as half-past four. We begin to work as soon as we get down. We get out after four, sometimes at five, in the evening. We work the whole time except an hour for dinner, and sometimes we haven't time to eat. I hurry by myself, and have done so for long. I know the corves are very heavy they are the biggest corves anywhere about. The work is far too hard for me; the sweat runs off me all over sometimes. I am very tired at night. Sometimes when we get home at night we have not power to wash us, and then we go to bed. Sometimes we fall asleep in the chair. Father said last night it was both a shame and a disgrace for girls to work as we do, but there was nought else for us to do. I have tried to get winding to do, but could not. I begun to hurry when I was seven and I have been hurrying ever since. I have been 11 years in the pit. The girls are always tired. I was poorly twice this winter; it was with headache. I hurry for Robert Wiggins; he is not akin to me. I riddle for him. We all riddle for them except the littlest when there is two. We don't always get enough to eat and drink, but we get a good supper, I have known my father go at two in the morning to work when we worked at Twibell's, where there is a day-hole to the pit, and he didn't come out till four. I am quite sure that we work constantly 12 hours except on Saturdays. We wear trousers and our shifts in the pit, and great big shoes clinkered and nailed. The girls never work naked to the waist in our pit. The men don't insult us in the pit. The conduct of the girls in the pit is good enough sometimes, and sometimes bad enough. I never went to a day-school. I went a little to a Sunday-school, but I soon gave it over. I thought it too bad to be confined both Sundays and week-days. I walk about and get the fresh air on Sundays. I have not learnt to read. I don't know my letters. I never learnt nought. I never go to church or chapel; there is no church or chapel at Gawber, there is none nearer than a mile. If I was married I would not go to the pits, but I know some married women that do. The men do not insult the girls with us, but I think they do in some. I have never heard that a good man came into the world who was God's Son to save sinners. I never heard of Christ at all. Nobody has ever told me about him, nor have my father and mother ever taught me to pray. I know no prayer: I never pray. I have been taught nothing about such things.

No. 115. *Eliza Coats*, aged 11 years, examined same day with the above, and working in the same pit: —

I hurry with my brother. It tires me a great deal, and tires my back and arms. I go sometimes at half past four and sometimes five; it's dark when I go; it often rains and we get wet, but we take off our top clothes when we get in the pit. They never lace or ill-use me in the pit. I can't read; I have never been to school. I do nought on Sundays. I have had no shoes to go in to school. I don't know where I shall go if I am a bad girl when I die. I think God made the world, but I don't know where God is. I never heard of Jesus Christ.

No. 116. *Sarah Gooder,* aged 8 years: —
I'm a trapper in the Gawber pit. It does not tire me, but I have to trap without a light and I'm scared. I go at four and sometimes half past three in the morning, and come out at five and half past. I never go to sleep. Sometimes I sing when I've light, but not in the dark; I dare not sing then. I don't like being in the pit. I am very sleepy when I go sometimes in the morning. I go to Sunday-schools and read Reading made Easy. [She knows her letters and can read little words.] They teach me to pray. [She repeated the Lord's Prayer, not very perfectly, and ran on with the following addition: — 'God bless my father and mother, and sister and brother, uncles and aunts and cousins, and everybody else, and God bless me and make me a good servant. Amen.'] I have heard tell of Jesus many a time. I don't know why he came on earth, I'm sure, and I don't know why he died, but he had stones for his head to rest on. I would like to be at school far better than in the pit.

No. 118. Mr. *John Clarkson Sutcliffe,* general agent for the Gauber colliery, belonging to the executors of Mr. Samuel Thorpe. Examined March 23, 1841: —
The children in our pit begin going down the shaft at half past four in the morning. They begin soon after to work; they leave off as an average at three o'clock. They do sometimes stop till five and in particular occasions they have staid till six in the evening, but this was when there was an accident or extra demand for coals. If we were hard pressed for coal we should keep them in the pit, colliers and all, but otherwise they come out when they like. Each collier works per piece, and delivers the coals he gets at the Bull stake, which is the place where the double rails terminate and the horse-gate begins. This point is removed further from the shaft as the workings advance. The men pay for hurrying down to this place themselves; we have no control over the hurriers ourselves except keeping order in the pit. If the men were to overwork the hurriers I should not interfere. We reckon one hour for dinner but if we are very busy we give order to stand only half an hour, as for instance to day. I think our corves are heavier than any about here they will weigh when full 12½ cwt. The journey made each way by the hurrier is 150 yards on the average; they will hurry 20 corves a-day at most, and the average number will be 16. I am certain 16 is the average of the journies both ways, making 32 backward and forward. They never have to hurry loaded corves up hill. I believe that a girl of 16 can hurry one of these corves very well, and do her day's work with ease.

Elizabeth Eggler does hurry alone. We cannot afford to pay the same wages as Lord Fitzwilliam, where you saw men employed to hurry. He gets more for his coal and can afford it better. It is much better for the hurriers to have the larger corf and to go less frequently. When the children are allowed to go in too little they are certainly tired, and from unfeeling parents this is sometimes the case.

As regards the working of girls in the pits, of whom we have 11, I should wish to see it abandoned altogether, but I am aware that some parents would suffer severely. The morals of the girls do suffer from it, especially from being together along with the lads. They all meet together at the Bull-stake, and it is the same as a rendezvous. Bastardy does not occur in our pit. Swearing and bad language occur, and the boys and girls meeting together hardens and encourages one another in acts of wickedness, more so than if they were only boys.

Children might begin to trap at nine and to hurry at ten as a double hurrier, and I should not object to a law to that effect. I could not conscientiously object to females being altogether prevented from going into pits. There ought to be due notice given of the prevention of girls going in. We have two men, Gooder and Eggler, the fathers of the girls you examined, are depending on the work of those girls to support their families. The education of the children is lamentably defective. The adults are as bad. There are but three men out of fifty in our pits who can sign their own names to our regulations. And it is lamentable to think that when trade improves they spend their money in drink and not in educating their children.

I think that pits might be allowed to work only 10 hours with half an hour included for dinner. This ought not to include the time necessary for letting the people down and drawing. It takes an hour to let down and an hour to take up our 106 people carefully. I wish particularly to observe that regulation ought to be made about the number of people drawn at once up the shaft; two men and two hurriers and no more ought to come up by a four and half inch flat rope; and six if a round rope, six inch circumference. Ropes are not changed often enough. The Government cannot be too particular in seeing that ropes are changed often enough.

No. 119. *Matthew Fountain*, under-ground steward at Darton colliery, belonging to Thomas Wilson, Esq.: —

The usual time of the children and men descending the pit is about six in the morning. They leave from three to five. Sometimes they will be to half past five. We have only one trapper, and the hurriers have to hurry from 150 to 400 yards, average 300 yards. The corves weigh eight and a half cwt. when full, and they have about 12 corves to hurry each way on an average. It is not hard work for the hurriers. I think hurriers have less to do here than at any other pit I know of. They will have to wait about four hours out of the eleven, including dinner-hour. There is no child in this pit overworked; if there were ill-usage we should interfere directly. We have not much gas. Every morning a man goes down to visit the workings. Particular care is taken of the machinery. My opinion decidedly is that women and girls ought not to be admitted into pits, though they work as well as the boys. In my belief sexual intercourse does take place, owing to the opportunities, and owing to lads and girls working together, and owing to some of the men working in banks apart, and having girls coming to them to fill the corves, and being alone together. The girls hurry for other men than their relations, and generally prefer it. Altogether it is very demoralising practice having girls in pits. It is not proper work for females at all. The girls are unfitted, by being at pits, from learning to manage families. Many could not make a shirt. I do not know whether the education of the children is sufficient or not.

I think it is better to have no limitation as to the time pits work at all. Let men work what time they like. I cannot speak as to overworking elsewhere; there is none in this pit. I think if children were prevented from coming till 10 years old they would be more likely to get schooling and to grow up strong men. They might begin to hurry with another elder one, and without hurting them, at 10 years old. The eldest hurrier always riddles as you did when we were in the pit, and they do nothing else than that. They do not fill. Riddling is easier than hurrying. We have no loaded corves to hurry up hill.

There are girls who work in our pit; the men will send them; I have tried to prevent their coming, but the colliers said they could not get others, or afford to pay men. If we were to give an order that no girls were permitted to descend the shaft, many of the best men would leave; we could not stop the practice so long as other pits were allowed to take girls.

19

Fraser's Magazine, whilst having a substantial readership among the country gentry, carried a number of articles on controversial social issues of the day, as well as publishing — with a certain reluctance — fiction which dealt with similar topics. Charles Kingsley's *Yeast*, describing hardship among the agricultural poor, appeared in it between July-December 1848 (published in novel form 1851), although John Parker, the editor, begged Kingsley to bring it to a speedy end, since it was upsetting his readers. This article, by the Mancunian Robert Lamb (1812-72), is typical of the moderate style of the magazine. It conveys a sense of dismay and horror that so much poverty should exist, and should remain outside the consciousness of the comfortably-off, yet it is anxious to temper this by optimistic glances towards England's industrial future, and by reassuring the readers that not all masters are exploitative, uncaring tyrants. Its classical reference indicates the educational, and hence social background which its readers may be assumed to share.

Unsigned article [Robert Lamb], 'The Manufacturing Poor', Fraser's Magazine for Town and Country, vol. XXXVII, January 1848.

(a) pp. 1-6

There is a homely saying, that 'one half of the world knows not how the other half lives.' Homely, however, as the adage is, it embodies an important truth, and suggests grave thoughts. Walk through the squares, or along the streets, the west end of the metropolis; mark the external magnificence of the buildings, and picture to yourself the costly luxuries within; enter the parks, and behold the gorgeous equipages rolling on like a stream which is too large for its channel; see the lazy postures and satiety-stamped faces of those who occupy the costly carriages. Then walk meditatively to the far east; and after you have arrived at the well-digested conclusion, that our nation is 'a mighty nation, an understanding people', take a survey of the surrounding neighbourhood. See those filthy streets and squalid dwellings, congenial habitations for the sons and daughters of misery. Look at those dirty, ragged children, who are enjoying themselves in their native gutters, and seem to be promising candidates for the Old Bailey. Mark that poverty-stricken mother who is standing at yonder door with the pale-faced child in her arms: from her vacant expression of countenance, she hears not the monotonous clack of the shuttle from within. Why should she? It is to her only the time-clock which ticks through the live-long day. Listen to the sounds which proceed from the wretched-looking house with the broken windows; they are the everyday noises of a father swearing in his drink, and children crying for their supper. Look on this picture, and on that. Verily, 'one half of the world knows not how the other half lives!' But ought it to be so?

In the large manufacturing towns of England the differences between classes are hardly less perceptible; the proverb is scarcely less true. There is one order of men, however, who have the privilege of being acquainted with the habits of both the rich and the poor. The clergy of the Established Church are a connecting link between the extremes of society. They are not above the poor, nor below the rich. They stand with one foot on the sanded floor of the cottage, and with the other on the Turkey carpet of the mansion. This is hardly a figure of speech. It frequently happens that, in less than an hour, the clergyman mixes with the extremes of wretchedness and of riches. He leaves the bedside of the sick — perhaps the father of a family whose earnings were the main support of the house; he leaves the close, foetid atmosphere of the sick-room, and the miserable habitation of indigent fellow-creatures, and, in the course of sixty short minutes, he is breathing the perfumed odours of the drawing-room, or sitting down to one of those distracting banquets — *cœnæ dubiæ* — where the appetite and judgment can hardly agree.

It may be, kind reader, that you belong to the class of mortals who are clothed in fine linen and fare sumptuously every day, and whose acquaintance with the poor is very limited. Now, we are of the intermediate order just mentioned. Be good enough, then, to accept our arm; you have probably nothing to do; and, for an hour or so, take a bird's eye view of a manufacturing population. And do not run away because the town is in Lancashire.

The district, you see, is not very inviting; the streets are narrow, and a heavy smoke hangs over the place to-day. The doors of the houses are, for the most part, wide open; some, you observe, have an appearance of cleanliness and comfort within, others are dirty in the extreme. Up those courts and alleys that

114

run out of the main street we will not venture. The atmosphere may not suit your well-bred nostrils, and your delicate taste may revolt at the idea of a family of eight having only one bedroom. But where do all these children spring from that are sprawling about the streets? We presume they had a like origin with your-self, though they are now left more to the liberal training of unrestrained nature. They grow up, nobody knows how; they push themselves upward through the dirt, like so many aspara-gus plants. Look at those girls of seven or eight years old carrying about their infant brothers or sisters, who are almost as large as themselves. Ask them what they are doing. 'Nossing choild' (nursing the child), is the answer.

'Holloa! my little girl, what are you about?' Down she has fallen, child and all. No matter, she picks up the bits and away she runs.

'Mother's at street end.'

What are these young children wanting who are coming up so demurely? They are going to make their 'cortsies' to 'the minister', after having done which they will run away and laugh, as if they had performed some wonderful feat. Now, what on earth can those women be after at the street corner? They are engaged in very earnest conversation: something important must have occurred to draw them from home before twelve o'clock in the day? Ordinarily a small matter, or no matter at all, will bring them out for a discussion at any given hour; but now an impor-tant event engages them. Peggy Jenkinson has had twins, 'a lad and a lass, fine children, uncommon, and as like their father as beans is beans.' Peggy has done the state some service: it is the second time that this duplicate visitation has befallen her. That fat, vivacious woman there in the check bed-gown and linsey-woolsey petticoat is launching out into a narrative about one of her own confinements, when she expected twins as a dead cer-tainty, but only the phenomenon, Billy, almost as big as two, put in his appearance. Then, after you have noticed the three or four hand-loom weavers, who are loitering about with their hands in their pockets, and the man with the donkey-cart, who is crying mussels, and cockles, and red herrings for sale; and the ragged trader with the wheelbarrow, who exchanges salt for antiquated linen, or carries on the respectable barter (as it is termed) of 'weight for weight', you have seen a fair specimen of the out-door life of a manufacturing district.

A manufacturing population is of a nomad character. A family changes its residence as easily as you change your coat. The young people go out from their old habitation in a morning, and return to dinner at a new one, as if nothing had happened. There is no carrying of sacred fire or clinging to household gods. But, perhaps, you would wish to see the indoor life of an operative's dwelling. Not that opposite: the people are dippers; and, if you enter, that jaundiced woman with the can of dirty water in her hand may dash it in your face, out of zeal for her peculiar doctrines. Nor this before us: the parents are, by religious profession, Teetotallers: the Temperance Hall is their church, and its noisy orators their ministers. Water seems to be so agreeable in its inward application, that it is all absorbed in such uses: it clearly finds its way very seldom either to the face of the woman or the surface of her floor.[1] A Roman Catholic family lives at No. 21; our reception might be courteous, or it might be the reverse: we will not venture. Come in here; we are acquainted with the household. You find every thing tidy; the floor has been lately scoured and sanded; the drawers are well polished; and the clock, with its painted face and clean mahogany case, bespeaks a considerable degree of regularity and providence.

'We're rayther rough, sir, this morning; but will you not sit down?' is the greeting of the mistress. A dinner of lobscouse is in preparation — a savoury dish, consisting of a little meat, many potatoes, and sundry onions, all mashed up and stewed together, after the fashion of Meg Merrilies. Of the family, the father, who is an overlooker, earns about 15*s*. a-week; two daughters, as steam-loom weavers each 10*s*,; and a boy, a 'short-timer,' about 3*s*. The two little girls, who are creeping into the corner there, attend the day-school, and the youngest is in the cradle. The family of eight live with great comfort on 38*s*. a-week; the young women maintain an undoubted respectability of character, dress in a becoming manner, and, though upwards of twenty years old, attend regularly their Sunday-school and church.

But lest you go away with a too favourable impression of an operative's household, please to step this way, and we will shew you another picture of indoor economy. The family consists either of church-people, 'if they go any where', or avowed Socialists, or plain, outspoken Ranters. The mother is about forty years old; and at the present time, you observe, she has a black eye. It was an accident in a slight skirmish with her husband, as they were taking some mild refreshment together. The pugnacious husband you do not see; he is a hand-loom weaver by

day, and a poacher by night, as that growling lurcher in the
corner testifies. There are four ragged, vacant-looking children,
roaming about the house, one of whom is very unconcernedly
receiving a volley of vile names from its mother. In the corner
there is a filthy shake-down chaff bed; a few bottomless chairs
and a three-legged table complete the furniture. Gracious
heavens! beneath that roof live a father and mother, and six
children, — human beings without a humanised feeling, grovel-
ling in the filth and sensuality of the swine, and exhibiting the
ferocity of the savage.

Between these two pictures, bear in mind, there are many
domestic gradations. We must leave your imagination to fill up
the hiatus.

But you might wish to walk through one of the mills, and see
the operatives at work. You have witnessed something of the kind
at the Polytechnic, have you not? We have just time to make a
short inspection before one o'clock, when 'the hands' leave for
dinner. The factory before us, with the very tall chimney, will suit
our purpose as being a well-regulated one. Within that enormous
pile of buildings, eleven or twelve hundred persons are engaged
in their daily employment. Under that roof the raw material,
which was grown thousands of miles away, is manufactured into
cloth, that it may be exported as an article of apparel to the very
spot where it was cultivated. Come along to the engine-room,
from whence is derived all the power that moves every wheel, and
spindle, and loom. How slowly and deliberately the leviathan
works! Every motion of those alternating beams carries with it the
power of two hundred horses, and yet the huge monster is as
docile as an elephant. Sometimes he breaks from his keeper, and
exhibits the Miltonic combination of

> Water with fire
> In ruin reconciled;

but, most generally, his steam-rumbling lungs testify by a
friendly snort, that

The waves and fire, old wranglers, have made peace
To do man service.
ξυνώμοσαν γὰρ, ὄντες ἔχθιστοι τὸ πρὶν,
πῦρ καὶ θάλασσα, καὶ τὰ πίστ᾽ ἐδειξάτην.[2]

117

We will now ascend to the topmost story of that large pile of buildings. This way: no, not by that circular staircase; there is a readier mode of ascent. Step into this box, and our friend here in the fustian jacket will place his finger on a spring, and we shall be raised up to the top by that cloud-compelling power we have just seen. Here we go; not, perhaps, in as elegant an apartment as that at the Regent's Park Collosseum, but in one equally expeditious and safe. What a strange scene opens out to us at the top! Wheels, rollers, straps, are around us, and below us, and above us. One overwhelming rattle stuns us for a moment. But take care, my dear sir; move cautiously along the slippery floor: should your coat-skirts be caught between those revolving cylinders, you would assuredly be dragged in like that heap of cotton, and come out mincemeat. On your appearance, we very much fear lest your metropolitan mother might not 'know you were out'. The process would undeniably derange your linen, and might slightly disfigure your features for your next ball in Park Lane: —

Not the mother that you bore
Would discern her offspring more;
That one moment would leave no trace
More of human form or face.

In an incredibly brief space you would be rolled out into 'the mangled Tybalt,' so graphically sketched in poor Seymour's *New Readings of Old Authors* —

> ὥστε μηδένα
> γνῶναι Φίλων ἰδόντ' ἂν ἄθλιον δέμας.³

Here the cotton undergoes its first process — that of cleaning. You see those large bundles in the corner: the cotton is there as it was packed up thousands of miles away. Look at that young woman spreading it carefully out, that it may be gradually drawn between those revolving cylinders. In its passage it is winnowed from the dust that is bound up in it. This is called 'scutching'; and it must be put through three separate processes of this kind, before it can be sufficiently clean for the further stages of its metamorphosis. Let us descend by this circular staircase; here you see the same material subjected to another dressing. After the cotton has been thoroughly cleaned, the fibres must be drawn out and arranged in lateral order. This is the work of the 'carding' machine. Then, in other rooms, the same material undergoes the processes of 'drawing' and 'roving', preparatory to its being spun into threads. But, if one may judge from your countenance, this jargon seems to be High Dutch to you. Scutching! carding! drawing! roving! We have, however, no time to spare: descend another flight of steps, and you behold ten thousand threads gathering round ten thousand spindles. Look at those self-acting 'mules' and 'throstles', they might be endowed with mind and volition:

Spiritus intus alit, totamque infusa per artus
Mens agitat molem, et magno se corpore miscet —

with seeming truth might it be said of those iron-nerved machines. How admirable is every arrangement! How calmly but accurately each operative goes through his particular duty! How quickly the eye perceives any broken thread, and how deftly the fingers piece or replace it! Seventy years ago it would have taken 300 men to do the work of that single set of fingers.[4]

But let us go down into the 'shed' (shade), where these threads are woven into cloth. What a magnificent sight! We enter a room, the end of which we can hardly see — it is so far off. It is on a groundfloor, and has no building above it. The windows are placed in the roof, that the 'hands' may have more light for their work. A truly *lucus a non lucendo* derivation for the term shade! Within it there are three or four hundred women, managing seven or eight hundred looms. Women, do you call them? They seem to be young girls. It is the circumstance of their having pinafores tied round their throats that suggests the juvenile appearance; but they vary in age from fifteen to forty, as you will perceive, if you mark them closely. Each is engaged on her work: there is no laughing, or giggling, or child's-play. Perhaps one here and there, recognising her 'minister', may convey the intelligence to her neighbour with a nod and a smile; but she becomes very demure again when she fancies she is observed. She probably begins to smooth her hair with the comb she has always near her, or to tidy some portion of her dress; for most of them have a proper sense of their 'becomings.' But why is she stopping her loom? Some thread has been broken, or some bad work made, during her absence of mind, and it is to be set right. The thread is pieced, a rod is touched, and the shuttle rattles on again, as if it were alternately shot from side to side out of two

119

fifty-pounders. Every thing is as orderly and neat as it can be, where there must necessarily be particles of dust and cotton fly-ing about. The ventilation is on the best principle, and the temperature not more than 65°. If there be a smell, it is the healthy one of oil. Such an employment for ten hours is not too fatiguing. The effort consists in mental attention, and in remain-ing long upon the legs. See that woman: a book is lying on her stool; she can take an occasional glance at some anecdote or narrative while her looms are going. Another, you remark, has her knitting by her side. These are very expert weavers. And, as you are a disciple of Lavater, do you not think that the intelligent eyes and interesting faces around you will bear a favourable com-parison with those of your London Graces? But how is this? The din of a thousand shuttles is yet ringing in our ears, but every loom is still in an instant. It is now one o'clock: the pinafores are thrown off; the shawls and bonnets hastily put on; and all the 'hands' are moving out in one continuous stream. Come along with the crowd: there is no rude remark to be heard; a mercurial boy or two may, perhaps, be talking louder than would beseem the deportment-room of a fashionable academy — that is all. The dense mass separates into its component parts as it reaches the street, to collect again at the same place about two o'clock.

We know not where the triumphs of the human mind are more distinctly traceable than within those four walls. We admire the classical scholar who can dig the rich ore out of the hidden mines of ancient learning. We reverence the astronomer, whose eye, guided by the laboured calculations of the mind, glances from this sublunary scene, and discovering a fresh planet among the unnumbered stars, 'lends the lyre of heaven another string'. We pay our homage to the naturalist, who classifies the myriads of animated beings that inhabit our globe, or arranges the varied species of plants that cover its surface, or penetrates in thought to its very heart and centre; and out of all his investigations can gather undoubted evidence of the wisdom and goodness of the Creator. We honour the poet, whose heart yearns after the beautiful and true, and whose mind can

Clothe whate'er his soul admires and loves
In language and in numbers.

But the discoveries of a Newcomen and a Watt, and the inven-tions of a Cartwright, a Kay, a Wyatt, and an Arkwright, excite in

120

our minds wonder more intense, and admiration more profound. Their thoughts have expanded into a practical and universal good; their ingenuity has triumphed over seeming impossibilities; and their triumphs, so far from resting in a theoretic truth, have produced the means of subsistence to thousands upon thousands, have opened a source of wealth and pre-eminence to our nation, and afforded an instrument wherewith to diffuse England's commerce, and England's civilisation, to the remotest corners of the earth.

1. Let us not be supposed to disparage the temperance movement *per se*; such characters, however, we have frequently met with.

2. Æschylus, *Agamemnon*, 633.

3. Sophocles, *Electra*, 755.

4. Dr. Darwin, in his *Botanic Garden*, thus describes these processes as they were found in Arkwright's establishment on the Derwent: —

First, with nice eye, emerging Naïads cull
From leathery pods the vegetable wool;
With wiry teeth revolving cards release
The tangled knots, and smooth the ravell'd fleece.
Next moves the iron hand with fingers fine,
Combs the wide card and forms th' eternal line;
Slow with soft lips the whirling can acquires
The tender skeins, and wraps in rising spires:
With quicken'd pace successive rollers move,
And these retain, and those extend, the rove;
Then fly the spokes, the rapid axles glow,
While slowly circumvolves the labouring wheel below.

(b) pp. 9-16

We have been frequently amused at seeing a factory described by one class of writers as somewhat worse than a Pandemonium, and by another as a trifle better than an Elysium. The descriptions of each party are equally unlike the truth. In a well-regulated mill, many of the young women might be envied by the wealthy for their high moral and religious tone of mind; some, again, maintain an unblemished character and a decent self-respect, without professing any very strict observance of religious duties; and others are doubtless very low both in profession and practice. An outward decorum, however, is for the most part observed, while they are at work; and the grades of character are as strictly defined, when they are off work, as the grades of rank and title during a London season.

The besetting sin of the poor is drunkenness. Not only is it an evil in itself, but it is the parent of almost every crime that comes before a court of justice. In Lancashire, at this moment, the phenomena of poverty and crime present a strange paradox. The several heads of the police force in the various divisions of the county, concur in this particular, that the committals to prison were never so few in the same period as they have been for the last six months; and yet the distress of the operative was never known to be greater. How is this? All the police superintendents give the same answer: with a decrease of wages, there has been a decrease of drunkenness; and with a decrease of drunkenness, there has been a decrease of crime. And take a more circumscribed view: fix upon any filthy dwelling, or ragged children, or sluttish mother, or brutal father, and the chances are ten to one that these miseries have either sprung out of, or go hand in hand with, habitual intoxication. The beer-shop, the ale-house, and the gin-palace, are the Pandora's box to the poor. Hunger, wretchedness, filth, disease, transgressions of the law in every shape, spring in broods out of these soul-destroying dens; and often even hope, that last solace of misery — 'hope that comes to all' — deserts the mind of him who frequents them.[1]

Let us not, however, deal too hardly with the poor. Indifferent to their moral and social duties, as many of them undoubtedly are, they are not wholly without excuse. Brought up without the rudiments of secular learning, and in ignorance of Christian truth, they can with difficulty be induced to see the advantage of the one, or to feel the consolations of the other. Working hard through the week, they claim the Sabbath as a day of leisure, and often turn it into a day of especial sin. Still there are many natural virtues in their dispositions. The Φυειχαὶ ἀϱιταὶ are broadly marked on their hearts. The difficulty lies in directing along a right channel the fountain of natural good; and the more so, inasmuch as it has already gathered mire and impurity in its course. The poor are almost invariably kind to each other in distress. Learn this lesson from them, ye wealthy! Being brothers and sisters in poverty, they often pinch themselves to relieve the pressing wants of a neighbour. 'Certainly', says Bacon, 'virtue is like precious odours, most fragrant where they are incensed or crushed'; and frequently have we seen the present pressure of the times elicit the perfume of this virtue among the poor. An industrious family, in full work, live in considerable comfort. But the manufacturer begins to 'work to stock'; he can find no market for his goods. He is at length obliged to 'start three days a-week'. The operative is now pinched; he returns home on the pay-night 'with the money light in his hand'. He makes his way, however, as best he can — perhaps gets a trifle into debt with the shop-keeper: he is now, to use his own phrase, 'running into bad'. But the worst has not yet come. Such is the commercial stagnation that the manufacturer must close his mill, or he would run the hazard of ruin. And now what becomes of 'the hands'? A family of eight, say, including parents, have to live without the regular income of a single farthing. Their Sunday clothes go one by one to the pawn-shop; and on these 'advances' they exist for a short time. Meanwhile they visit — but with great reluctance — the poor-office; and the board of guardians allow them, probably, 6*s*. a-week. But what are 6*s*. among so many? House-rent is 3*s*. weekly, and firing 1*s*. 3*d*.; so that 1*s*. 9*d*. remain for food. The clergyman, it may be, lends his aid; but he cannot keep the family, for he has fifty such cases under his charge. In this emer-gency the neighbours and friends step in, and are frequently able, by timely assistance, to keep the candle of life burning till work is procured, and better days come.

We may mention another characteristic of the poor — we hope we may rank it in the category of virtues — a grateful reliance on the clergyman in times of distress. Among such heterogeneous materials as constitute the mass of the lower orders, considerable numbers will ever be found whose especial calling it seems to be to abuse the Church and her ministers. Nay, we have seen a fair smattering of this leaven among parties who claim for themselves the title of 'good Churchmen' *par excel-lence*. But, as a body, the poor are inclined to look up to the clergy with respect. They are most irregular church-goers; or, more properly, most regular church-absentees; but they entertain a notion, after all, that the ministers of the Establishment have their interest at heart, and in difficulties are willing to place the most implicit confidence in their advice.

It would surprise many of our fair readers were we to relate with what unreserved freedom the clergyman is admitted into the secrets of all family ailments. The poor seem to think he is entitled to the full privilege of the doctor. We have ourselves made a point of declining — with many grateful acknowledge-ments — all the delicate investigations which old women would have pressed upon us. From the non-observance of this rule, a clerical friend of ours, not long ago, was placed in a singular predicament. We heard the tale from his own mouth, and can vouch for its truth. He has a country living — surrounded, however, by manufacturing towns, and inhabited chiefly by hand-loom weavers. He acts not only as their spiritual physician, but takes equal pride in administering to the relief of their bodily ailments. He is consulted by the old women far and wide, and is considered unrivalled in his knowledge of the *Pharmacopœia.* Being an old soldier — a Waterloo officer — it is supposed that he picked up his skill somewhere abroad, or on the field of battle. Some go so far as to say that on one occasion he was shut up four-and-twenty hours with an Egyptian necromancer. One night last winter he was retiring to rest about eleven o'clock: his house was quiet, and his household in bed; when he was startled by a thundering rap at his door.

'Holla! who's there?' he inquired from his bedroom window.

'James Jackson', was the laconic answer. 'Mother's badly.'

'Does your mother want me tonight?'

'Ay, directly!' was the stubborn reply.

Our friend was decidedly sulky as he contrasted the warmth of his bed with the 'cold without'; but, being too good a disciplin-arian to break ecclesiastical canons, he re-adjusted his coat and waistcoat, muffled up his throat, threw on his veteran roquelaure, and started off with his parishioner — a lubberly lad of nineteen. It was a frosty, moonlight night; on the two trudged over the crisp snow; when, after walking about half a mile, our friend's temper began to cool by degrees; and, turning round to his companion, he said, in his usual kind tone, —

'Well, and is your mother very poorly?'

'Ay, hoo's (she's) vara badly at present.'

'But she is likely to get better, I hope?'

'Ay, ay, hoo'll mend, happen (perhaps), after a bit.'

'What's the matter with her, do you know?'

'O, ay, I know. Hoo's labboring (in labour).'

'Labboring! labboring!' shrieked our friend, turning round fiercely upon his fellow-traveller. 'What do you mean by coming for me? Labboring! go for Dr. Potts this instant. Labboring! Am I a man-midwife, think you?'

'Well, well,' was the imperturbable reply. 'Folks says ye're vara skilfu' in chymistering, and' — scratching his head, and looking his pastor imploringly in the face — 'a labbor's ten and sixpence!'

Patience under suffering, again, is a broadly-marked characteristic of the poor. Though, perhaps, more the result of habit than reflection, it still deserves our warmest admiration. They only who associate with the lower orders, and see them in their secret struggles after bare existence, can tell how much they have to endure in times of commercial depression. It would be an appalling spectacle, could we behold in one mass the aggregate of human suffering among the Lancashire poor during the last eight months. Provisions of all kinds at famine prices, and the operatives unemployed one-half their time! The potato was never seen at their tables for many months. Butchers' meat, ham, and bacon, were equally unattainable. Oatmeal-porridge, milk, tea greatly diluted, and bread thinly covered with butter, were their chief articles of food. And at the time of our writing their condition was never worse. 'We're like to clam hard' (we are obliged to suffer much hunger), was the unsophisticated remark of a little girl to us a few days ago. And yet they have hitherto borne their sufferings with singular endurance. Their present conduct is in remarkable contrast with their turbulence of 1842. Then their privations were comparatively trifling; and yet, from the instigation of desperate men, they rose against the manufacturer, jeopardised his property, desecrated churches, took forcible possession of populous towns, and resisted even unto blood. If the present difficulties continue, we know not, indeed, to what the *duris urgens in rebus egestas* may not impel the people; but as yet we see no shadows of coming disorder. Hardly pressed as the operative is, he is fully aware that his master is suffering no less severely; he concludes that the ruin of the manufacturer must be to his own loss; he sees that the interests of the one are bound up in the interests of the other; and, understanding this, he possesses his soul in patience, waiting for better times. And that those times be not far distant, is our fervent hope and sincere prayer!

In speaking of the praiseworthy endurance of the distressed operative, our remarks, be it understood, are not intended to apply universally. There are noisy idlers and mischief-making mouthers in every community, however small. Herein lies the mistake of almost all the writers on our manufacturing population. They deduce an universal conclusion from the induction of a few facts, and that conclusion, probably, a preconceived one. Take, for instance, Dr. Cooke Taylor's *Notes of a Tour in the Manufacturing Districts of Lancashire*, written in 1842. Every suffering operative is indiscriminately an object of admiration, and the stern endurance of the Saxon would bear a favourable com-

parison with the iron-hearted Spartan dying on his shield. Every
foul-mouthed Chartist is invested with the dignity of a noble
minded patriot struggling for the freedom of his country. The
Corn-law is the ogre that stops the loom, locks up food, and
devours the people. Alas! how unlike are the facts, and how false
is the reasoning! Dr. C. Taylor is addressing Archbishop
Whately. Has the Doctor ever read the 'Fallacies' of his friend? If
our Oxford memory does not deceive us, there is one classed
under the head of 'Undue Assumption' — the logical *non causa
pro causâ*. Into this has the doctor fallen. The restrictions on corn
are removed; but trade is far more prostrated than in 1842. We
do not presume to offer in this place an opinion on the removal of
the Corn-law. We ourselves have no faith in the promises which
brought it about; and entertain but little hope that it may eventu-
ate in the good of commerce and the comfort of the poor. But, to
our mind, the great fallacy consists in attributing our commercial
stagnations to any existing law. Examine the instances of manufacturing depression which have recurred at intervals during the
last thirty years, and you will find that they are almost universally
traceable to incidental circumstances over which the law, as it
exists, has but little influence. And here lies the great danger of
fixing upon any obnoxious statute, and holding it up as the sole
cause of distress: but the passions of an uneducated people are far
more likely to break forth into outrage, when they are concen-
trated on a single point which they are led to regard as the
fountain-head of all their misery.

We know how difficult it is to convey an accurate idea of the
manufacturing poor to the mind of a person who has never
resided among them. The descriptions of them by casual visitors
are mostly in extremes: the pictures are much larger than life.
This is easily accounted for. Among the operatives, there are
greater extremes of good and evil than in a rural population; in
the average, the difference would be found very trifling. In order,
therefore, to arrive at an accurate estimate of their qualities, your
induction of facts must be very extended; your acquaintance with
their habits must be at the same time very minute and very
enlarged. Of manufacturing towns themselves, the characteristics
are widely different. Some are marked by a general cleanliness
and moral order; others are notorious only for turbulence and
filth. In the same town, again, there are mills which have not two
properties in common, so far as relates to their moral or social

condition. One belongs to a master who has a proper sense of his responsibility; and, while he provides every thing requisite for the comfort and well-being of his work-people, insists at the same time that they in their turn shall observe a certain degree of decency and order in their general behaviour. Another is owned by some sordid fellow (one of a class we are happy to believe now rapidly diminishing) who regards his 'hands' in the same light as his iron machinery; and if they have only turned off so much work on a Saturday night, cares not a straw though they be swine-drunk throughout the Sunday. In the same factory, again, the difference of character among the operatives is as great as light and darkness. Some of the working-class might be fit models for the idle rich, while others are lost to every gentle feeling of our nature. Wherefore, in examining into the social, intellectual, and moral condition of the manufacturing poor, the danger is, lest a stranger should arrive at some sweeping conclusion, which may be correct from his own limited induction, but which would represent the whole truth as accurately as a brick of Babylon would represent the entirety of that departed city.

A noble county, believe us, kind reader, is that of Lancaster, notwithstanding its tall chimneys, and black-mouthed coal-pits, and smoke-begrimed faces, and swarthy artizans, and cotton-covered operatives. The Southern shrinks from it as a pestilence. 'Only think of Manchester, your royal highness!' was Brummell's exclamation, when his regiment was ordered thither. Even the bishopric went begging for awhile. The Londoner would almost as soon be stuck up to the neck in a Tipperary bog, as be fixed in a manufacturing town. But, over the wide world, point out to us a district of the same extent as Lancashire with the same properties of greatness. In this much-maligned county there are fields as green, and landscapes as fair, as eye can rest on. Nowhere is agriculture, in its science and practice, advancing more rapidly. From beneath its surface coal is dug out by brawny arms to turn the machinery of the monster factory, and to cheer the fireside of the humble cottage. From its mountain-sides the stone is quarried in abundance. Along its picturesque valleys the dancing waterfall is made available for turning the wheels of the mill, and the wild beauties of nature are trained to the service of the practical and useful. Railways intersect the county like net-work, affording unusual facilities of transit. On its rivers float the argosies of a hundred lands; and from its ports are borne its manufactures to the four corners of the earth. Its inhabitants are characterised by a sterling intellect of Saxon parentage, polished and whetted by the daily attrition of commercial dealings. Many a strong mind has struggled up from the weaver's loom, till it has enriched the literature of the day, or increased the comforts of man by its practical inventions. A noble county, indeed, with all its failings! — a country 'whose merchants are princes', whose women are 'witches', and whose working men are strong enough to 'whip the world'!

1. It is calculated that more than 65,000,000*l.* sterling are annually expended in the United Kingdom in intoxicating drink! — ten times the usual amount of the English poor-rates! — more, by 5,000,000*l.*, than the declared value of our exports! Impossible as this may, at first sight, appear, on consideration it becomes perfectly credible. We have the best reason for saying that *the male labourers* of England — using the term in its largest sense — including members of teetotal and temperance societies, spend, on the average, twenty-five per cent of their earnings in drink.

Part Two
London

20

In *Bleak House*, the 'black, dilapidated street' of Tom-all-Alone's, with its crumbling, collapsing tenements, its 'maggot numbers' of inhabitants crawling in and out of gaps in walls and boards (Chapter 16) is presented as a carefully worked set of images, evoking the horrors of slum dwelling, and the disgusted recoil such horrors produce. Since it is in Chancery, its dilapidation emphasises still further the pernicious tentacles of this institution. Despite offering an extreme contrast to the gloomy opulence of Chesney Wold, the plot binds it to the world of the Dedlocks, thus reinforcing Dickens's theme of the ultimate interdependence of all parts of society.

This particular slum is not, in the novel, explicitly made representative of others like it in those central London areas which contained the worst housing. But inescapably, Dickens's evocations would have been read in the context of the growing exposure of intolerable living conditions in both daily and periodical press reports, and in the increasing number of accounts, part horrific investigation, part voyeuristic, which were published in book form. Dickens's own *Sketches by Boz* (1833-6; published in volume form, 1st series 1836; 2nd series 1837) provided an early, lively model for such journalistic revelations. As Sheila Smith has shown in *The Other Nation* (pp. 52-60), both Dickens's style and his topographical choice of St Giles considerably influenced other writers. Notable among these was Douglas Jerrold, author of *St Giles and St James*, a text, and a phrase, which gave authority called upon by Thomas Miller in opening his chapter on 'St Giles's' in *Picturesque Sketches of London*, London, 1852: '... we will stride from splendour to squalor — from St James's to St Giles's, whose names Douglas Jerrold has rendered inseparable in his fearless and life-like novel' (p. 229).

(a) An early example of fascination with the capital's contrasting social conditions is the six-volume *London*, edited by Charles Knight, 1841-4. The section on St Giles, written by W. Weir, can be compared with Dickens's *Meditations in Monmouth Street* (1836). When Knight's *London* was reprinted in 1875, this passage changed into the past tense, and the formation of New Oxford Street, Endell Street and other thoroughfares was noted.

W. Weir, *'St Giles, Past and Present'*, London, *edited by Charles Knight, 6 vols, London, 1841-4, vol. III, 1842, pp. 266-7.*

Whoever has passed along Monmouth Street must have been struck with the redundant drapery of the old-clothes' shop, intermingled with stores of second-hand boots and shoes, enough, it would seem, to fit out whole Spanish legions, were they again required. Doubtless good part of them finds a retail sale on the spot: it is not easy to escape the importunities of their eloquent vendors. But in addition to these, a large export trade is driven with Ireland. It is understood that Mr. O'Connell's patriotic attempt to promote the domestic manufactures of Ireland has failed mainly from the circumstance that nine-tenths of the population have contracted a habit of wearing in preference second and third-hand clothes, and that the remaining tenth cannot with their best will wear out their new clothes quick enough to provide the rest with a constant supply of their favourite wear.

The classical reader may possibly retain from his schoolboy days a recollection of a race of people called Troglodytes — dwellers in caves, an intermediate species between the man and the rabbit. Their descendants still flourish in great force in Monmouth Street. Cellars serving whole families for 'kitchen and parlour and bed-room and all' are to be found in other streets of London, but not so numerous and near to each other. Here they cluster like cells in a convent of the order of La Trappe, or like onions on a rope. It is curious and interesting to watch the habits of these human moles when they emerge, or half emerge, from their cavities. Their infants seem exempt from the dangers which haunt those of other people: at an age when most babies are not trusted alone on a level floor, these urchins stand secure on the upmost round of a trap-ladder, studying the different conformations of the shoes of the passers-by. The mode of ingress of the adults is curious: they turn their backs to the entry, and, inserting first one foot and then another, disappear by degrees. The process is not unlike (were such a thing conceivable) a sword sheathing itself. They appear a short-winded generation, often coming, like the otter, to the surface to breathe. In the twilight which reigns at the bottom of their dens you can sometimes discern the male busily cobbling shoes on one side of the entrance, and the female repairing all sorts of rent garments on the other. They seem to be free feeders: at certain periods of the day tea-cups and saucers may be seen arranged on their boards;

at others, plates and pewter pots. They have the appearance of being on the whole a contented race. At present, when the cold north-easter of the income-tax is about to sweep cuttingly across the face of the earth, we often feel tempted to envy those who, in their subterranean retreats, will hear it whistle innocuously far above their heads, with the feelings of the travellers in 'Mary the Maid of the Inn':

'Tis pleasant, says one, seated by the fireside,
   To hear the wind whistle without.

There are some features common to both divisions of this region, which will be best understood and appreciated after we have introduced our readers to 'the Rookery'. Here is the genuine unsophisticated St Giles's. Its limits are not very precisely defined, its squalor fades into the cleanness of the more civilised districts in its vicinity, by insensible degrees, like the hues of the rainbow, but we shall not be far from the mark if we describe it as the triangular space bounded by Bainbridge Street, George Street, and High Street, St Giles's. It is one dense mass of houses, 'so olde they only seemen not to falle', through which narrow tortuous lanes curve and wind, from which again diverge close courts innumerable, all communicating with those nearest them. It is one great maze of narrow crooked paths crossing and intersecting in labyrinthine convolutions, as if the houses had been originally one great block of stone eaten by slugs into innumerable small chambers and connecting passages. There is no privacy here for any of the over-crowded population; every apartment in the place is accessible from every other by a dozen different approaches. Only at night, when they are asleep — and not always at night — can their redundant numbers find room; for so long as they are lively enough to turn and be aware that anything presses them, there is squeezing and jostling, and grumbling and cursing. Hence whoever ventures here finds the streets (by courtesy so called) thronged with loiterers, and sees through the half-glazed windows the rooms crowded to suffocation. The stagnant gutters in the middle of the lanes, the accumulated piles of garbage, the pools accumulated in the hollows of the disjointed pavement, the filth choking up the dark passages which open like rat-holes upon the highway — all these, with their indescribable sights and smells, leave scarcely so dispiriting an impression on the passenger as the condition of the houses. Walls of the colour of bleached soot — doors falling from their hinges — door-posts worm-eaten and greasily polished from being long the supports of the shoulders of ragged loungers — windows where shivered panes of dirty glass alternate with wisps of straw, old hats, and lumps of bed-ticken or brown paper — bespeak the last and frailest shelter that can be interposed between man and the elements. It is a land of utter idleness. Groups of women, with dirty rags hung round them, not put on, cower round the doors — the old with wrinkled parchment skins, the young with flushed swollen faces and heavy eyes. The men lean against the wall or lounge listlessly about, sometimes with pipes in their mouths. In this region there are no birds or flowers at window or on wall; the inmates can scarcely muster liveliness sufficient to exchange words, or perpetrate the practical joke of pushing each other into the kennel. Shops are almost unknown — in the interior of the district quite unknown. Half-way up Bainbridge Street is one in which a few withered vegetables are offered for sale; in George Street another, where any kind of rags, with all their dirt, are purchased; along Broad Street, St Giles's, are some provision shops, one or two of those suspicious deposits of old rusty keys called marine stores, and opposite the church a gin-shop, Here a few miserable women may be seen attempting to help each other to arrange their faded shawls, when by any means they have procured liquor enough to stupify themselves — exhilaration is out of the question. Such is the aspect of this place by day.

(b) Thomas Beames, *The Rookeries of London*, 1850, focuses far more specifically than does Knight on London's less salubrious quarters. He defines a rookery thus: 'We speak of human masses pent up, crowded, thrust together, huddled close, crammed into courts and alleys, where, as by a fatal attraction, opposite houses grow together at the top, seem to nod against one another, conspiring to shut out the little air which would pierce through for the relief of those beneath' (p. 5), and goes on to describe their growth, before delineating St Giles, Saffron Hill and Bermondsey in detail. In conclusion, chapters discuss the way in which such living conditions overthrow all the decencies of life and foster immorality. Above all, Beames stresses the fact that they pose a political threat, since the very real grievances provide a fertile breeding ground for revolutionary ideas: 'under the cloak of lectures on science, their political grievances are magnified, one system of government decried, and men's worst passions roused by the invectives of artful demagogues ... schools are established for the rising generation in connection with these hot-beds of sedition' (p. 177). An analogical reading of *Bleak House* uncovers something of the same fear of social eruption among those who live in appalling slums. Krook's death by spontaneous combustion, however bizarre and unpleasant, is a contained event. But Dickens uses it as a metaphor for the spontaneous combustion which must inevitably take place within a corrupt body politic: 'The Lord Chancellor of that Court ... has died the death of all Lord Chancellors in all Courts, and of all authorities in all places under all names soever, where false pretences are made, and where injustice is done ... it is the same death eternally — inborn, inbred, engendered in the corrupted humours of the vicious body itself' (Chapter 32). If one looks back to the description of Tom-all-Alone's, with the 'crowd of foul existence ... maggot numbers ... fetching and carrying fever' it contains, the seat of such potential combustion may well be located within this specific rotting body, as well as in the sphere inhabited by the legal profession, themselves already referred to in unsavoury terms, residing, in Lincoln's Inn Fields, 'like maggots in nuts' (Chapter 10).

The Reverend Thomas Beames was the spiritual force behind the Society for Improving the Dwellings of the Working and Poorer Classes, an admirer of Henry Mayhew's investigative work, and author of the first analytic study of London's slums.

Thomas Beames, The Rookeries of London, *London, 1850, pp. 25-43.*

... the worst sink of iniquity was The Rookery, — a place or rather district, so named, whose shape was triangular, bounded by Bainbridge street, George street, and High street, St Giles's. While the New Oxford Street was building, the recesses of this Alsatia were laid open partially to the public, the *débris* were exposed to view; the colony, called The Rookery, was like an honeycomb, perforated by a number of courts and blind alleys, *culs de sac,* without any outlet other than the entrance. Here were the lowest lodging houses in London, inhabited by the various classes of thieves common to large cities, — the housebreaker, who did not profess to have any other means of livelihood; the tramp and vagrant, whose assumed occupation was a cloak for roguery; the labourer who came to London to look for work; the hordes of Irish who annually seem to come in and go out with the flies and the fruit, — were here banded together: driven by their various necessities to these dens, they were content to take shelter there, till the thief had opportunity to repair his fortune, and the labourer means to provide better lodging. The streets were narrow; the windows stuffed up with rags, or patched with paper; strings hung across from house to house, on which clothes were put out to dry; the gutters stagnant, choked up with filth; the pavement strewed with decayed cabbage stalks and other vegetables; the walls of the houses mouldy, discoloured, the whitewash peeling off from damp; the walls in parts bulging, in parts receding, — the floor covered with a coating of dirt. In the centre of this hive was the famous thieves' public house, called Rat's Castle; this den of iniquity was the common rendezvous of outcasts. In the ground floor was a large room, appropriated to the general entertainment of all comers; — in the first floor, a free and easy, where dancing and singing went on during the greater part of the night, suppers were laid, and the luxuries which tempt intoxication freely displayed. The frequenters of this place were bound together by a common tie, and they spoke openly of incidents which they had long ceased to blush at, but which hardened habits of crime alone could teach them to avow. Even by day it was scarcely safe to pass through this district! Did not the loathsome sights appal you, it was crowded with loiterers, whose broken hats and ragged shooting jackets were in keeping with their dwellings; round them, lounged boys with dogs, birds, and other appurtenances; these being their only visible means of support, it was possible, though very improbable, that they lived solely by the sale of them: by day, then, you might inspect the dingy alley with its thievish population; women with short pipes in their mouths and bloated faces and men who filled every immediate occupation between greengrocer and bird-catcher. Thieves lurk here now, their very semblances worn to conceal a less reputable calling; dog-breakers, dealers in birds, marine store-keepers, water-cress sellers, costermongers (*i.e.* small greengrocers), sellers of sprats and herrings, hawkers of prints and toys, street sweepers, dealers in coffee, lozenges, and other kinds of confectionery; men, whom indolence and dissipation unfit for more regular employment, throng these haunts even by day; there the bill-stickers retire, there go the bands of placard carriers who have obstructed the causeway, marching in column shouldering their weapons of offence; there beggars throng to count, divide, and spend their gains, — but night alone witnesses the real condition of our Rookeries. Then the stream of vagrants who have driven their profitable trade return to their lair — trampers come in for their night's lodging; the beggar's operas, as they were wont to be called, then open their doors to those whom necessity or crime has made skulkers or outcasts; no questions are asked, it is sufficient that the money is forthcoming, — and they, who are driven to such dens, are seldom in a condition to ask questions. Not in St Giles's alone, but in most London parishes, are rooms where chance lodgers are gathered at nightfall; these are crammed by those whom poverty assembles, and the landlord derives a large revenue from the necessities of his customers; so that you cannot judge by the daylight aspect of the Rookery, what face it wears by night. In St Giles's, especially, rooms are opened as night lodgings, where, as a general rule, several men sleep who have never met before; in many cases, there are double beds, where married couples sleep, five or six pairs, in the same room: you would be startled to witness the crowding of inmates even in favoured localities; to see the industrious mechanic, his wife, and his children huddled into a single apartment, — by day, the common sitting room, by night, the common dormitory; you would be startled to find that such is the rule among the working classes, the meed of honesty and diligence, so that it has few exceptions. In the genuine Rookery, even this remnant of decency, this slender rag, which betokens a lingering regard to the proprieties of social life is removed; men and women are brought together in the same apartment whom no marriage tie unites, and who have no other bond than that of common want; children of all ages sleep with their parents; and even the miserable boon of laying the head in such places as these, though paid for, is often made of none effect, through the cries of infants, which break the silence of the night. In some of these places, bedsteads are supplied, — in some only straw, — and the charge, of course, varies with the accommodation. In these houses there is generally, on the ground floor, a common room, answering to the coffee room of an inn, or rather combining coffee room and kitchen; this is sometimes hung round with beds at the side, but not always; here is a good fire; spirits and beer are brought in, bacon fried, meals prepared; boys and girls are lying on the floor gambling or playing with marbles, sometimes exercising their ingenuity in tricks with dirty cards.

Because all are taken in who can pay their footing, the thief and the prostitute are harboured among those whose only crime is poverty, and there is thus always a comparatively secure retreat for him who has outraged his country's laws. Sums are here paid, a tithe of which, if well laid out, would provide at once a decent and an ample lodging for the deserving poor; and that surplus, which might add to the comfort and better the condition of the industrious, finds its way into the pocket of the middleman.

We have lately had an opportunity of visiting the worst district of St Giles's — George street and Church lane; through this part of the parish runs the New Oxford street, and they are thus the remains of the famous Rookery — the still standing plague-spots of that colony. You cannot gain an idea of what The Rookery was without visiting these streets. Rows of crumbling houses, flanked by courts and alleys, *culs de sac*, &c. in the very densest part of which the wretchedness of London takes shelter. You seem for a time to leave the day, and life, and habits of your fellow-creatures behind you — just to step out of the din and bustle of a crowded thoroughfare — to turn aside from streets whose shops teem with every luxury — where Art has brought together its most beautiful varieties, — and you have scarce gone a hundred yards when you are in The Rookery. The change is marvellous: squalid children, haggard men, with long uncombed hair, in rags, most of them smoking, many speaking Irish; women without shoes or stockings — a babe perhaps at the breast, with a single garment, confined to the waist by a bit of string; wolfish looking dogs; decayed vegetables strewing the pavement; low public houses; linen hanging across the street to dry; the population stagnant in the midst of activity; lounging about in remnants of shooting jackets, leaning on the window frames, blocking up the courts and alleys; with young boys gathered round them, looking exhausted as though they had not been to bed. Never was there so little connection between masses of living beings and their means of livelihood. And then these dens, the fronts of a small court — square you can scarce call it — more wretched, more utterly destitute of all that is needed for the purposes of life, than the lanes of which they are the background. These alleys were thickly populated, as though a close atmosphere had more attractions, and drew by a sympathetic cord more lodgers than the open thoroughfares; you could scarcely have an idea of the number of persons crowded together in a single room. At first, when the average proportion of

sleepers is stated to you, you feel inclined to calculate the number
of square feet contained in the area of the room, to see whether it
is possible that so many human beings can lie down there. You
begin to fancy that the process so familiar to the prisons of the
middle ages must take place here; that persons do not sleep in a
recumbent posture, but by leaning against the walls; or perhaps,
at night, some purgatory like a steamer's cabin is erected, and
men sleep in tiers, as in one of those marine Pandemoniums.
Thus in one room, measuring six feet by five broad, we were
assured that eight people, some of them, of course, children,
slept. You will tell us this must be exaggeration; however, the
tendency amongst the inhabitants, was to conceal, or qualify; for
the landlords had made wholesale clearances in many houses,
where they had reason to believe that information on the subject
of lodgings had been given by the tenants. The landlords were
alarmed at the inquiries made of late, and determined to elude
them. In one house 100 persons have been known to sleep on a
given night. In a particular instance, we ascertained that three
rooms were thus occupied — first room, by eight persons, second
by fifteen, third by twenty-four. We ourselves saw as many as
twenty-four persons in the same room; they were assembled
there even in the daytime, and yet you are assured that night
alone affords a fair criterion. In these rooms are piled the wares
by which *some* of the inhabitants gain their precarious living, —
oranges, herrings, water-cresses, onions, seemed to be the most
marketable articles; and there were sweepers, cadgers or beggars,
stray luggage porters, &c. lounging about. In another house, the
average number of persons who slept in a room was twelve; in
others, of course, larger, forty persons are known to have slept in
a single night.

In a back alley, opening into Church street, was a den which
looked more like a cow-house than a room for human beings —
little, if any light, through the small diamond panes of the
windows; and that, obstructed by the rags which replaced the
broken glass — a door whose hinges were rotting, in which time
had made many crevices, and yet seventeen human beings eat,
drank, and slept there; the floor was damp and below the level of
the court; the gutters overflowed; when it rained, the rain gushed
in at the apertures. On a wretched mattress lay a poor young
man, with a fearful racking consumptive cough; he was quite
naked, had not a rag to his back, but over him was thrown a thin
blanket, and a blue rug like a horse cloth, — these he removed to

let us see there was no deception. This room was so low, that a tall man could not stand upright in it — the rest of the inhabitants slept on shavings; the ceiling was broken, several of the inhabitants were ill, and had all suffered more or less. In Church lane, it has been computed that from 1000 to 1100 persons live; our informant thinks, even at present, there are more than 800; and he has long known it, and indeed, from what we saw, this is likely to be accurate; in another room, about 8 feet by 12, twelve people slept.

We asked several questions respecting the inhabitants, and in one house some information was given us, which, in many points, was corroborated by our companion — that in an upper room as many as seventeen juvenile thieves had been collected, and used to live together; that one of these had been transported, and their ages ranged from six to twelve. It seems unlikely that sentence of transportation should have been carried out in the case of one so young; perhaps sentence was passed, and he was sent to a model prison in virtue of that sentence: but, substantially, the account was no doubt true; the extreme youth of the criminals, their habits, their plan of clubbing together, we fear, cannot be misstated. Many of the houses are so far below the level of the street, that, in wet weather, they are flooded; perhaps this is the only washing the wretched floorings get; the boards seem matted together by filth.

The aspect of these rooms is singular; in some, heaps of bedding — that is to say, blanket and mattress are tied up in a bundle, and placed against the wall so as to leave the middle of the room clear for meals; little bags, containing the whole of their small stock, are hung on a nail; shavings carefully gathered into a heap, occupy one corner; old hats, reaping hooks, bonnets, another — some sick child moaning in another part of the room. These peculiums[1] are arranged with some neatness; there is an individuality about them, the idea of a *meum* and *tuum*, the little stake in the country's welfare, which is not altogether lost; there seemed something like attachment to these shadows, which we wished we could see exercised on more substantial comforts; some clinging still as to a home, miserable as it was, enough to show that reformation was not quite hopeless. Many, perhaps most of the inhabitants, were Irish; how strong their attachment to their native country! One old man, breaking fast, was about to return, to lay his bones in the 'ould country'. Those about him spoke with warm enthusiasm of his return; their eyes glistened, and some of them, we ascertained, had wrung a little horde even from the wretchedness around them, as a fund on which to subsist in their native land. Seldom have we seen the love of country so strong; and strong it must be to survive long separation, the wrongs they had suffered before they had left their native shore, the demoralising air of Rookeries, and the ties they had formed in England. In several of the rooms four and five distinct families lodged together; in the time of the cholera, this induced fearful suffering. It was warm weather; those who were well, were engaged either in their daily business, or in their out-door lounge. In one room a benevolent man told us he saw three persons dying at the same time of the epidemic; there were several cases where, because the disorder was sudden, or they had no connections, or perhaps from fear, those stricken were left to die alone, untended, unheeded, 'they died and made no sign', without mentioning their relatives, without a word which betokened religious feeling on their lips, without God in the world, poor hapless outcasts, acclimatised long to the atmosphere they breathed, reckless from want of knowing better!

In these lodging-houses many of the families are stationary, that is, comparatively so, remaining for the week, the month, or the quarter; but we have said trampers come in, and the poverty of the inhabitants makes them glad to receive these chance customers. We were curious to know the charge for the night's lodging, and found it to be 1*d.* per night upon the bare boards, 3*d.* per night on a mattrass. The habits of the dwellers in these Rookeries are of course strange. Women will be seen crawling out to beg, who have been only two days confined. Marriage is too often dispensed with; men leave their wives, and wives their husbands, in Ireland, and come over here with other partners, or else pick them up in England. Thus, some years since, in our noviciate, we paid the passage of a poor woman, who was very ill, to Ireland. She left her husband, he intending to join her; she soon returned, and found him provided with a partner; and it is difficult to convince them this is wrong; indeed, when anything happens, which, in higher circles, would lead to a divorce, the working classes generally take the law into their own hands, separate from their erring wives, and live with some other woman; and they justify themselves on religious grounds, — defend, as they think, this breach of morality. Among these people, superstition abounds. We saw a sick child, whose sufferings were severe; we asked why it was not in the infirmary? The answer was, it had been there, but the mother took her babe away, conveyed it to Mile End, that it might be *charmed*, and thus restored to health. In another house was a young man who said he had been 'in trouble'; in other words, he had just returned from the House of Correction. He said he had stolen a desk purposely, that he might be committed, for he was starving; that he would now willingly work, but that he had pawned his shoes, and therefore must resort to the old trade for a livelihood. He could read and write; we asked why he did not enlist before he took to thieving? and he answered, that his arm had been broken. Prostitution prevailed here to a fearful extent. In one large house it is said that £.10, in a smaller that £.5 per week, are cleared by this traffic; the most open and shameless immorality is carried on; the middle classes contribute to the evil. Six or seven houses in one street are applied to this nefarious trade, and there are from 200 to 300 fallen females here, for mothers send out their own daughters on these errands, and live on the proceeds.

Juvenile theft is also recruited by the same means, and there are parents in this neighbourhood, training their children to this iniquity, punishing them severely when they return home empty-handed, and living on the fruits of their success. Yet Ragged Schools are not wanting in the neighbourhood, nor do they labour in vain, although scarcely a tenth part of the juvenile population is educated.

We have said that a large majority of the inhabitants are Irish; they fly from starvation and thus colonies are formed, not merely Hibernian in all their attributes, but separate colonies from different parts of the country, or plough lands, as they call them: thus, when an emigration takes place, the emigrants on arriving in London drop into the places prepared for them, as much as if they were billeted on the different wards of a hospital or a barrack. In one wretched room where eleven beds were ranged against the wall, two of them double beds, the landlady of the house was confined, and the occupants witnessed the pains of labour. When asked if she was not ashamed, her answer was, she had no other room in which to live.

This description will startle you, gentle reader: you thought, perhaps, as we did, that New Oxford Street had superseded The Rookery. Was any colony of old worse than this — more thoroughly wretched and demoralising? Will any one now say we don't want an Act of Parliament to regulate the number of families per house, of inmates per room, and public prosecutors to see that the law is enforced? A religious society employ an Irish missionary in this district. When he first sent in his journal, the committee complained that he had only selected cases of open vice and extraordinary ignorance: his answer was, that he had passed over the worst cases; yet, that if his journal was to be a fair criterion of his labours, it could contain nothing, but details of ignorance and vice — that in such a district anything else was impossible. But nine-tenths of the inhabitants are Irish; do we, then, set down to Irish nurture this amount of wretchedness and immorality? God forbid! We believe that examples of female profligacy are more rare in Ireland than England, though poverty is more excessive, and accompanied with more utter prostration of the individual than among us; yet the Irish coming to London seem to regard it as a heathen city, and to give themselves up at once to a course of recklessness and crime. Some regulations then should be framed to meet this great and pressing evil. Rookeries, at least such as Church Lane, should at once be proscribed; it would be difficult, with our free institutions, to stop these descents of Irish upon our great towns; but the names of those who land here should be entered in a book, their progress observed, and, if they did not get work within a certain time, they should be sent back to their own Unions; or, at any rate, not be allowed to congregate in such masses in the worst parts of our towns: they bring their bad habits with them, and leave their virtues behind. The misery, filth, and crowded condition of an Irish cabin, is realised in St Giles's. The purity of the female character, which is the boast of Irish historians, here, at least, is a fable. Rookeries are bad, but what are they to Irish Rookeries? Within the ordinary boundaries of a district, we are assured, on the authority last mentioned, there is scarcely a family which is not Irish.

We do not aim in this sketch at describing minutely the condition of those who inhabit Rookeries, and have therefore contented ourselves with few details. We must otherwise, in the cause of truth, enter upon inquiries, whose results are too disgusting for our pages. Such descriptions very properly fill the reports of Sanatory Commissioners, for, if they were left out, many an evil would be unchecked. *The Times*, *The Morning Chronicle*, and, above all, Mr Mayhew, have told the naked tale. Thus, in the following pages, though much to the uninitiated may seem exaggeration, not one tithe of the nuisances which disgrace Rookeries, has been enumerated. Yet still a few facts, and they not the most startling, may prepare us for further investigation; and, as we have derived them from official sources, we are less likely to be misled.

In the report of the Statistical Society, we have the following remarks, respecting the district visited by its members, which was one of the most densely populated in St Giles's: —

The inhabitants may be classed as follows: —

1st. Shopkeepers, lodging-house keepers, publicans, and some of the under-landlords of the houses, who make a considerable profit by letting the rooms, furnished and unfurnished.

2nd. Street dealers in fruit, vegetables, damaged provisions, and sundries; sweeps, knife-grinders, and door-mat makers.

3rd. Mendicants, crossing sweepers, street singers, persons who obtain a precarious subsistence, and country tramps.

4th. Persons calling themselves dealers, who are probably thieves, and the occupants of houses of ill-fame.

5th. Young men and lads, of ages varying from ten to thirty, known as pickpockets, and thieves of various degrees.

About one half of the inhabitants are Irish, chiefly natives of Cork, who for the most part have been long resident in London. About one eighth are of Irish descent, born in England; the remainder consist of English, some of whom have been in better circumstances.

This last remark must be taken with some allowance, because of the obvious difficulty attending such classifications.

You are much struck in visiting the rooms and houses where the working classes live, by the absence, not merely of the comforts, but almost the necessaries of life. Take, for instance, a family consisting of man and wife, and five children; they are lucky if they have one bedstead and three beds; in many instances, there are no bedsteads; in some cases, in the worst districts, as we have seen, straw furnishes the bed, and the day clothes the covering by night. The houses of the poor are, for years together, guiltless of paint; and even whitewash, cheap as it is, is sparingly laid on. The inmates suffer much, too, from the want of water, with which these courts are very inadequately supplied, even where it is turned on; and this takes place, in many instances, only twice a-week, though the companies have a plentiful supply at command; and few investments have turned out so profitable as those made in the shares of these different societies.

We need not wonder that such dens exist, that several persons unconnected by birth or even similar occupation are massed together in the same room, when the independent labourer, the artisan, the mechanic, seldom rent more than a single apartment severally for themselves and their families. Below them in the scale of society are several degrees; — the man of uncertain occupation, the beggar, the thief, the felon, each a grade in itself, and that grade distinguished, not only by more reckless habits than the one above it, but also worse clothed and lodged.

The Rookery is no more! a spacious street is in its stead; but will you tell us that any poor man has gained by the change — that any section of the working classes has reaped an advantage — that any band of ruffians is dispersed — that middlemen have felt a mortal blow — that vagabondism, pauperism, alms-asking, or any other unlicensed trade has been broken up? Certainly not; there must be poor, and they lodged and fed; how or where the Legislature must provide. The effects of the late removal are thus shown in the Report of a Committee of the Council of the Statistical Society: —

The Council consider that a main cause of this evil is what are falsely called the improvements, which have recently taken place in this part in the formation of New Oxford Street. It would seem to raise a suspicion of the sanatory value of that kind of improvement which consists in occupying, with first or second-rate houses, ground previously covered by the tenements of the poorer classes. The expelled inhabitants cannot, of course, derive any advantage from new erections, and are forced to invade the yet remaining hovels suited to their means; the circle of their habitations is contracted while their numbers are increased, and thus a large population is crowded into less space. Church Lane consists of twenty-seven houses. The Council proceeded in their examination from No. 1 to No. 18, passing over No. 1 as a corner house and shop, and 11, 12, 13, 15, and 16, as lodging-houses, and therefore no fair specimens of the ordinary population. The number of houses examined were thus reduced to twelve, and the population of each was compared with that of the census of 1841 — the great increase of overcrowding since is exhibited in the following most remarkable table:-

			Population in 1841	1847
No. 2	.	.	33	61
No. 3	.	.	14	49
No. 4	.	.	27	61
No. 5	.	.	35	47
No. 6	.	.	29	32
No. 7	.	.	29	62
No. 8	.	.	13	48
No. 9	.	.	25	26
No. 10	.	.	17	13
No. 14	.	.	17	19
No. 17	.	.	12	26
No. 18	.	.	26	17

The increase of population in twelve houses being thus 186. Dividing the number of cubic feet of air in these twelve houses by the number of individuals found in them, the average supply for each individual was only 175 feet — while 1000 is the number deemed necessary for a single prisoner in England. The largest supply of air in these twelve houses was 605 cubic feet, and the smallest was as low as fifty-two.

The conclusion is obvious: if Rookeries are pulled down, you must build habitable dwellings for the population you have displaced, otherwise, you will not merely have typhus, but plague; some fearful pestilence worse than cholera or Irish fever, which will rage, as the periodical miasmata of other times were wont to do, numbering its victims by tens of thousands!

1. 'Peculium' — private or exclusive possession or property.

21

On 5 July 1849, *The Times* published a letter from fifty-four residents of Church Lane, Carrier Street and other dwellings in the rookery which lay directly behind New Oxford Street. The building of this thoroughfare, whilst it had meant the demolition of some of the worst housing in the area, had led to the redispersal of its occupants. This had intensified the problems of overcrowding and sanitation in the neighbourhood.

This area had been notorious even before *The Times* correspondence. See the unsigned article (probably by W.A. Guy), 'Church Lane, St Giles", *Frasers' Magazine*, 37, March 1848, pp. 257-60.

A connection between the Sanitary Remonstrance letter and *Bleak House* is made by Trevor Blount, 'Dickens's Slum Satire in *Bleak House*', *Modern Language Review*, LX, 1965, pp. 340-51.

(a) The Times, *5 July 1849, p. 5.*

'A SANITARY REMONSTRANCE'

THE EDITUR OF *THE TIMES* PAPER

Sur, — May we beg and beseech your proteckshion and power. We are Sur, as it may be, livin in a Wilderniss, so far as the rest of London knows anything of us, or as the rich and great people care about. We live in muck and filth. We aint got no priviz, no dust bins, no drains, no water-splies, and no drain or suer in the hole place. The Suer Company, in Greek St., Soho Square, all great, rich and powerfool men, take no notice watsomdever of our complaints. The Stenche of a Gully-hole is disgustin. We all of us suffer, and numbers are ill, and if the Colera comes Lord help us.

Some gentlemans comed yesterday, and we thought they was comishioners from the Suer Company, but they was complaining of the noosance and stenche our lanes and corts was to them in New Oxforde Street. They was much surprized to see the seller in No. 12, Carrier St, in our lane, where a child was dyin from fever, and would not believe that Sixty persons sleep in it every night. This here seller you couldent swing a cat in, and the rent is five shillings a week; but theare are greate many sich deare sellars. Sur, we hope you will let us have our complaints put into your hinfluenshall paper, and make these landlords of our houses and these comishioners (the friends we spose of the landlords) make our houses decent for Christians to live in.

We are your respeckfull servents in Church Lane, Carrier St., and the other corts.

Teusday, Juley 3, 1849

John Scott	Hanna Crosbie
Ewen Scott	Edward Copeman
Joseph Crosbie	Richard Harmer
John Barnes	John Crowe
William Austin	James Crowe
Elen Fitzgerald	Thomas Crowe
William Whut	Patrick Fouhey
Ann Saunderson	William Joyce
Mark Manning	Michal Joyce
John Turner	John Joyce
William Dwyre	Thomas Joyce
Mary Aiers	John Sullivan
Donald Connell	Timothy Sullivan
Timothy Driscoll	Cathrin Trice
Timothe Murphy	James Ragen
John O'Grady	Timothy Brian
Marie O'Grady	James Bryan
John Dencey	Philip Lacey
John Crowley	Edward brown
Margaret Steward	Mrs. brocke
Bridget Towley	Nance hays
John Towley	Jeryh fouhey
Timothy Crowley	Jeryh fouhey
John Brown	Marey fouhey
Catherine Brown	Jerey Aies
Catherine Collins	Timothy Joyce
Honora Flinn	John Padler

(b) Unsigned article, The Times, *9 July 1849, p. 3. 'Our Sanitary Remonstrants'.*

It is but seldom that the public attention is called to the misery and disease that exist in the metropolis, except through the medium of police reports, inquests, the returns of sanitary commissioners and medical officers; and these even convey but a slight idea of the horrors that really prevail. The subjoined description may convey some notion of the incredible misery, destitution, and filth, that often prevail near the proudest localities in this great city:-

On Thursday last a rather curious letter or remonstrance, addressed to the Editor of *The Times,* was laid before the public, complaining of the miserable state of two streets called Church

Street and Carrier Street, which are situate on the extreme verge
of St Giles's, and within twenty yards of the handsome buildings
recently erected in New Oxford Street. It would be neither desirable nor safe to prosecute any inquiries in this locality alone and
unaided, the inhabitants being of the very lowest order — perhaps a degree more respectable on one side of the street than on
the other — and our reporter, having secured the assistance of a
police sergeant well acquainted with the street, and with many of
the unfortunate residents, went from room to room, and from
house to house, — not to witness an endless repetition of filth and
degradation, but in each house to see some additional wretchedness, or at least an aggravation of former scenes.

The street itself is about fifteen feet wide, very ill-paved, and
containing ruinous houses, having generally five rooms, but
sometimes more. These houses are let by the owners to men and
women, who again let out the rooms singly and by twos, and
these rooms are again sub-let by the occupants to those outcasts
and trampers who are in want of a night's shelter. These are
charged 1*d.*, and sometimes 2*d.* per night, and many are admitted
for 'anything they can give', or for nothing, according to their
state of poverty and destitution. No limit is placed to the number
of persons so admitted, except the capacity of the room; and
men, women, and children, more or less naked, repose nightly in
these places, occasionally on old beds stuffed with straw, sometimes on straw and shavings, without covering, but by far the
larger part sleep on the bare boards, and in the back rooms,
which are destitute of boards, on the bare earth.

In the house No. 3, Church Street, there are five rooms, which
are let and sub-let as before mentioned. The number of its
inhabitants varies each night. The landlord or occupier of the
ground floor stated the average in summer to be thirty, but much
more in winter. There are no drains, and there is no privy, the
door leading to the space dignified with the name of a yard
having been locked to make room for the 'improvements'. The
inmates of this and the two adjoining houses go to a privy at a
shop at the corner of the street, at which shop they sometimes
leave the rent. The stairs are so incrusted with dirt that weeds
might grow upon them, and are also so dilapidated as to make it
a matter of risk to ascend them. The rooms vary from six to seven
feet in height. It is scarcely possible for them to be dirtier, and the
atmosphere is unendurable. The filth and offal are thrown into
the street or court, from which it is swept by a man who is

engaged for the purpose. All the inmates joined in condemning the atmosphere as 'enough to poison anybody', and in a hearty wish that something might be done to alleviate their sufferings from this cause. Any inquiry as to the existence of fever was met by the reply, "Oh, they are all taken to the hospital!" but the mephitic[1] air was often too sudden in its action to allow of these cases being taken in time, as will hereafter be seen.

The house No. 6 also contains five rooms, in a similar state of filth to those of No. 3. Two of these rooms project over the back yard, where there is or was a very good privy, but this place also is locked up, the inhabitants going to the corner shop. The smell in these premises is very offensive, caused partly by the utter absence of drainage, and by the number of persons living under the same roof. The rent of these rooms varies from 2*s*. to 3*s*. per week. The back rooms on the ground floor had not a vestige of boarding, the furniture being composed of some old tubs for seats, and one or two bottomless chairs. It is absolutely impossible to detect whether the walls or ceilings were ever painted or whitewashed; the filthy state of the occupants of the rooms and the loaded atmosphere having reduced everything to a dull earthy tint. In the front room of the ground floor there was some appearance of cleanliness, that is, comparatively speaking. It was inhabited by a man with his wife and family; they had lived there for some time. The man was in the last stage of pulmonary consumption, and complained much of the poisonous atmosphere generated by the want of drainage, and by the number of persons sleeping in the house. He declined attempting to estimate the number, but it was ascertained from some of the other inmates that in a room not nine feet square from eighteen to twenty-three slept nightly. The window of this room scarcely admitted daylight, and could only be opened about eight inches.

In No. 7 the back yard was not locked up; it was an imperfectly flagged space, eight yards long by three feet six inches in width, and on each side of it were the entrances to the back rooms. In these rooms from eighteen to twenty-three people slept on the average; sometimes the number was greater. The privy had been taken away, and the cesspool just covered with boards and earth. The soil underneath oozed up through the boards, saturating the earth with fetid matter. In one of the back rooms several Irish families lived. One girl supported herself by selling watercresses, which she purchased in Fleet Market, and afterwards retailed. A little girl was sitting on a basket making up small bundles of these watercresses from a heap which lay beside her on the floor. The Catholic clergyman sometimes came to visit the sick there, and, as the woman said, 'there were plenty of them'. The room opposite was occupied by only three families in the day, but as many as could be got into it at night. The price varied from 'anything they could give', to 1*d.* and 2*d.* per night. This room fetched 2*s.* per week. Two cases of fever had been taken away from it. The window slid back about eight inches — that was the only means of ventilation. Although this room was not more than nine feet square, daylight did not reach the back of it. It was scarcely high enough for an ordinary man to stand upright in. The person who took the rents came to the door for them every Monday morning.

These three houses are a fair sample of all on one side of Church Street. The houses on the St Giles's side are, strange as it may appear, much cleaner, — nearly all have privies, which they do not permit the other inhabitants to use, and there is in some a supply of water, of which the opposite houses are entirely destitute.

Carrier Street contains about twenty houses, and is perhaps the most disgustingly filthy spot that exists anywhere in London. A few facts only will serve to show the nature of the place, and these facts, incredible as they may seem, are by no means so frightful as many that commonly occurred in this locality. At the corner of the street, or rather, a few yards from it, there is a narrow bricked alley, — not wider than a doorway. On going down it, as soon as the eye is enabled to perceive anything in the dim light, an opening is seen on either side, each being the entrance to a staircase so filthy, so offensive, so repulsive to every sense, as to render it impossible to give any idea of it. On going up one of these — a matter of risk and difficulty — five or six different doors are perceived leading to as many rooms, and each of these again let to as many families. In one room, not ten feet long, and less than five wide, lived four families, comprising in all sixteen persons — eight adults and eight children. One corner of the room was occupied by a heap of straw used as a bed, and near it, on some old rags, was lying a child suffering apparently from fever. The mother was crying near it, and pointing to a small mouldy biscuit from which a small portion had been taken, said that that was all she had had to give her child for many days. A man who was lying on the floor in a corner of the room corroborated this statement, and said that he would be very glad to work for anything instead of starving in that den. The appearance of the inmates was a guarantee for the truth of their assertions, want being to be seen in every countenance. A stout young Irish-woman, who seemed better off and more intelligent than the rest, complained bitterly of the smell which pervaded the house (it was so bad in this room as to render it difficult to breathe). There was no water in the place. Some medicine had been given to the mother of the child by a dispensing surgeon to whom she took it. The medicine when brought into the room in the evening was quite red; in the morning it had turned quite black. It was, no doubt, the air which had changed it, poisoned as it must be by the breathing of so many persons in one room. It appeared, at the first sight of this room, to be physically impossible that sixteen persons could sleep in it; and, indeed, there could not be room unless some of them rested in a sitting position in the angles of the wall with their children on their knees. The police sergeant, who heard the statement, on being appealed to as to its truth, said that there was nothing either impossible or improbable; he had seen many such cases. In the room next or next but one to this, and of much the same size, three families resided. There were not so many to sleep in at night — the number stated was eight or ten persons. On a bed of shavings, and covered only with a sack and some cotton fragments sewn together, lay another child, also suffering from low fever and diarrhoea. It was a boy about seven years old. He was quite naked. The father could get no work, and they had nothing to give him. The poor child seemed to suffer much from the fever. In a room above these, and nearly as large as two of them put together, several Irish families resided. The room was not so bad as the lower ones as to cleanli-ness, and the window admitted both air and light. It was, how-ever, a most deplorable scene of misery. In a corner, with only a few rags to support her hand, in her day-dress, and with a sack thrown loosely over her, lay a woman, whose features indicated the rapid approach of death. She was unable to speak English, and on being questioned by the residents in the Irish language, she said that she was a stranger — a poor widow with one child. She had applied to the inhabitants of the room for shelter on the previous night. They said that she had 'not long to live by the looks of her; but they could not refuse her'. No one had sent for the doctor. They had sent for the Roman Catholic clergyman of the district, and he was shortly expected. Her child, a girl of about fifteen, sat by her side crying as if her heart would break.

The clergyman, on his arrival, glanced at the woman, and, as if assured that there was but little time to spare, he turned the people out of the room whilst he administered the last offices to the dying. This woman laboured under the symptoms of cholera. In another corner of the room was a long bag stuffed with straw, and on this a woman, her husband, and two children slept. One boy in the room was pointed out as having slept on the stairs for the last twelve nights. He was a 'strange boy', no one knew where he came from. He had had nothing to eat for two days, except a crust of bread given to him by a woman who pitied him, though she could ill spare the morsel she gave from her own children. This woman said that they seldom tasted meat — hardly ever. They did not expect it. They were glad to get bread, and they had not often enough of that. At the bottom of the staircase, and about two feet below the landing, from which it was entered by a door, was the bedroom of a tailor named John Crow. This room had a bed in it. It was about six feet square, with no window; and it was impossible to see anything in it without a candle, even on the most sunny day. This unfortunate man complained that the landing outside his room-door was used by the residents as a privy. The poor man spoke very angrily of the annoyance he was put to by the soil running into his room. It came in at night under the door; the smell was almost suffocating; and he was obliged often to rise and clean out his room — at least to clear away the soil — before he or his wife could sleep. The next house to this was, with the exception of the cases of fever, &c., a repetition of the last. There were four or five houses at the extreme end of the street, which were a degree better than those described. The man who was the landlord of them pointed in triumph to a clock and some crockery in one of the rooms — a miserable place enough in itself, but a paradise compared to many near it.

The cellars in this street are the next object of attention. A flap in the pavement being opened, it rather surprised the bystanders to find that the cavern below was inhabited. It was about 11 feet square, and when the flap or lid was down must have been quite dark. There were women and children in it, and the atmosphere was thick and moist with offensive effluvia and exhalations. The woman had seen or heard of the letter which had appeared in the *Times*. She was much enraged, and said that her cellar was the one referred to as having accommodated sixty people. It was certainly impossible that sixty people could have slept in it; and, indeed, it was a matter of doubt and difficulty how any person could have lived in it at all, when the number of this woman's tenants — which she stated to be twelve — were there. There were two beds filled with shavings in the corners; and when the tenants came in, shavings were spread over the floor generally, and they lay down to sleep. There are ten or twelve of these cellars.

It would be too disgusting to enter into many *minutiæ* observed in this horrible place. In spite of the demoralizing influence which this locality must have, many of its poorest inhabitants seemed to desire cleanliness. In nearly every house some women were engaged in rinsing or washing the miserable rags which covered their children or their beds. Many of the better class of the residents live by hawking cabbages, onions, and other ordinary vegetables. These they keep in their rooms at night. All of them complained of the poisonous smells that often arose, and said it was hard that they should have no drains or water, and but little light and air.

The foregoing description falls rather short of the reality, as any venturous person may at once see if disposed to enter this locality. The police at Clarke's Buildings station will afford every facility for those who have some better motive to lead them than mere curiosity and the desire of seeing the extent to which misery and dirt can grow there — unknown and almost uncared for, in this great city.

A list in the possession of the police sergeant returns the average of the inmates in this locality at from sixteen to eighteen per room. The same sergeant states that in fourteen small rooms he counted one night 150 people — men, women, and children, nearly all naked, and sleeping in promiscuous heaps. At many of the houses the sergeant (whose name is, we believe, Fowler) was obliged to assure the inmates that 'no harm was meant' before those who went on this sorrowful expedition were admitted.

It is worthy of observation, that the Rev. Mr. Watts, a clergyman who resides in Endell Street, and officiated at the new church there, died about eight months since in consequence of visiting this locality.

The subject was taken further by Joseph Banks Durham, a cutler from New Oxford Street and, according to Blount (p. 348) a living analogue for Snagsby. He communicated copiously with the General Board of Health about the state of the locality; they referred the matter on to the Metropolitan Commission of Sewers. There is no evidence that Durham's correspondence produced any direct results: indeed, the Board of Health assured him that no existing legal provision could remedy the gross overcrowding. 'The situation was an apt, if deplorable, instance of the callousness that resulted from the reluctance of bureaucracy to act, and it provides further corroboration of the relevance of Dickens's satire' (Blount, p. 348). But Durham's protest reached a wider public when his correspondence was published, together with *The Times* material, in Charles Purton Cooper, *Pamphlet Respecting the Sanitary State of Church Lane and Carrier Street*, London, 1850.

1. 'Mephitic' — offensive smelling, pestilential, noxious.

(c) Joseph Banks Durham to Charles Purton Cooper, 13 August 1850, reprinted in Charles Purton Cooper, Pamphlet Respecting the Sanitary State of Church Lane and Carrier Street, *London, 1850, pp. [11]-13.*

456, *Oxford Street,*
August 13, 1850.

SIR,
On comparing the account of the state of Church Lane and Carrier Street, which appeared in the *Times* in July, 1849, with the present condition of these streets and their courts, I have no hesitation in saying that it is as substantially true of them now as it was then; and, from an intimate acquaintance with the locality, I believe it is quite impossible for any description, however full, to give to any one an adequate idea of its filth and misery, and the moral degradation of its inhabitants.

It must however be stated that the cellars mentioned in the *Times* are now closed, which is the only improvement observable. In the Report of Carrier Street there is also an error, there being only in it nine houses instead of twenty, as stated; but of these the account is by no means overdrawn; in fact, it is much understated with respect to two of them especially.

As regards the south side of Church Lane the Report is much too favourable, as there are on that side many houses as bad, if not worse, than any on the north side. In a room, about thirteen feet square and seven feet high, on the ground floor of one of these houses, and opening into the yard, I have seen at midnight

155

thirty human beings sleeping on straw and shavings on the ground, many of them without a rag to cover them, a woman with a new-born infant in one corner, the infant born in this room with all its inhabitants present, and a dead child at the further end: in this room have I twice seen such a scene (and from my experience I can say that it is no uncommon occurrence in these places). The yard of this house contains a privy, and is in so disgusting a state that I will not attempt to describe it. At the back of Church Lane, on St. Giles's side, is a row of houses known as Kennedy's Court, which must, I imagine, have been overlooked by the *Times* reporter, it being ten times more vile and disgusting than Carrier Street, and, as might have been expected, not a single house in it escaped the cholera, each one of them having lost some of its inhabitants.

I took the following account of No. 8, Church Lane, very recently, therefore I can vouch for its correctness, and it may be taken as a very fair sample of these houses generally.

In the yard, which is merely a narrow passage about 4 feet wide, are four rooms. The two lower ones are about 10 ft. square, 6 ft. 4 in. high, and are so dark that you can scarcely see daylight in them. The two upper rooms are smaller. The four contain twenty-three regular inhabitants. The rent of the lower ones 2*s.* 6*d.* per week each, of the upper, 2*s.* 3*d.* each.

The first floor, 13 ft. by 11 ft. 4 in. and 7 ft. 6 in. high; rent 3*s* per week; contains eighteen men, women, and children.

Second floor same size as first; rent 3*s.* per week; fifteen men, women, &c.

Third floor 13 ft. by 11 ft. 4 in., 6 ft. high; rent 3*s.* per week; twenty-four men, women, &c.

The parlour 10 ft. square; rent 3*s.* per week; twelve men and women.

Thus making a total of ninety-two inhabitants, and producing a rental of £55 18*s.* per annum.

The house is destitute of furniture, and has no water or convenience of any kind.

The above were stated to be its regular inhabitants, and were they counted at night there can be no doubt that their number would be found much greater.

It should be observed, that besides the numerous inhabitants of these houses there is at all times to be seen in the rooms large quantities of vegetables, fruit, or shell fish, according to the season of the year, thus still further vitiating the air, and affording a ready means of disseminating the infectious disorders so frequent in these places.

I have the honour to be,
    Sir,
    Your obedient servant,
               JOSEPH BANKS DURHAM

22

The notorious condition of London graveyards added to the city's health problems. They were highlighted in *Bleak House* through Dickens's descriptions of Nemo's last resting place, a foot or two beneath the surface of 'a hemmed-in churchyard, pestiferous and obscene, whence malignant diseases are communicated to the bodies of our dear brothers and sisters who have not departed ...' (Chapter XI). Esther's narrative, in Chapter LIX, speaks of the burial-ground as 'a dreadful spot', with 'heaps of dishonoured graves and stones', the surroundings oozing damp and soaked with humidity. When Jo shows Lady Dedlock the rat-infested burial ground, he is more specific about the process of interment: 'He was put there ... Among them piles of bones, and close to that there kitchen winder! They put him wery nigh the top. They was obliged to stamp upon it to git it in. I could unkiver it for you with my broom, if the gate was open' (Chapter XVI).

Dickens's rhetorical practices — his majestic indignation; his employment of Jo's cockney tones — serve as a partial mask of the vileness of the circumstantial details: details as reported in, for example, G.A. Walker's four *Series of Lectures on the Actual Condition of the Metropolitan Graveyards*. These consist of attacks on 'the hundreds of burying-places of this huge metropolis, permitted to exist in the midst of its living population [which] are so many centres of infection, laboratories of malaria, whence issue most offensive and deadly compounds, the gaseous products of human putrefaction, the food, if not the principles, of malignant disease and premature death'. G.A. Walker, *The First of a Series of Lectures on the Actual Condition of the Metropolitan Graveyards*, 1846, p. 1. Dickens possessed copies of these lectures (*Catalogue of the Library of Charles Dickens from Gadshill,* ed. J.H. Stonehouse, London, 1935, p. 89), in addition to the *Report on a General Scheme for Extramural Sepultre,* 1850, and J.D. Parry, *Urban Burial: the London Churchyards, with Suggestions for joint Parochial Cemeteries in Town and Country,* 1847.

G.A. Walker, The Second of a Series of Lectures on the Actual Condition of the Metropolitan Graveyards, *London, 1847, pp. 6-9.*

Let us now enter upon the examination of a locality that first excited my attention, and led to my subsequent inquiries: —

The Portugal Street burial-ground, known also by the singular name of the 'Green-ground', is a small patch of land about one-third of an acre in superficial extent. In this place the father of jokes, Joe Miller, has a gravestone erected to his memory. Situated at the top of Clement's Lane, Strand, in the vicinity of Clare Market and a shambles, and immediately behind one of our metropolitan hospitals, it has been used as a burying-place beyond the memory of man.

As the numbers annually buried in this ground are nearly ten times as many as they ought to be, you will not be surprised to hear that it is saturated with human putrescence, — that the necessity of obtaining room gives rise to the most revolting indecencies. Of some of them I have been an eye-witness. I have seen the heaps of coffin wood — of wood with perfectly fresh cloth covering; I have seen bones on the surface ready for removal; and I have experienced the effects of the effluvia which the ground almost constantly throws off from its surface. Others have witnessed similar desecration. A writer in the *Times,* who states that twelve of his nearest and dearest relations were buried in that ground, saw two men employed in carrying baskets of human bones from one portion of the burial-place to a small gate; and pertinently asks, where does this gate lead to?

James Lane, of No. 30, Clements Lane, who gave evidence before the Parliamentary Committee (question 717), being asked, What is the mode of interment practised? answered, digging a shallow grave at times, and then a few weeks afterwards they will go a good depth. There was one occasion when my wife noticed it more than at any other time; there was a corpse buried on a Sunday from the hospital; there were two females following it; what made us take particular notice of it was, that they came from the hospital, and went out at the gate across the ground towards Clare Market, and then came back again to the hospital. In the course of about a month afterwards they opened this grave again, and when they opened it they brought the coffin up in pieces, not split, but the sides were taken from the head and foot-board; they brought it up without splitting, just as you might take a case to pieces, or the lid off a box. After they had brought up the lid, and laid it on the ground, they brought up the bones with the flesh hanging in tatters upon it; then about four shovels full of soft substance came up, and my wife called to the person in the next room to witness the thing; they called out to the men; the men made them no answer, but turned their backs towards the houses to try to avoid the people seeing it, but the window being high, we could see every thing that came out of the grave as plainly almost as if we had been close to them; they were not far off.

Lane also stated that he has been repeatedly awakened in the morning by the noise of men breaking up the coffins in order to make room for the dead and fire-wood for the living. Many times he and his wife have seen a coffin disturbed; that is to say, cut through and broken up within six weeks after it was put down. Colonel Fox asked him, 'What became of the contents of the coffin?' The answer is worthy of record, — 'It is mixed with the mould. The body, which was brought up piece-meal, with the flesh hanging to the bones, and stuff brought up in shovels with-out bones, was let down in a solid lump again on the top of the coffin; and the women called out to the men, and told them they had better take people's money out of their pockets, and not bury the dead at all, or bury them without a coffin. It is a shocking place for disturbing the dead.'

Michael Pye, the grave-digger, fully corroborated the evidence given by Lane; and, here let me remark, that if reference is so fre-quently made to grave-diggers, it is because persons of that class are precisely those most likely to be acquainted with the *day* and *night* doings of the 'managers' of the dead. This Pye proved that in the 'Green-ground' the diggers were compelled to find a grave, no matter how, or where, or what lay beneath the spade. When even these wretched men evinced some compunction, some faint glimmering of decency or moral feeling, epithets the most dis-gusting and approbious were applied to them.

William Chamberlain, who was connected with this same ground for many years, enables us to reveal its secrets still more completely. The evidence of this man, an eye-witness of all that he relates, is so crushing that I must beg permission to refer to it at some length. For seven years Chamberlain never opened a grave in the Portugal Street ground 'without coming into other coffins of children, grown persons, and what are termed in grave-yard *parlance*, "odd sizes"'. These were indiscriminately cut through, and the bodies in them so perfect that males were distinguishable from females, were chopped and cut up, with tools specially made for the purpose. Oftentimes were the mutilated remains thrown up behind the boards on which the mourners were supported, and after the farce of burial was concluded, the flesh was thrown into the recent grave, and the coffins taken away for fire-wood. This abominable practice, it seems, was peculiarly applied to children.

'I have taken up', says Chamberlain, 'the children and moved them within a week after they were buried, and placed them in a different spot, not above a foot-and-a-half deep; sometimes I have placed them nowhere. It was done by orders.'

This placing 'nowhere' consisted in breaking up the coffins, cutting the flesh into pieces, and then burying it wherever a hole could be found. For the above horrid purpose, there were, as I have informed you, suitable instruments provided, instruments never required for digging a grave.

In 1843, a disgraceful scene, which nearly gave rise to an outbreak of public violence, occurred in this ground. The body of a man named Jacob Burns, respectable and once wealthy, was brought for interment; as he was poor, the grave-diggers thought that 'a hole' would suffice instead of a grave. They endeavoured by means of heavy logs of wood to force the coffin into the place they had prepared for it, but were prevented by the spectators, whose indignation became aroused; and no wonder that indignation should manifest itself, for when the eldest daughter of the deceased, with tears in her eyes, implored the grave-digger not to insult the remains of her father, the only reply she received was, 'where is your black?'

Fearing violence from the excited multitude, they thrust the coffin upright into the hole, and having covered it with a sprinkling of earth, left it with the head close to the surface. This unseemly method of disposing of an old and respectable inhabitant of the parish so irritated the numbers who had crowded into the church-yard, that the officials became alarmed, sent for the authorities, and gave a public promise that the body of Mr. Burns should be interred on the following day in a decent manner. The grave-diggers were at work before daylight on the following morning; yet, with their best 'management', the lid of the coffin was only one foot eight inches from the surface.

Such is the condition of the 'Green-ground', — such the deeds perpetrated in a so-called sanctuary of the dead. Yet at one extremity of this ground, so situated that the living invalids are compelled to breathe the putrid miasmata of this charnel-house, has an hospital been established for the cure of disease.

How long will those in authority violate the simplest laws of Public Health? If the atmosphere of a grave-yard be disgusting to persons in health, and injurious to all who inhale it, what shall we say of the policy that exposes the sick and the dying to its influence?

23

Bermondsey, particularly the area known as Jacob's Island, was another district of London which contained notorious living conditions. The decrepit, crowded houses of Jacob's Island occupied the site of an old Grange which had adjoined Bermondsey Abbey. They were surrounded not by a running stream, but by a stagnant ditch, into which Thames water was sparingly introduced a couple of times a week. As Beames emphasises, 'this circumambient pond is *the common sewer of the neighbourhood, and the only source from which the wretched inhabitants can get the water which they drink — with which they wash — and with which they cook their victuals*' (*The Rookeries of London*, p. 81). Unsurprisingly, the earliest fatal cases in the cholera epidemics of 1832 and 1849 occurred there.

Jacob's Island, 'the filthiest, the strangest, the most extraordinary of the many localities that are hidden in London' (*Oliver Twist*, Chapter 50), provided Dickens with a melodramatic setting for Sykes's death. Yet though he describes the abhorrent practice of obtaining domestic water supplies from the ditch, the squalor and tainted air of the tiny rooms, and speaks of 'every repulsive lineament of poverty, every loathsome indication of filth, rot, and garbage', the focus of the chapter falls not so much on social protest as on the excitement of the search for the murderer of Nancy, and the desperation of the murderer himself.

But the description came to have a wider currency. It was borrowed wholesale by J. Saunders, writing on 'Modern Bermondsey' in Charles Knight's *London*, III, p. 20; 'the features which this spot presents are described so vividly, and with such close accuracy, that we cannot do better than quote the passage ...'

The degree to which the area was, as Dickens claimed at the opening of Chapter 50, 'wholly unknown, even by name, to the great mass of [London's] inhabitants' was emphasised by a meeting of the Marylebone vestry in 1850, where Sir Peter Laurie, Master of the Saddler's Company, a former Lord Mayor, and satirised by Dickens in *The Chimes*, referred to a recent speech which the Bishop of London had made when chairing the first meeting of the Metropolitan Sanitary Association, at which Dickens himself had been the principle speaker. '"The Bishop of London, poor soul", said Sir Peter "in his simplicity, thought there really was such a place ... whereas it turned out that it only existed in a work of fiction, written by Mr Charles Dickens ten years ago."' For a full account of the relevant meeting of the Metropolitan Sanitary Association, see *The Speeches of Charles Dickens*, edited by K.J. Fielding, Oxford, 1960, pp. 104-10.

The fullest exposé of the district was made by Henry Mayhew, in his article 'The Cholera Districts of Bermondsey', *Morning Chronicle*, 24 September 1849. Charles Kingsley was moved and inspired by this as he worked on the novel which was to become *Alton Locke*. He travelled up to London to see the cholera districts of Bermondsey with his own eyes, and wrote to his wife:

Oh, that I had the tongue of St. James, to plead for those poor fellows! To tell what I saw myself, to stir up some rich men to go and rescue them from the tyranny of the small shopkeeping landlords, who get their rents out of the flesh and blood of these men ... Oh, that one-tenth part of the money which has been spent in increasing, by mistaken benevolence, the cruelties of the slave-trade, had been spent in buying up these nests of typhus, consumption, and cholera, and rebuilding them into habitations fit — I do not say for civilised Englishmen — that would be too much, but for hogs even (Charles Kingsley: *His Letters and Memories of his Life*, edited by his wife, 2 vols, London, 1877, I, pp. 216-17).

He asked his wife to use family connections in order to apply pressure in Parliament; involved himself with the establishment of a cart to supply fresh water in the Bermondsey streets, and corresponded with Lord Carlisle, known for his concern over public health and sanitation, Lord John Russell, the Bishop of Oxford, and other public figures. Additionally, he incorporated a lurid description of Jacob's Island in Chapter XXXV of *Alton Locke*. This, however, culminates in an impassioned rhetorical plea — 'Go through Bermondsey or Spitalfields, St Giles's or Lambeth, and see if *there* is not foul play enough already — to be tried hereafter at a more awful coroner's inquest than thou thinkest of!' The mannered anger of this counter-productively distances the impact of such specific details as Mayhew provides.

Henry Mayhew (1812-87) began his writing career as a dramatist, and, in addition to the sociological and philanthropic writing for which he is best known, produced travel books, biographies, novels and treatises on popular science. Writing first for the *Morning Chronicle*, between September 1849 and February 1850, and then collecting further material which went to form his mammoth *London Labour and the London Poor*, reissued in 1861, 1862, 1864 and 1865 with numerous additions and supplementary volumes, Mayhew's methodology combined statistics, minute social observation, and portraits of individual men and women, written up as though he were directly transcribing their speech in answer to his questions.

See the introductory chapters to *The Unknown Mayhew: Selections from the 'Morning Chronicle' 1849-1850*, edited and introduced by E.P. Thompson and Eileen Yeo, London 1971, and Anne Humphreys, *Travels into the Poor Man's Country: The Work of Henry Mayhew*, London, 1977.

Unsigned article [Henry Mayhew], 'A Visit to the Cholera Districts of Bermondsey', Morning Chronicle, 24 September 1849, p. 4.

There is an Eastern fable which tells us that a certain city was infested by poisonous serpents that killed all they fastened upon; and the citizens, thinking them sent from Heaven as a scourge for their sins, kept praying that the visitation might be removed from them, until scarcely a house remained unsmitten. At length, however, concludes the parable, the eyes of the people were opened; for, after all their prayers and fastings, they found that the eggs of the poisonous serpents were hatched in the muck-heaps that surrounded their own dwellings.

The history of the late epidemic, which now seems to have almost spent its fatal fury upon us, has taught us that the masses of filth and corruption round the metropolis are, as it were, the nauseous nests of plague and pestilence. Indeed, so well known are the localities of fever and disease, that London would almost admit of being mapped out pathologically, and divided into its morbid districts and deadly cantons. We might lay our fingers on the Ordnance map, and say here is the typhoid parish, and there the ward of cholera; for as truly as the West-end rejoices in the title of Belgravia, might the southern shores of the Thames be christened Pestilentia. As season follows season, so does disease follow disease in the quarters that may be more literally than metaphorically styled the plague-spots of London. If the seasons are favourable, and typhus does not bring death to almost every door, then influenza and scarlatina fill the workhouses with the families of the sick. So certain and regular are the diseases in their returns, that each epidemic, as it comes back summer after summer, breaks out in the self-same streets as it appeared on its former visit, with but this slight difference, that if at its last visitation it began at the top of the street, and killed its way down, this time it begins at the bottom, and kills its way as surely up the lines of houses.

Out of the 12,800 deaths which, within the last three months, have arisen from cholera, 6,500 have occurred on the southern shores of the Thames; and to this awful number no localities have contributed so largely as Lambeth, Southwark and Bermondsey, each, at the height of the disease, adding its hundred victims a week to the fearful catalogue of mortality. Any one who has ventured a visit to the last-named of these places in particular, will not wonder at the ravages of the pestilence in this malarious quarter, for it is bounded on the north and east by filth and fever, and on the south and west by want, squalor, rags and pestilence. Here stands, as it were, the very capital of cholera, the Jessore of London — JACOB'S ISLAND, a patch of ground insulated by the common sewer. Spared by the fire of London, the houses and comforts of the people in this loathsome place have scarcely known any improvement since that time. The place is a century behind even the low and squalid districts that surround it.

In the days of Henry II, the foul stagnant ditch that now makes an island of this pestilential spot, was a running stream, supplied with the waters which poured down from the hills about Sydenham and Nunhead, and was used for the working of the mills that then stood on its banks. These had been granted by charter to the monks of St Mary and St John, to grind their flour, and were dependencies upon the Priory of Bermondsey. Tradition tells us that what is now a straw yard skirting the river, was once the City Ranelagh, called 'Cupid's Gardens', and that the trees, which are now black with mud, were the bowers under which the citizens loved, on the sultry summer evenings, to sit beside the stream drinking their sack and ale. But now the running brook is changed into a tidal sewer, in whose putrid filth staves are laid to season; and where the ancient summer-houses stood, nothing but hovels, sties, and muck-heaps are now to be seen.

Not far from the Tunnel there is a creek opening into the Thames. The entrance to this is screened by the tiers of colliers which lie before it. This creek bears the name of the Dock Head. Sometimes it is called St Saviour's, or, in jocular allusion to the odour for which it is celebrated, Savory Dock. The walls of the warehouses on each side of this muddy stream are green and slimy, and barges lie beside them, above which sacks of corn are continually dangling from the cranes aloft. This creek was once supplied by the streams from the Surrey hills, but now nothing but the drains and refuse of the houses that have grown up round about it thickens and swells its waters.

On entering the precincts of the pest island, the air has literally the smell of a graveyard, and a feeling of nausea and heaviness comes over any one unaccustomed to imbibe the musty atmosphere. It is not only the nose, but the stomach, that tells how heavily the air is loaded with sulphuretted hydrogen; and as soon as you cross one of the crazy and rotting bridges over the reeking ditch, you know, as surely as if you had chemically tested it, by the black colour of what was once the white-lead paint upon the door-posts and window-sills, that the air is thickly charged with this deadly gas. The heavy bubbles which now and then rise up in the water show you whence at least a portion of the mephitic compound comes, while the open doorless privies that hang over the water side on one of the banks, and the dark streaks of filth down the walls where the drains from each house discharge themselves into the ditch on the opposite side, tell you how the pollution of the ditch is supplied.

The water is covered with a scum almost like a cobweb, and prismatic with grease. In it float large masses of green rotting weed, and against the posts of the bridges are swollen carcasses of dead animals, almost bursting with the gases of putrefaction. Along its shores are heaps of indescribable filth, the phosphoretted smell from which tells you of the rotting fish there, while the oyster shells are like pieces of slate from their coating of mud and filth. In some parts the fluid is almost as red as blood from the colouring matter that pours into it from the reeking leather-dressers' close by.

The striking peculiarity of Jacob's Island consists in the wooden galleries and sleeping-rooms at the back of the houses which overhang the dark flood, and are built upon piles, so that the place has positively the air of a Flemish street, flanking a sewer instead of a canal; while the little ricketty bridges that span the ditches and connect court with court, give it the appearance of the Venice of drains, where channels before and behind the houses do duty for the ocean. Across some parts of the stream whole rooms have been built, so that house adjoins house; and here, with the very stench of death rising through the boards, human beings sleep night after night, until the last sleep of all comes upon them years before its time. Scarce a house but yellow linen is hanging to dry over the balustrade of staves, or else run out on a long oar where the sulphur-coloured clothes hang over the waters, and you are almost wonderstruck to see their form and colour unreflected in the putrid ditch beneath.

At the back of nearly every house that boasts a square foot or two of outlet — and the majority have none at all — are pig-sties. In front waddle ducks, while cocks and hens scratch at the cinder-heaps. Indeed, the creatures that fatten on offal are the only living things that seem to flourish here.

The inhabitants themselves show in their faces the poisonous influence of the mephitic air they breathe. Either their skins are white, like parchment, telling of the impaired digestion, the languid circulation, and the coldness of the skin peculiar to persons suffering from chronic poisoning, or else their cheeks are flushed hectically, and their eyes are glassy, showing the wasting fever and general decline of the bodily functions. The brown, earthlike complexion of some, and their sunk eyes, with the dark areolae round them, tell you that the sulphuretted hydrogen of the atmosphere in which they live has been absorbed into the blood; while others are remarkable for the watery eye exhibiting the increased secretion of tears so peculiar to those who are exposed to the exhalations of hydrosulphate of ammonia.

Scarcely a girl that has not suffusion and soreness of the eyes, so that you would almost fancy she had been swallowing small doses of arsenic; while it is evident from the irritation and discharge from the mucous membranes of the nose and eyes for which all the children are distinguished, that the poor emaciated things are suffering from continual inhalation of the vapour of carbonate of ammonia and other deleterious gases.

Nor was this to be wondered at, when the whole air reeked with the stench of rotting animal and vegetable matter; for the experiment of Professor Donovan has shown that a rabbit, with only its body enclosed in a bladder filled with sulphuretted hydrogen, and allowed to breathe freely, will die in ten minutes. Thénard also has proved that one eight hundredth part of this gas in the atmosphere is sufficient to destroy a dog, and one two hundred and fiftieth will kill a horse; while Mr Taylor, in his book on poisons, assures us that the men who were engaged in excavating the Thames Tunnel suffered severely during the work from the presence of this gas in the atmosphere in which they were obliged to labour. 'The air, as well as the water which trickled through the roof,' he tells us, 'was found to contain sulphuretted hydrogen. This was probably derived from the action of the iron pyrites in the clay. By respiring this atmosphere the strongest and most robust men were, in the course of a few months, reduced to a state of extreme exhaustion and died. They became emaciated, and fell into a state of low fever, accompanied with delirium. In one case which I saw,' he adds, 'the face of the man was pale, the lips of a violet hue, the eyes sunk and dark all round, and the whole muscular system flabby and emaciated.' To give the reader some idea as to the extent with which the air in Jacob's Island is charged with this most deadly compound, it will be sufficient to say that a silver spoon of which we caught sight in one of the least wretched dwellings was positively chocolate-coloured by the action of the sulphur on the metal.

On approaching the tidal ditch from the Neckinger-road, the shutters of the house at the corner were shut from top to bottom. Our intelligent and obliging guide, Dr Martin, informed us that a girl was then lying dead there from cholera, and that but very recently another victim had fallen in the house adjoining it. This was the beginning of the tale of death, for the tidal ditch was filled up to this very point. Here, however, its putrefying waters were left to mingle their poison with the 267 cubic feet of air that each man daily takes into his lungs, and this was the point whence the pestilence commenced its ravages. As we walked down George-row, our informant told us that at the corner of London-street he could see, a short time back, as many as nine houses in which there were one or two persons lying dead of the cholera at the same time; and yet there could not have been more than a dozen tenements visible from the spot.

We crossed the bridge, and spoke to one of the inmates. In answer to our questions, she told us she was never well. Indeed, the signs of the deadly influence of the place were painted in the earthy complexion of the poor woman. 'Neither I nor my children know what health is', said she. 'But what is one to do? We must live where our bread is. I've tried to let the house, and put a bill up, but cannot get any one to take it.' From this spot we were led to narrow close courts, where the sun never shone, and the air seemed almost as stagnant and putrid as the ditch we had left. The blanched cheeks of the people that now came out to stare at us, were white as vegetables grown in the dark, and as we stopped to look down the alley, our informant told us that the place teemed with children, and that if a horn was blown they would swarm like bees at the sound of a gong. The houses were mostly inhabited by 'corn-runners', coal-porters, and 'longshore-men', getting a precarious living — earning some times as much as 12s. a day, and then for weeks doing nothing. Fevers prevailed in these courts we were told more than at the side of the ditch.

By this way we reached a dismal stack of hovels called, by a strange incongruity, Pleasant-row. Inquiring of one of the inmates, we were informed that they were quite comfortable now! The stench had been all removed, said the woman, and we were invited to pass to the back-yard as evidence of the fact. We did so; the boards bent under our feet, and the air in the cellar-like yard was fœtid to positive nausea. As we left the house a child sat nursing a dying half-comatose baby on a door step. The skin of its little arms, instead of being plumped out with health, was loose and shrivelled, like an old crone's, and had a flabby monkey-like appearance more than the character of human cuticle. The almost jaundiced colour of the child's skin, its half paralyzed limbs, and state of stupor told it was suffering from some slow poison; indeed the symptoms might readily have been mistaken for those of chronic poisoning from acetate of lead. At the end of this row our friend informed us that the last house on either side was *never* free from fever.

Continuing our course we reached 'The Folly', another street so narrow that the names and trades of the shopmen were

painted on boards that stretched, across the street, from the roof
of their own houses to that of their neighbour's. We were here
stopped by our companion in front of a house 'to let'. The building was as narrow and as unlike a human habitation as the
wooden houses in a child's box of toys. 'In this house', said our
friend, 'when the scarlet fever was raging in the neighbourhood,
the barber who was living here suffered fearfully from it; and no
sooner did the man get well of this than he was seized with
typhus, and scarcely had he recovered from the first attack than
he was struck down a second time with the same terrible disease.
Since then he has lost his child with cholera, and at this moment
his wife is in the workhouse suffering from the same affliction.
The only wonder is that they are not all dead, for as the man sat
at his meals in his small shop, if he put his hand against the wall
behind him, it would be covered with the soil of his neighbour's
privy, sopping through the wall. At the back of the house was an
open sewer, and the privies were full to the seat.'

One fact, says an eminent writer in toxicology, is worthy of the
attention of medical jurists, namely, that the respiration of an
atmosphere only slightly impregnated with the gases emanating
from drains and sewers, may, if long continued, seriously affect
an individual and cause death. M. D'Arcet had to examine a
lodging in Paris, in which three young and vigorous men had
died successively in the course of a few years, under similar
symptoms. The lodging consisted of a bed-room with a chimney,
and an ill-ventilated ante-room. The pipe of a privy passed down
one side of the room, by the head of the bed, and the wall in this
part was damp from infiltration. At the time of the examination
there was no perceptible smell in the room, though it was small
and low. M. D'Arcet attributed the mortality in the lodging to the
slow and long-continued action of the emanations from the pipe
(Ann. d'Hyg., Juillet, 1836).

We then journeyed on to London-street, down which the tidal
ditch continues its course. In No. 1 of this street the cholera first
appeared seventeen years ago, and spread up it with fearful virulence; but this year it appeared at the opposite end, and ran
down it with like severity. As we passed along the reeking banks
of the sewer the sun shone upon a narrow slip of the water. In the
bright light it appeared the colour of strong green tea, and positively looked as solid as black marble in the shadow — indeed it
was more like watery mud than muddy water; and yet we were
assured this was the only water the wretched inhabitants had to

drink. As we gazed in horror at it, we saw drains and sewers emptying their filthy contents into it; we saw a whole tier of door-less privies in the open road, common to men and women, built over it; we heard bucket after bucket of filth splash into it, and the limbs of the vagrant boys bathing in it seemed, by pure force of contrast, white as Parian marble. And yet, as we stood doubting the fearful statement, we saw a little child, from one of the galleries opposite, lower a tin can with a rope to fill a large bucket that stood beside her. In each of the balconies that hung over the stream the self-same tub was to be seen in which the inhabitants put the mucky liquid to stand, so that they may, after it has rested for a day or two, skim the fluid from the solid particles of filth, pollution, and disease. As the little thing dangled her tin cup as gently as possible into the stream, a bucket of night-soil was poured down from the next gallery.

In this wretched place we were taken to a house where an infant lay dead of the cholera. We asked if they *really did* drink the water? The answer was, 'They were obliged to drink the ditch, without they could beg a pailfull or thieve a pailfull of water.' But have you spoken to your landlord about having it laid on for you? 'Yes, sir; and he says he'll do it, and do it, but we know him better than to believe him.' 'Why, sir', cried another woman, who had shot out from an adjoining room, 'he won't even give us a little whitewash, though we tell him we'll willingly do the work ourselves: and look here, sir', she added, 'all the tiles have fallen off, and the rain pours in wholesale.'

We had scarcely left the house when a bill caught our eye, announcing that 'this valuable estate' was to be sold!

From this spot we crossed the little shaky bridge into Providence-buildings — a narrow neck of land set in sewers. Here, in front of the houses, were small gardens that a table-cloth would have covered. Still the one dahlia that here raised its round red head made it a happier and brighter place. Never was colour so grateful to the eye. All we had looked at had been so black and dingy, and had smelt so much of churchyard clay, that this little patch of beauty was brighter and greener than ever was oasis in the desert. Here a herd of children came out, and stared at us like sheep. One child our guide singled out from the rest. She had the complexion of tawed leather, and her bright, glassy eyes were sunk so far back in her head, that they looked more like lights shining through the hollow sockets of a skull than a living head, and her bones seemed ready to start through the thin layer of skin. We were told she had had the cholera twice. Her father was dead of it. 'But she, sir', said a woman addressing us, 'won't die. Ah! if she'd had plenty of victuals and been brought up less hardy she would have been dead and buried long ago, like many more. And here's another', she added, pushing forward a long thin woman in rusty black. 'Why I've know'd her eat as much as a quartern loaf at a meal, and you can't fatten her no how.' Upon this there was a laugh, but in the woman's bloodless cheeks and blue lips we saw that she like the rest was wasting away from the influence of the charnel-like atmosphere around her.

The last place we went to was in Joiner's-court, with four wooden houses in it, in which there had lately been as many as five cases of cholera. In front, the poor souls, as if knowing by an instinct that plants were given to purify the atmosphere, had pulled up the paving-stones before their dwellings, and planted a few stocks here and there in the rich black mould beneath. The first house we went to, a wild ragged-headed-boy shot out in answer to our knock, and putting his hands across the doorway, stood there to prevent our entrance. Our friend asked whether he could enter, and see the state of the drainage? 'No; t'ain't con-venient', was the answer, given so quickly and sharply, that the lad forced some ugly and uncharitable suspicion upon us. In the next house, the poor inmate was too glad to meet with any one ready to sympathise with her sufferings. We were taken up into a room, where we were told she had positively lived for nine years. The window was within four feet of a high wall, at the foot of which, until very recently, ran the open common sewer. The room was so dark that it was several minutes before we could see anything within it, and there was a smell of must and dry rot that told of damp and imperfect ventilation, and the unnatural size of the pupils of the wretched woman's eyes convinced us how much too long she had dwelt in this gloomy place.

Here, as usual, we heard stories that made one's blood curdle, of the cruelty of those from whom they rented the sties called dwellings. They had begged for pure water to be laid on, and the rain to be shut out; and the answer for eighteen years had been, that the lease was just out. 'They knows its handy for a man's work', said one and all, 'and that's the reason why they impose on a body.' This, indeed, seems to us to be the great evil. Out of these wretches' health, comfort, and even lives, small capitalists reap a petty independence; and until the poor are rescued from the fangs of these mercenary men, there is but little hope either for their physical or moral welfare.

The extreme lassitude and deficient energy of both body and mind induced by the mephitic vapours they continually inhale leads them — we may say, *forces* them to seek an unnatural stimulus in the gin-shop; indeed, the publicans of Jacob's Island drive even a more profitable trade than the landlords themselves. What wonder, then, since debility is one of the predisposing conditions of cholera, that — even if these stenches of the foul tidal ditch be not the *direct* cause of the disease — that the impaired digestive functions, the languid circulation, the depression of mind produced by the continued inhalation of the noxious gases of the tidal ditch, together with the intemperance that it induces — the cold, damp houses — and, above all, the quenching of the thirst and cooking of the food with water saturated with the very excrements of their fellow creatures, should make Jacob's Island notorious as the Jessore of England.

24

Henry Mayhew's investigations of the London tailoring trade influenced Charles Kingsley's writing of *Alton Locke*, as well as directly informing Kingsley's pamphlet attacking the slop system, *Cheap Clothes and Nasty*, published in 1850 under the pseudonym of Parson Lot. Chapters II and X of *Alton Locke* are those which deal most extensively with the tailors' grievance. The danger of contagion spreading from the conditions in which garments are made is built into the plot. Locke's cousin dies of typhus fever, its infection spread by his new coat, which had earlier been used to cover three corpses in the Bermondsey house where it was made. This detail came from a report about the conditions of their trade instituted by the tailors themselves in 1844, and quoted by Mayhew in the 18th of his series of letters 'Labour and the Poor: The Metropolitan Districts' in the *Morning Chronicle*, 18 December 1849, pp. 4-5. In December 1849, Kingsley wrote to J.M. Ludlow, barrister and philanthropist: 'Borrow or buy the *Morning Chronicle* articles, and send me them, and I will reimburse you; at least send me the *Tailor* one by return of post' (*Letters and Memorials of his Life*, I, p. 224). Ludlow's own piece based on the

Morning Chronicle articles, 'Labour and the Poor', appeared in *Fraser's Magazine*, XLI, January 1850, pp. 1-18.

Kingsley's pamphlet, as well as providing evidence of working and living conditions, makes several suggestions about how things may be improved. First, 'no man who calls himself a Christian — no man who calls himself a man — should ever disgrace himself by dealing at any show-shop or slop-shop' (Charles Kingsley, 'Cheap Clothes and Nasty', *The Life and Works of Charles Kingsley*, Library Edition, London, 1901-3, VII, p. 75). Second, he advocates a dozen, or fifty, or a hundred journeymen saying to one another: 'It is competition that is ruining us, and competition in division, disunion, every man for himself, every man against his brother. The remedy must be in association, co-operation, self-sacrifice for the sake of one another' (*Life and Works*, p. 76), establishing a workshop and retail outlet of their own with prices as low as in the shops. This is the very type of scheme which is praised so warmly by Eleanor to Locke towards the end of the novel (Chapter XL), left 'as seed, to grow by itself in many forms, in many minds' (Charles Kingsley to J.M. Ludlow, August 1850, in Thomas Hughes, 'Prefatory Memoir', *Life and Works*, VII, p. 20). In *Cheap Clothes and Nasty*, Kingsley played on the same sense of fear as motivated Beames when he begged for urgent change:

The continual struggle of competition, not only in the tailors' trade, but in every one which is not, like the navigator's or engineer's, at a premium from its novel and extraordinary demand, will weaken and undermine more and more the masters, who are already many of them speculating on borrowed capital, while it will depress the workman to a point at which life will become utterly intolerable; increasing education will serve only to make them the more conscious of their own misery; the boiler will be strained to bursting pitch, till some jar, some slight crisis, suddenly directs the imprisoned forces to one point, and then —
What then?
Look at France, and see.
(*Life and Works*, VII, pp. 79-80)

Unsigned article [Henry Mayhew], Letter VI, Morning Chronicle, 6 November 1849, pp. 4-5.

I had seen so much want since I began my investigation into the condition of the labouring poor of London that my feelings were almost blunted to sights of ordinary misery. Still I was unprepared for the amount of suffering that I have lately witnessed. I could not have believed that there were human beings toiling so long and gaining so little, and starving so silently and heroically, round about our very homes. It is true, one or two instances of the kind had forced themselves into the police reports, and songs and plays had been written upon the privations of the class; still it was impossible to believe that the romance of the song-writer and the fable of the playwright were plain, unvarnished, everyday matters of fact — or, even admitting their stories to be individually true, we could hardly credit them to be universally true. But the reader shall judge for himself. I will endeavour to reproduce the scenes I have lately looked upon — and I will strive to do so in all their stark literality. It is difficult, I know, for those who are unacquainted with the misery hiding itself in the by-lanes and alleys of the metropolis to have perfect faith in the tales that it is my duty to tell them. Let me therefore once more assure the sceptical reader, that hardly a line is written here but a note was taken of the matter upon the spot. The descriptions of the dwellings and the individuals I allude to have all been written with the very places and parties before me; and the story of the people's sufferings is repeated to the public in the self same words in which they were told to me. Still it may be said that I myself have been imposed upon — that I may have been taken to extreme cases, and given to understand that they are the ordinary types of the class. This, I am ready to grant, is a common source of error; I will therefore now explain the means that I adopted, in this instance in particular, to prevent myself being deluded into any such fallacy.

My first step was to introduce myself to one of the largest 'slop-sellers' at the East-end of the town; and having informed the firm that I was about to examine into the condition and incomings of the slopworkers of London, I requested to know whether they would have any objection to furnish me with the list of prices that they were in the habit of paying to their workpeople, so that on my visiting the parties themselves — as I frankly gave them to understand I purposed doing — I might be able to compare the operatives' statements as to prices with theirs, and thus be able to check the one with the other. Indeed, I said I thought it but fair that the employer should have an opportunity of having his say as well as the employed. I regret to say that I was not met with the candour that I had been led to expect. One of the firm wished to know why I singled their house out from the rest of the trade. I told him I did so merely because it was one of the largest in the business, and assured him that, so far from my having any personal object in my visit, I made it a point never to allude by name to any employer or workman to whom I might have occasion to refer. My desire, I said, was to deal with principles rather than persons; whereupon I was informed that the firm would have no objection to acquaint me with the prices paid by *other* houses in the trade. 'If you merely wish to arrive at the principle of the slop business, this,' said one of the partners, 'will be quite sufficient for your purpose.' Though I pressed for some more definite and particular information from the firm, I could obtain nothing from them but an assurance that a statement should be written out for me immediately as to the general custom of the trade, and that, if I would call at any time after sunset on Saturday evening, it should be at my disposal. I soon saw that it was useless seeking to obtain any further information from the parties in question — so, taking my departure, I made the best of my way to the workmen in the neighbourhood. My time being limited, I consulted with a gentleman who is thoroughly conversant with the character of several of the operatives, as to the best and fairest means of taking an unprejudiced view of the state of the slopworkers of London; and it was agreed between us, that as the work was performed by both males and females, it would be better first to direct my attention to the state of the male 'hands' employed by the trade; while, in order to arrive at an accurate estimate as to the incomings and condition of the class generally, it was deemed better to visit some place where several of the operatives were in the habit of working together, so that the opinions of a number of individuals might be taken simultaneously upon the subject.

Accordingly I was led, by the gentleman whose advice I had sought, to a narrow court, the entrance to which was blocked up by stalls of fresh herrings. We had to pass sideways between the baskets with our coat-tails under our arms. At the end of the passage we entered a dirty-looking house by a side entrance. Though it was midday, the staircase was so dark that we were forced to grope our way by the wall up to the first floor. Here, in a small back room, about eight feet square, we found no fewer than seven workmen, with their coats and shoes off, seated cross-legged on the floor, busy stitching the different parts of different garments. The floor was strewn with sleeve-boards, irons, and snips of various coloured cloths. In one corner of the room was a turn-up bedstead, with the washed out chintz curtains drawn partly in front of it. Across a line which ran from one side of the apartment to the other were thrown the coats, jackets, and cravats of the workmen. Inside the rusty grate was a hat, and on one side of the hobs rested a pair of old cloth boots, while leaning against the bars in front there stood a sackful of cuttings. Beside the workmen on the floor sat two good-looking girls — one cross-legged like the men — engaged in tailoring.

My companion having acquainted the workmen with the object of my visit, they one and all expressed themselves ready to answer any questions that I might put to them. They made dress and frock coats, they told me, Chesterfields, fishing-coats, paletots, Buller's monkey jackets, beavers, shooting coats, trousers, vests, sacks, Codringtons, Trinity cloaks and coats, and indeed, every other kind of woollen garment. They worked for the ready-made houses, or 'slopsellers'. 'One of us,' said they, 'gets work from the warehouse, and gives it out to others. The houses pay different prices. Dress coats, from 5s. 6d. to 6s. 9d.; frock coats the same; shooting coats, from 2s. 6d. to 2s. 9d. In summertime, when trade is busy, they pay 3s. Chesterfields, from 2s. 6d. to 3s., some are made for 2s.; paletots, from 2s. 6d. to 3s.' 'Aye, and two days' work for any man', cried one of the tailors with a withered leg, 'and buy his own trimmings, white and black cotton, gimp, and pipe-clay.' 'Yes,' exclaimed another, 'and we have to buy wadding for dress coats; and soon, I suppose, we shall have to buy cloth and all together.' Trousers, from 1s. 6d. to 3s.; waistcoats, from 1s. 6d. to 1s. 9d. Dress and frock coats will take two days and a half to make each, calculating the day from six in the morning till seven at night; but three days is the regular time. Shooting coats will take two days; Chesterfields take the same as dress and frock coats; paletots, two days; trousers, one day.

'The master here' (said one of them scarcely distinguishable from the rest) 'gets work from the warehouse at the before-mentioned prices; he gives it out to us at the same price, paying us when he receives the money. We are never seen at the shop. Out of the prices the master here deducts 4s. per week per head for our cup of tea or coffee in the morning, and tea in the evening, and our bed. We sleep two in a bed here, and some of us three. In most places the workmen eat, drink, and sleep in one room; as

many as ever the room will contain. They'd put 20 in one room if
they could.' 'I should like to see the paper this'll be printed in,'
cried the man with the withered leg. 'Oh, it'll be a good job, it
should be known. We should be glad if the whole world heard it,
so that the people should know our situation. I've worked very
hard this week, as hard as any man. I've worked from seven in the
morning till 11 at night, and my earnings will be 13s. this week;
and deducting my 4s. out of that, and my trimmings besides —
the trimmings comes to about 1s. 9d. per week — which makes
5s. 9d. altogether, and that will leave me 7s. 3d. for my earnings
all the week, Sunday included. It's very seldom we has a Sunday
walking out. We're obliged to work on Sunday all the same. We
should lose our shop if we didn't. Eight shillings is the average
wages, take the year all through. Out of this 8s. we have to deduct
expenses of lodging, trimming, washing, and light, which comes
to 5s. 9d. We can't get a coat to our backs.'

I inquired as to the earnings of the others. 'Well, it's nearly
just the same, take one with another, all the year round. We work
all about the same hours — all the lot of us. The wages are lower
than they were this time twelvemonth, in 1848 — that they are,
by far, and heavier work too. I think there's a fall of 6d. in each
job at the lowest calculation.'

'An, that there is', said another; 'a 3s. job we don't have 2s. 6d.
for now.'

'Yes, it's causing half of the people,' cried a third, 'to be thieves
and robbers. That's true. Wages were higher in 1847 — they're
coming down now every year. The coats that they used to pay 5s.
for this time two years, they are making for 3s. 6d. at present —
the very same work, but a deal heavier than it was two years ago.
This time twelvemonth we made coats for 7s., and 5s. this year is
all we has for the same. Prices have come down more than a
quarter — indeed about half, during these last 10 years. I'm sure
I don't know what's the cause of it. The master first says, I can't
give no more than such a price for making such an article. Then
the man objects to it, and says he can't live by it; as soon as he
objects to it, the master will give him no more work. We really are
the prey of the master, and cannot help ourselves. Whatever he
offers we are obliged to accept, or else go starve.' 'Yes, yes', said
they all, 'that's the real fact. And if we don't take his offer, somebody else will, that's the truth, for we have no power to stand out
against it. The workhouse won't have us — we must either go
thieve, or take the price in the long run. There's a standing price

in the regular trade, but not in this. The regular trade is 6d. an hour. The regulars work only from six in the morning till seven at night, and only do 'bespoke' work. But we are working for the slop shops or warehouses, and they keep a large stock of ready-made goods. We're called under-the-bed workers, or workers for the "sweaters". All the persons who work for wholesale houses are "sweaters". Single workmen cannot get the work from them, because they cannot give security — £5 in money, or a shop-keeper must be responsible to that amount. Those who cannot give security are obliged to work for "sweaters". The reason for the warehouses requiring this security is, because they pay so badly for the work they are afraid to trust the journeyman with it. But in the regular trade, such as at the West-end, they require no security, whatever. In the slop trade the journeymen do not keep Monday — they can't do it, Sunday nor Monday either — if they do they must want for food. Since we've been working at the slop trade we find ourselves far worse off than when we were working at the regular trade. The journeymen of the slop trade are unable to earn 13s. where the regular journeyman can earn 30s., and then we have to find our own trimmings and candlelight. I'd sooner be transported than at this work. Why, then, at least, I'd have regular hours for work and for sleep; but now I'm harder worked and worse fed than a cab-horse.'

During my stay in this quarter an incident occurred, which may be cited as illustrative of the poverty of the class of slop-workers. The friend who had conducted me to the spot, and who knew the workmen well, had long been striving to induce one of the men — a Dutchman — to marry one of the females working with him in the room, and with whom he had been living for many months. That the man might raise no objection on the score of poverty, my friend requested me to bear with him half the expense of publishing the banns. To this I readily consented, but the man still urged that he was unable to wed the girl just yet. On inquiring the reason we were taken outside the door by the Dutchman, and there told that he had been forced to pawn his coat for 6s., and as yet he had saved only half the amount towards the redemption of it. It would take him upwards of a month to lay by the remainder. This was literally the fact, and the poor fellow said, with a shrug of his shoulders, he could not go to be married in his shirt sleeves. He was told to make himself easy about the wedding-garment, and our kind-hearted friend left delighted with the day's work.

I now wished to learn from some of the female operatives what prices they were paid, and requested my friend to introduce me to some workwoman who might be considered as one of the most provident, industrious, and best conducted in the trade. The woman bears, I understand, an excellent character, and she gave the following melancholy account of her calling: — She makes various kinds of garments. Scarcely a garment that is to be made but what she makes; works for various slop-sellers; makes shirts, drawers, trousers, blouses, duck frocks, sou'-westers, and oilskin waterproof coats, some in a rough state in the calico before they're oil'd, and others after they're oil'd. Works first hand. For shirts she gets 2s. to 6s. a dozen, that's the highest; there are some lower than that, but she generally refuses those. The lowest are 1s. a dozen, or only a penny each. Of the 2s. a dozen she can make about three in the day — the day being from eight in the morning to ten in the evening. She usually makes 18 in the week. Shirtmaking is generally considered the worst work — has to find all her own trimmings, all the thread and cotton, everything, excepting the buttons, out of the 2s. a dozen. The price is paid for rowing shirts, called 'rowers', with full bosoms put in, just the same as the 6s. a dozen ones, only the work is not so good. Of the 6s. a dozen she can't make more than one in the day. They're white collars and wristbands. Has to find her own trimmings. Is forced to give security for about £5. Those who cannot get security must work for 'sweaters'. Flannel drawers are some 2s. 6d. a dozen, and some 3s. Some are coloured, and some are white flannel; the white are 3s., the coloured 2s. 6d. Has to find her own thread. Can do three pairs in a day — making 9d. at best work, or $7\frac{1}{2}$d. at worst, out of which there is to be deducted $1\frac{1}{2}$d. for one ounce of thread. Moleskin trousers, and beaverteen, like the other articles, vary in price. The lowest price for moleskin trousers is 6s. a dozen pair — the highest, 10s. The beaverteen the same. Can't make more than one pair of either the high or low priced ones in the day. The trimmings for each dozen pair come to 1s. 6d. The highest priced ones are all double stitched. Blouses are from 5s. to 7s. a dozen. Can't make two of the lowest price in the day. Might make one of the highest. Trimming for a dozen comes to about 6d., because it's chiefly cotton that is used in blouses. Duck frocks are 2s. to 2s. 6d. a dozen. May make about a dozen and a half of those in a week if she sits very close to it. 'During the course of years,' she said, 'that I have worked at the business, I find it's all alike. You can't earn much more at one kind of work than you can at another.' Sou'-westers are 10d. a dozen; from that to 3s. Can make one in a day of those at 3s., and of those at 10d. she makes half a dozen in the day. Oilskin water-proof coats, ready-dressed, are 1s. 6d. each; and the others, undressed, from 4s. to 6s. per dozen. She has to find all her trim-mings out of that. Can make one of those that are dressed in two days, and of those that are in the undressed state, a dozen in the week.

'Upon the average,' she says, 'at all kinds of work, excepting the shirts, that I make, I cannot earn more than 4s. 6d. to 5s. per week — let me sit from eight in the morning till ten every night; and out of that I shall have to pay 1s. 6d. for trimmings and 6d. candles every week; so that altogether I earn about 3s. in the six days. But I don't earn that, for there's the firing that you *must* have to press the work, and that will be 9d. a week, for you'll have to use half a hundredweight of coals. So that my clear earnings are a little bit more than 2s., say 2s. 3d. to 2s. 6d. every week. I consider the trousers the best work. At the highest price, which is 10s. a dozen, I should make no more than eight of them in a week; that would give me 6s. 8d. The trimmings of that eight pair would cost me 1s., the candles 6d., and the coals 9d., for pressing, leaving 4s. 5d. clear — and that is the very best kind of work that can be got in the slop trade. Shirt work is the worst work — the very worst, that can be got. You cannot make more of those at 6s. a dozen than one a day, yielding 3s. a week. The trimmings would be about 3d. for the shirts, and the candles 6d., as before, making 9d. to be deducted, and so leaving 2s. 3d. per week clear. I have known the prices much better when I first began to work at the business, some nineteen years ago. The shirts that they now give 6d. for were then 1s.; and those now at 2d., were 8d. The trousers were 1s. 4d. and 1s. 6d. a pair, the best — now they give only 10d. for the best. The other articles are down equally low.'

'I cannot say,' she added, 'what the cause may be. I think there are so many to work at it, that one will underwork the other. I have seen it so at the shop. The sweaters screw the people down as low as they possibly can, and the masters hear how little they can get their work done for, and cut down the sweaters, and so the workpeople have to suffer again. Every shop has a great number of sweaters. Sometimes the sweaters will get as much as 2d. or 3d.; indeed, I've known 'em take as much as 4d. out of each garment. I should suppose one that has a good many people to work for her — say about a dozen — I suppose that she'll clear from £1 to £1 5s. per week out of their labour. The workpeople are very dissatisfied, and very poor indeed — yes, *very* poor. There is a great deal of want, and there is a great deal of suffering amongst them. I hear it at the shop when I go in with my work. They have generally been brought up regularly to the trade. It requires an apprenticeship. In about three months a person may learn it, if they're quick; and persons pay from 10s. to £1 to be taught it, bad as the trade is. A mother has got two or three daughters, and she don't wish them to go to service, and she puts them to this poor needlework; and that, in my opinion, is the cause of the destitution and prostitution about the streets in these parts. So that in a great measure I think the slop trade is the ruin of the young girls that take to it — the prices are not sufficient to keep them, and the consequence is, they fly to the streets to make out their living. Most of the workers are young girls who have nothing else to depend upon, and there is scarcely one of them virtuous. When they come on first they are very meek and modest in their deportment, but after a little time they get connected with the others and led away. There are between 200 and 300 of one class and another work at my shop. I dare say of females altogether there are upwards of 200. Yesterday morning there were seventy-five in the shop with me, and that was at eight in the morning, and what there may be throughout the day it's impossible to form an idea. The age of the females in general is about fourteen to twenty.

'My daughter is a most excellent waistcoat hand. I can give you an account of her work, and then, of course, you can form an idea of what everybody else gets. The lowest price waistcoat is 3s. per dozen, and the highest 9s. They are satin ones. She can make one satin one per day, and three of the 3s. ones. She earns, upon an average, about 4s. per week; deduct from this, trimmings about 6d. for the lowest, and 1s. per week for the highest price. As we both sit to work together, one candle does for the two of us, so that she earns about 3s. per week clear, which is not sufficient to keep her even in food. My husband is a seafaring man, or I don't know what I should do. He is a particularly steady man, a tee-totaller, and so indeed are the whole family, or else we could not live. Recently my daughter has resigned the work and gone to service as the prices are not sufficient for food and clothing. I never knew a rise, but continual reductions. I know a woman who has six children, and she has to support them wholly on slop work. Her husband drinks, and does a day's work only now and then, spending more than he brings home. None of her children are able to work. I don't know how on earth she lives, or her little ones either. Poor creature, she looked the picture of distress and poverty when I last saw her.'

This woman I had seen away from her home, so I requested my friend to lead me to the dwelling of one of the shirt workers, one that he knew to be a hard-working, sober person, so that I might judge of the condition of the class.

The woman lived over a coal and potato shed, occupying a small close room on the 'second floor back'. It did not require a second glance either at the room or the occupant to tell that the poor creature was steeped in poverty to the very lips. In one corner of the apartment was rolled up the bed on the floor. Beside the window was an oyster tub, set upon a chair. At this she was busy washing, while on the table a small brown pan was filled with the newly washed clothes; beside it were the remains of the dinner, a piece of dry coarse bread, and half a cup of coffee.

In answer to my inquiries, she made the following statement: —

'I make the "rowers", that is the rowing shirts. I'm only in the shirt line. Do nothing else. The rowers is my own work. These (she said, taking a cloth off a bundle of checked shirts on a side table) is 2d. a piece. I have had some at 2½d., and even 3d., but them has full linen fronts and linen wristbands. These are full-fronted shirts — the collars, wristbands, and shoulder-straps are all stitched, and there are seven button-holes in each shirt. It takes full five hours to do one. I have to find my own cotton and thread. I gets two skeins of cotton for 1d., because I am obliged to have it fine for them; and two skeins will make about three to four shirts. Two skeins won't quite make three-and-a-half, so that it don't leave above seven farthings for making each of the shirts. If I was to begin very early here, about six in the morning, and work till nine at night, I can't make above three in the day at them hours. I often work in the summer time from four in the morning to nine or ten at night — as long as I can see. My usual time of work is from five in the morning till nine at night, winter and summer; that is about the average time throughout the year. But when there's a press of business, I work earlier and later. I often gets up at two and three in the morning, and carries on till the evening of the following day, merely lying down in my clothes to take a nap of five or ten minutes. The agitation of mind never lets one lie longer. At the rowers work I don't reckon I makes 5s. a week at the best of times, even working at the early and late hours; and working at the other hours I won't make above 3s. 6d. Average all the year round I can't make more than 4s. a week, and then there's cotton and candles to buy out of that. Why, the candles will cost about 10d. or 1s. a week in the depth of winter, and the cotton about 3d. or 4d. a week, so that I clears about 2s. 6d. a week — yes, I reckon that's about it! I know it's so little I can't get a rag to my back. I reckon nobody in the trade can make more than I do — they can't — and there's very few makes so much, I'm sure. It's only lately that I found a friend to be security for the rowing shirts, or else before that I only received 1½d. for the same shirts as I now have 2d. for, because I was forced to work for a sweater. These prices are not so good as those usually paid in the trade; some houses pays 3s. a dozen for what I have 2s. for. A few weeks — that is, about six weeks ago — the price was 2s. 6d. a dozen; but they always lowers the price towards winter. Never knew them to raise the prices. I have worked at the business about eight years, and when I first began the "rowers" were at 3s. 6d. a dozen — the very same article that I am now making for 2s. They in general keep the sweaters employed in winter — some call them the "double hands", and they turn off the single hands first, because it's the least trouble to them. The sweaters, you see, take out a great quantity of work at a time. The sweaters, many of them, give security to £20. I've known some of them take out as much as a chaise-cart full of various sorts of work, according to the hands they've got employed. One that I knows keeps a horse and cart, and does nothing himself — that he don't. I suppose he's got near upon a hundred hands, and gives about £50 security. He was a potboy at a public-house, and married a shirt-maker. The foremen at the large shops generally marry a shirt-maker, or someone in the line of business, and then take a quantity of work home to their wives, who give it out to poor people. They take one-fourth part out of the price, let it be what it will.'

She produced an account-book, of which the following is a copy: —

1842					£	s.	d.
July	2	Nine at 2d.	...	...	0	1	6
July	4	Nine at 2d.	...	...	0	1	6
July	7	Three at 2d.	...	...	0	0	6
July	10	Nine at 2d.	...	...	0	1	6
July	12	Seven at 2½d.	...	...	0	1	5½
July	17	Nine at 2½d.	...	...	0	1	10½

					£	s	d
July	19	Nine at 2½d.	...	...	0	1	10½
July	21	Six at 2d.	...	...	0	1	0
July	24	Twelve at 2¼d.	...	...	0	2	3
July	26	Six at 2¼d.	...	...	0	1	1½
July	27	Six at 2½d.	...	...	0	1	3
July	28	Six at 2½d.	...	...	0	1	3
July	31	Six at 2½d.	...	...	0	1	3
Aug.	2	Three at 3d. (bespoke)	...	...	0	0	9
Aug.	2	Nine at 2½d.	...	...	0	1	10½
Aug.	6	Nine at 2½d.	...	...	0	1	10½
Aug.	11	Six at 2½d.	...	...	0	1	3
Aug.	14	Twelve at 2½d.	...	...	0	2	6
Aug.	16	Four at 2d.	...	...	0	0	3
Aug.	17	Six at 2½d.	...	...	0	1	3
Aug.	21	Eight at 2½d.	...	...	0	1	8
Aug.	23	Eight at 2d.	...	...	0	1	4
Aug.	25	Eighteen at 2d.	...	...	0	3	0
Aug.	31	Seventeen at 2d.	...	...	0	2	10
Sept.	11	Nine at 2d.	...	...	0	1	6
Sept.	13	Nine at 2d.	...	...	0	1	6
Sept.	17	Twelve at 2d.	...	...	0	2	0
Sept.	25	Eight at 2¾d.	...	...	0	1	10
Sept.	27	Eight at 2½d.	...	...	0	1	8
Sept.	29	Twelve at 2d.	...	...	0	2	0
Oct.	6	Twelve at 2d.	...	...	0	2	0
To be in by 12 Tuesday, or not to be paid for: —							
Oct.	9	Nine at 2d.	...	...	0	1	6
Oct.	16	Twelve at 2d.	...	...	0	2	0
Oct.	29	Nine at 2d.	...	...	0	1	6
					£2	12	4

Hence it will be seen that the average earnings were 2s. 10¼d. per week, from which are to be deducted cotton and candles, costing say, 10½d. a week, and so leaving 2s. per week clear for 17 weeks. These prices are all 'first-handed'.

She can't say why they get so little — supposes it's owing to the times. But one cause is the Jews going to those in the trade and making their brag how little they can get the shirts done for. The original cause of the reduction was their being sent to the unions[1] and the prisons to be made. This is now discontinued. 'I find it very hard times,' she said, 'oh, very hard indeed. If I get a bit of meat once a week, I may think myself well off.' (She drew a bag from under the table.) 'I live mostly upon coffee, and don't taste a cup of tea not once in a month, though I am up early and late; and the coffee I drink without sugar. Look here, this is what I have. You see this is the bloom of the coffee that falls off while it's being sifted after roasting; and I pays 6d. for a bagfull holding about half a bushel.'

The next party I visited was one who worked at waistcoats,

184

and here I found the keenest misery of all. The house was unlike
any that I had seen in the same trade: all was scrupulously clean
and neat. The old brass fender was as bright as gold, and worn
with continued rubbing. The grate, in which there was barely a
handful of coals, had been newly black-leaded, and there was not
a cinder littering the hearth. Indeed, everything in the place
evinced the greatest order and cleanliness. Nor was the suffering
self-evident. On the contrary, a stranger, at first sight, would have
believed the occupant to have been rather well to do in the world.
A few minutes' conversation with the poor creature, however,
soon told you that the neatness was partly the effect of habits
acquired in domestic service, and partly the result of a struggle to
hide her extreme poverty from the world. Her story was the most
pathetic of all I had yet heard: — 'I work for a slop-house — waistcoat work,' she said; 'I don't make sleeve waistcoats, but body
waistcoats, and the lowest price I get is 4d.; I have had 'em as
high as 1s. 3d. I take the run, such as they have got to give me —
sometimes one thing and sometimes another in the waistcoat
way. Some have better work than others, but my eyesight won't
admit of my doing the best work. Some waistcoats are as much as
1s. 9d., some 2s. I have worked twenty-six years at the same warehouse. The general price for the waistcoats I have now is 6d., 8d.,
and 10d. I can make one a day sometimes, and sometimes three
in two days — just as it happens — for my health is very bad.
Sometimes I don't earn more than 2s. 6d. a week, and sometimes
I have earned 3s. 6d. and 4s. That's the most I have earned for
this several years. I must work very close from about nine in the
morning to eleven at night to earn that. Prices have come down
very much indeed since I first worked for the warehouse — *very
much*. The prices when I was first employed there were as much
as 1s. 9d. for what I get now 1s. 1d. for. Every week they have
reduced something within these last few years. Work's falling
very much. The work has not riz — no, never since I worked at it.
It's lower'd, but it's not riz. The masters seem to say that the
work is lowered to them — that they can't afford to pay a better
price, or else they would. The parties for whom I work lay it to
the large slop-houses. They say it's through them that the work
has lowered so. I find it very difficult to get sufficient to nourish
me out of my work. I can't have what I ought to have. I think my
illness at present is from over-exertion. I want more air than I can
get. I am wholly dependent on myself for my living, and never
made more than 4s. a week. Several times I have had my work

thrown back upon my hands, and that has perhaps made me ill, so that I've not been able to do anything. I am obliged to work long, and always — sick or well — I must do it for my living, to make any appearance at all. My sight is very bad now from over-work, and perhaps other difficulties as well — I suffer so bad with my head. My greatest earnings are 4s. per week, my lowest 2s. 6d., and I generally average about 3s. Many weeks I have been wholly without working — not able to do it. Young people that have got good health and good work might, perhaps, earn more than I do; but at the common work I should think they can't make more than I can. I never was married. I went out to service when I was younger, and to waistcoating after quitting service; so that I might be at home with mother and father, and take care of them in their old age. I rent the house. It's where I buried mother and father from; and as such, I've kept it on since they've been dead. I let the two rooms, but I don't gain anything by it. I stand at about ten-pence a week rent when I live in the top room and let the others; but sometimes it's empty, and I lose by it. Some time ago, too, a party ran away, and left £3 10s. in my debt. That nearly ruined me. I've not got the better of it yet. I've been very short — very short indeed, sir; in want of common necessaries to keep my strength and life together. I don't find what I get by my labour sufficient to keep me. I've no money anywhere, not a farthing in the house; yes — I tell a story — I've got a penny. If I were to be taken ill I don't know what I should do. But I should be obliged to do as I've often done before. The Almighty is my only support. For my old age there is nothing but the workhouse. After six and twenty years' hard work I've not a penny to the fore — nothing to depend upon for an hour. If I could have saved, I should have been very glad to have done so. Take one week with another, I have earned 3s., and that has been barely sufficient to keep me. I've sold several things to make up, when I've come short. The things here belonged to father and mother. I've sold a great many that they left me. Many people who follow the same business I think are worse off, if anything, than I am; because I've got a home, and I strive to keep it together, and they've not.'

It seemed difficult to believe that there could be found women suffering more keenly than this poor creature; and yet the gentle-man who had kindly undertaken to introduce me to the better class of workpeople in the trade, led me to a young woman, most ladylike in her appearance and manners, from whom I gathered the following pitiable tale: —

She works at waistcoat business; at the best kind of work. Gets 10d. each waistcoat, sometimes 8d., and sometimes 6d.; some she has heard of being as low as 2½d. There are shilling ones but there's a great deal of work in them. Black satin waistcoats are 10d., stitched all round; and out of the 10d. trimmings are to be found. The trimmings for each waistcoat cost 1d., sometimes 1½d., and occasionally 2d. 'Those I am making now at 10d.', she said, 'have a quantity of work in them. They would take me the whole day, even if I was well enough to sit so long at 'em. Besides this, there's half a day lost each time you take your work in. And sometimes every other day — and often every day — they'll drag you up to the warehouse for the little bit of work. They give out four at a time mostly. We have to give housekeeper's security for £5 before we can get work. Some weeks I don't do more than four. Some weeks I don't do that. Last week I had a hard matter to do four; but then I wasn't well. When I was apprentice we used to have 5s. for making the very same as those that I now get 10d. for. At 2s. apiece one might live, but as it is now, *I am starving*; if it wasn't for my friends helping me a little, I don't know what would become of me, I'm sure. Frequently the work is returned upon our hands, and recently I have had 9s. to pay out of my earnings for some waistcoats that were sent back to me because they were kept out too long. They were kept out longer than they should have been, because I was ill; I wasn't able to make them. I sat up in my bed, ill as I was, and basted them myself, and then a girl that I got did what she could to them, and I finished them; but, owing to the delay, the foreman grew spiteful and returned them on my hands. I have been suffering for this ever since, and I couldn't subsist upon what I get now, were it not for some kind friends. I've got a spirit, and wouldn't like to be under an obligation, but I am forced to live as I do. While I was ill my rent went back, and I've left part of my things where I was living before I came here, because I couldn't pay up what I owed for my lodging. There is my doctor's bill to be paid — for I haven't paid it yet, and I have been obliged to get rid of the waistcoats that were returned to me; I sold them for a trifle, as I could, with the exception of one that I've pledged. I got 1s. upon that, and I sold the others at 1s. 6d. each, though they charged me at the shop 3s. 3d apiece for them. I was glad to get rid of them anyhow, just then.

'The waistcoats that they pay a shilling for to have made are like jackets — they have sleeves and flaps to pockets like coats. I don't know what they are like. It would take anyone two days to make them. It takes me two days. My average earnings are from 3s. to 4s. a week, and out of that I have to pay 2s. for the waistcoats returned on my hands, and about 6d. for trimmings, per week, leaving me about 1s. 6d. to live upon. Some persons say they can earn at waistcoating 14s. to 15s. per week, and they tell the master so; but then they have people to help them — girls who probably pay them something to learn the business, or who are very young, and have 1s. per week for doing the inferior parts. I don't know why the prices are so low. I have found prices continually going down since I came from the west-end of the town. I never knew an advance. If they took 2d. or 1d., I never heard of their putting it on again. The prices have fallen more within the last two or three years — much more than ever they did before. I don't think they can get very much lower. If they do, persons *must* starve. It is almost as bad as the workhouse now. I was apprenticed to the waistcoating at the West-end, and was paid a little different then. I could earn 15s. a week at that time. The business has materially injured my health; yes, that it has. My eyesight and health have both suffered from it. It has produced general debility; the doctor says it's sitting so long in the house. Sometimes all night I used to sit up to work. I've known many people that have had strong constitutions, and after they've worked at it many years they've gone like I have. There are persons who get even lower prices than I do — oh, yes, sir, a great deal lower! Some I know get three-pence, and even four-pence for a waistcoat.'

I asked whether she kept any account of her earnings, and she immediately produced the book in which her work was *entered by her employers*. On one side was a statement of the work given out to her, and on the other that of the work brought home, together with the price paid for it, and the amount deducted from the earnings for the waistcoats which had been returned upon the poor girl's hands. The following is the account of the prices paid to, and the sums received by, the waistcoat maker: —

					s.	d.
		Four vests returned, 9s. to pay				
Sept.	12	Four at 10d.	...	...	3	4
Sept.	13	One at 10d.	...	...	0	10
					4	2
		To pay for waistcoats				
		returned	...	...	2	0

		Paid	...	...	2	2
Sept.	28	Five at 10d.	...	...	4	2
		To pay for waistcoats returned	...	...	2	0
		Paid	...	...	2	2
Oct.	10	Two at 1s.	...	...	2	0
Oct.	17	Three at 6d.	...	...	1	6
Oct.	18	One at 1s.	...	...	1	0
					4	6
		To pay for waistcoats returned	...	...	1	6
		Paid	...	...	3	0
Oct.	22	Four at 9½d.	...	...	3	2
Oct.	26	Two at 10d.	...	...	1	8
					4	10
		To pay for waistcoats returned	...	...	1	6
		Paid	...	...	3	4
Oct.	30	Three at 10d.	...	...	2	6
Oct.	31	One at 10d.	...	...	0	10
					3	4 .
		To pay for waistcoats returned	...	...	1	0
		Paid	...	...	2	4

Total receipts from Sept. 13 to Oct. 31 (seven weeks), 13s., averaging 1s. 10¼d. per week.

On my way home from these saddening scenes, I called at the wholesale slop warehouse for the promised statement as to the prices paid by the generality of the trade. After waiting a considerable time, one of the principals and foreman came to communicate to me the desired information.

The usual sum earned by a person working at the slop trade is; they told me, *three-pence per hour!!*

Women working at moleskin trousers, they said, would earn, upon an average, 1s. 10d. every day of ten hours' labour.

At waistcoats females would earn generally at the rate of 2s. per day of ten hours' labour.

The foreman and the principal then wished to know in what state I had found the workpeople generally. I told them I had never seen or heard of such destitution. 'Destitution!' was the exclamation. 'God bless my soul, you surprise me!' 'And I think it but right, gentlemen,' I added, 'to apprise you that your statement as to prices differs most materially from that of the workpeople'; and so saying, I took my departure.

1. A workhouse, under the terms of the 1834 Poor Law.

25

In Chapter VIII of *Alton Locke*, the tailor-poet and the bookseller Mackaye visit the garret of seamstresses working at home:

> upon a few rags on the floor lay a girl, ugly, small-pox marked, hollow-eyed, emaciated, her only bedclothes the skirt of a large handsome riding-habit, at which two other girls, was an tawdry, were stitching busily, as they sat right and left of her on the floor.

The most graphic accounts of women's work in the clothing trade come in the Second Report of the Children's Employment Commission, published at the end of February 1843. Extracts from Parliamentary reports about the condition of seamstresses appeared in periodicals from 1842, and the subject was frequently taken up in newspaper reports of the decade. 'Because almost all women sewed, the seamstress seemed at least as much woman as worker. She was, therefore, a perfect working-class symbol for writers who wished to see class relations entirely in terms of family relations' (Catherine Gallagher, *The Industrial Reformation of English Fiction: 1832-1867*, Chicago and London, 1985, p. 130), and formed the basis for a variety of writing: Thomas Hood's 'The Song of the Shirt' (*Punch*, Christmas 1843):

> O, men with sisters dear!
>   O, men, with mothers and wives!
> It is not linen you're wearing out,
>   But human creatures' lives,

and a range of fiction, such as Francis Paget, *The Pageant* (1843);

Elizabeth Stone, *The Young Milliner* (1843); J.M. Rymer, *The White Slave: A Romance for the Nineteenth Century* (1844) and G.W.M. Reynolds, *The Slaves of England: No. 1, The Seamstress* (1850).

The Second Report of the Children's Employment Commission was one of the few Commissions to which Dickens referred when writing his fiction. His imagination and compassion were stirred by the report. He wrote to Thomas Southwood Smith[1] on 6 March 1843 that he was 'so perfectly stricken down by the blue book you have sent me' that he thought of bringing out a cheap pamphlet entitled 'An Appeal to the People of England, on Behalf of the Poor Man's Child' (*The Letters of Charles Dickens*, III, 1842-3, edited Madeline House, Graham Storey and Kathleen Tillotson, Oxford, 1974, p. 459). Although this pamphlet never materialised, the report lay behind elements of certain of Dickens's subsequent works, especially *The Chimes*, where the profession of seamstress is part of Meg's downward spiral which Trotty Veck sees in his gloomy vision of the future.

Evidence collected by R.D. Grainger Esq, 'Evidence on the London District: Dress-makers and Milliners', Appendix to the Second Report of the Commissioners Inquiring into the Employment of Children in Trades and Manufactures, 1843, pp. 204-6.

No. 525 — February 9, 1841. *Miss H. Baker.*

Is in business as a milliner, and has been altogether acquainted with the business several years. Came to London at the age of 16 as 'an improver', having previously learnt the business in the country. The young women who come as improvers are generally 16 or 17 years of age; they have in most cases served an apprenticeship previously either in London or the country. The apprenticeship is usually for 2 years; for this, if board and lodging are included, 30*l* or 40*l* are paid. There are many young women employed after their apprenticeship as journeywomen, receiving from 15*l* to 50*l* a-year and board and lodging. The journeywomen and the improvers are worked the longest; the apprentices, being beginners and not knowing the business so well, are sent to bed earlier. Has been herself in several houses in London. In some of the establishments the hours of work are regulated; in others not. The common hours, where they are regulated, are from 8 A.M. till 11 P.M. The breakfast is eaten as quick as possible at about half-past 8; about 20 minutes are allowed for dinner, which is also taken as quickly as possible, the hour being half-past 1. For tea, at 5, no time is allowed; it is taken as quick as the other meals. Supper is at 9 or 10. In the houses which are regulated, by which is meant those which do not make a practice of working all night, it happens that if any particular order is to be executed they go on later than 11, often till 2 and 3 in the morning, and, if requisite, all night. In those houses which are not so well regulated they often work all night; in the season they usually go on till 1 or 2 in the morning. In the summer it is common to commence at 5 in the morning. In one establishment where witness formerly worked, during 3 months successively, she had never more than 4 hours' rest, regularly going to bed between 12 and 1, and getting up at 4 in the morning. On the occasion of the general mourning for His Majesty William IV. witness worked without going to bed from 4 o'clock on Thursday morning till half-past 10 on Sunday morning; during this time witness did not sleep at all: of this she is certain. In order to keep awake she stood nearly the whole of Friday night, Saturday, and Saturday night, only sitting down for half an hour for rest. Two other young persons worked at the same house for the same time; these two dozed occasionally in a chair. Witness, who was then 19, was made very ill by this great exertion, and when on Sunday she went to bed, she could not sleep. Her feet and legs were much swelled, and her feet seemed to overhang the shoes. No difference is made as to the time of beginning in the morning, when the work has been carried on very late the night before. In some houses they work on the Sunday. The young persons are often so much fatigued, that they lay in bed so late on Sunday as not to be able to go to church. In some few houses the work is not carried on so late at night, and the young women go to church. Generally speaking, the hours are longer in London than in the country; but there are many exceptions, some country houses working very late. Nothing is paid for extra work.

Witness's health was seriously injured by the long hours of work and sitting so long. When she first came to London she often fainted once or twice in the day. Is short-sighted, and at night sees very indifferently. Working with black articles, especially black velvet, tries the sight very much. It oftens happens from the present fashion that young women are employed for many weeks in succession at black work. It was more common than not that the young girls and women were subject to fainting fits. When they first come their health is more liable to suffer than afterwards. Pain in the side and between the shoulders is very common; has sat so long in one position as to suffer great pain in the back. Various other complaints are caused. Some suffer from the coldness of the workshop; knows a young girl who was obliged to leave in consequence of rheumatism.

There are always plenty of workwomen who go out, and who might be procured to assist whenever any particular order is to be executed, so as to relieve those belonging to the establishment. Although these persons are, in general, inferior milliners and dressmakers, yet there are in every dress plainer parts which they could execute. Thinks certainly, that if it were the custom on sudden emergencies to employ these extra hands, that the hours of labour might be very much shortened. Is decidedly of opinion that by proper regulations, applicable to all, there is nothing connected with the business itself which requires longer hours than other occupations. Knows it would be a great boon to a large number of young persons, now totally unprotected, if the hours were shortened, and night-work prohibited. If any become sick, they must either go on with their work, or leave the house. 'They often sit at work when they are so ill as to be scarcely able to stick to their needle.' Employers in general pay little or no attention to the health of the young people who work for them.

(Signed) HARRIET BAKER.

No. 526 — February 12, 1841. Miss *O'Neil*, Welbeck-street.

Has been a dress-maker and milliner several years, and has been employed in several of the London houses. Is now in business for herself. The hours of work in the spring season are longer than those in the autumn season; in the former they are unlimited. The common hours are from 6 A.M. till 12 at night; sometimes from 4 A.M. till 12. Has herself often worked from 6 A.M. till 12 at night for 2 or 3 months together. It is not at all uncommon, especially in the dress-making, to work all night; just in 'the drive of the season' the work is occasionally continued all night, 3 times a-week. Has worked herself twice in the week all night. 'In some houses which profess to study the health of their young people, they begin at 4 A.M., and leave off at 11 P.M., never earlier.' Has heard there are houses in London which work on Sundays. In some houses to prevent late hours on Saturday they work all night on Friday; they frequently lay in bed on Sunday to rest themselves. Sometimes the young persons are called up at 2 on Monday morning, and continue till the usual hour, 11 or 12 at night. The hours are considered short if they do not exceed from 7 A.M. till 11 P.M. The time for meals is very short; 10 minutes for breakfast, 15 for dinner, and 10 for tea; in most houses there is no supper till the work is finished, although that is not till 11 or 12 at night. In some establishments the food is insufficient in quantity and inferior in quality; salt beef is frequently used and hard puddings. Has been obliged to buy food in consequence of the insufficient allowance, and has known others who have been obliged to do the same.

The hours of work are decidedly longer in the fashionable houses than in any others. It is very common in those to work all night. There are no relays on these occasions; the same who work by day work by night. Thinks that if it be possible the French houses are worse than the English; the work people are of both nations. In some of the French houses believes there are relays, night and day workers, and that they go on night and day. If they get very sleepy they lie on the floor, 'on the cuttings if there are any.' This indulgence depends on the kindness of the head of the room.

The business is conducted by a forewoman; the employer, having little to do with the workroom, has regular hours of rest.

Has known two young women, one not more than 16, who fainted generally once or twice in the day; one of these left the house in a deep decline, and witness believes she afterwards died.

The usual age at which young girls begin to work is from 14 to 16 years. They very frequently come from the country, and are then healthy and strong. The effects upon the health are, in the first place, lassitude, and debility, with loss of appetite; pain in the back, either between the shoulders or in the loins, is universal; should think there is not one in 20 who does not suffer from this affection. Indigestion is very common. Pulmonary affections, such as cough and tightness in the breath are also frequent. Head ache is very common; 'you would never be in a work-room half an hour without some one complaining of that'. If they become ill, unless it be dangerous, they must continue at their work; they do this for months together; the employers taking very little care of the health of the young women. If they are seriously ill they must go home; it is a very rare thing for them to remain in the house. Many go into the country in a state threatening a fatal result and 'never return.' Out of all the young women known to witness, has only known one who had retained her health; believes that this one began later in life than general, at 20. Does not think it would be possible to keep up the system which is adopted in the dress-making establishments in London, if there were not a constant succession of fresh hands from the country. Does not think that men could sustain the labour which is imposed on these young and delicate women. Witness can only account for these young persons submitting to such labour from the fact of their bread depending on their having employment; this applies to the journeywomen. As regards the apprentices, they have no chance, because if they complained, 'their indentures would be brought against them.' Has known the indentures to be so brought against apprentices who have objected to working on Sunday; 'the principal saying the time of the apprentice was theirs.' A case of this kind happened some years ago in Maidstone. Thinks that in the principal houses in a country town there is frequently as much hardship as in London.

If any general regulations for ordering the hours of work were enforced, considering that there are always an abundance of hands to be had in London, no interruption to the efficient carrying on the business could arise. Such regulations would tend to the employment of some hundreds of workwomen who now are out of work. A restriction of the hours of labour would be a blessing to thousands of girls and young women, who are now utterly taxed beyond their health and strength. Witness's health is seriously affected, and she has been under the treatment of a physician for 3 months. Has bad sight; it is common for the eyes to become affected. Feels that as the young men employed in linen-drapers and other shops have their hours regulated, not exceeding 12, in the busiest time of the year, that young women have a stronger claim to protection, their occupation being so much more unhealthy.

(Signed) MARGARET FOULKEN O'NEIL.

(*Note.* — I saw Miss O'Neil at the suggestion of the physician under whose care she was, in consequence of illness brought on by long continued application. She is in a very delicate state of health, and her constitution is permanently and seriously impaired.)

1. Thomas Southwood Smith, 1788-1861: physician, sanitary reformer and, together with Thomas Tooke, Leonard Horner and Robert John Saunders, one of the four Infant Labour Commissioners appointed to enquire into conditions in the mines.

26

The source for the specific troubles of Meg Veck in *The Chimes* — her employment as a seamstress; her attempt to drown herself and a child in the Thames — was derived by Dickens from the case of Mary Furley, tried and sentenced for infanticide on 16 April 1844. Her death sentence caused a public outcry, in which Dickens joined: it was subsequently commuted to seven years' transportation.

(a) The Times, *17 April 1844, p. 8. The case was heard at the Central Criminal Court, April 16 1844, under Mr Justice Maule.*

Mary Furley, aged 40, was indicted for the wilful murder of her infant child, George Furley.

From the statements made by the witnesses it appeared that for some time previous to the commission of the dreadful crime the prisoner with her two children had remained in the Bethnal-green workhouse. On the 20th of March she left the workhouse voluntarily, taking her children with her, having obtained a small pecuniary supply. She went then and lived for a few days with some of her friends; to all of whom she complained of the treatment which her children had received. She did not appear in any way incapable of taking care of them, but said that she was in great distress of mind. She was heard several times to say that she and her children would meet a watery grave. She made use of this expression to many of her friends. On Sunday, the day of the murder, she washed her children at the house of a friend named Mary Butler, and remarked that all her troubles would end that day. She then went out and dined at the house of a woman called Wheeler. She left this place at 20 minutes past 8 o'clock in the evening, taking only her youngest child with her. At about 9 o'clock, the attention of William Gardner, a boatman at the

Regent's-canal, was called to one of the wharfs, near Mile-end bridge, from which he heard a faint moaning. He went round, and on going to the place whence the sound proceeded he saw something floating in the water, about 15 feet from the side. He drew it to the bank with a boathook, and found that it was the prisoner. On being taken out she exclaimed, 'Oh my child!' and on being asked where it was, she said that it was in the water. The child, however, dropped from under her arm as she was speaking. The boatman then took it to the Globe Tavern, where it was attended by Mr New, a surgeon, who pronounced it to be quite dead. The prisoner said, on being removed, that she had committed the act through distress and ill-treatment.

The prisoner, who was undefended, on being called upon at the conclusion of the evidence said that, while she and her children were in the Whitechapel workhouse, they were well treated, but on going to Bethnal-green workhouse the eldest child became ill from some affection of the head. It was removed from the infirmary, and sent down again to her, and its head became a second time so bad that it was ordered to be shaved. The barber who performed this operation was drunk, and in consequence he cut pieces of flesh from the head of the child. The wounds became very bad, and continued so for some time, and on their being cured the child's eyes became sore. An eruption also appeared all over its body, which she attributed solely to the child being fed at the workhouse on hard beef. She requested that this might be changed for mutton, but this was refused. She then came to the determination of leaving the house, and after having obtained a loan of 6s. from the guardians, she went about amongst her friends, and by small contributions from them she got a few shillings. She obtained some employment at shirt-making, but as they only allowed 1¾d. for a shirt, and by working hard she could only make three shirts a day, she was compelled to relinquish it and seek some more profitable employment. She then determined to lay out the small stock of money she had in the purchase of a few ribands, &c., to make up dress caps and sell them, to try and eke out a slight subsistence for her infant. She accordingly set out to do so, but, on arriving at the shop, found that a little green silk purse, containing her money, had been lost or stolen from her pocket. This occurrence increased, if possible, her distress of mind, as she had then no friend in the world who could assist her, and no other prospect before her than to re-enter the workhouse, to which she entertained such an aversion, that she preferred death to herself and her child. (The prisoner faltered at this part of her statement, and spoke in so low a tone, that nothing but the words, 'I fell off the plank at the wharf', were heard, she then sat down, much affected.)

Mr Justice MAULE summed up, and explained to the jury the difference between cases of murder and manslaughter. The learned judge said that, in this case he could see no cause or provocation which could bring the crime under the denomination of manslaughter; on the contrary, the act appeared to have been perfectly premeditated, as was proved by the threats used by the prisoner to other persons. The crime was not altered at all by the fact of her having attempted her own life at the same time that she destroyed that of her infant.

After a few minutes' consultation, the jury returned a verdict of *Guilty*.

The prisoner was called up for judgement. She said that she had nothing to urge against the sentence of the law.

The learned JUDGE then put on his black cap, and addressing the prisoner, said — You have been convicted of the crime of wilful murder, which crime is proved to have been committed under circumstances of evident premeditation — Your act, which would have been at any time cruel, is rendered more so by the fact of the crime being committed by you — the mother of the child. I do not wish to excite your feelings by prolonging this painful scene, but I earnestly recommend you to turn your attention to your spiritual affairs, which are now of infinitely more importance to you than any worldly consideration, for you have but a short interval, I fear, before the sentence I am about to pass will be carried into execution. I therefore entreat you to turn your attention to your God, and to fortify your mind against the time when your sentence will be carried into effect. His Lordship then passed sentence of death in the usual form.

The prisoner, who was much affected, was then removed.

(b) *[Charles Dickens], 'Threatening Letter to Thomas Hood, from an Ancient Gentleman, by favor of Charles Dickens',* Hood's Magazine and Comic Miscellany, *I, May 1843, pp. 409-10.*

Ah! governments were governments, and judges were judges, in *my* day, Mr Hood. There was no nonsense then. Any of your seditious complainings, and we were ready with the military at the shortest notice ... Then, the judges were full of dignity and firmness, and knew how to administer the law. There is only one judge who knows how to do his duty, now. He tried that revolutionary female the other day, who, though she was in full work (making shirts at three-halfpence a piece), had no pride in her country, but treasonably took it in her head, in the distraction of having been robbed of her easy earnings, to attempt to drown herself and her young child; and the glorious man went out of his way, sir — out of his way — to call her up for instant sentence of Death; and to tell her she had no hope of mercy in this world — as you may see yourself if you look in the papers of Wednesday the 17th of April. He won't be supported, sir, I know he won't; but it is worth remembering that his words were carried to crowds in every political parlour, beer-shop, news-room, and secret or open place of assembly, frequented by the discontented working men; and that no milk-and-water weakness on the part of the executive can ever blot them out. Great things like that, are caught up, and stored up, in these times, and are not forgotten, Mr Hood. The public at large (especially those who wish for peace and conciliation) are universally obliged to him.

27

Bethnal Green was one of the poorer areas of London, where many seamstresses, and others engaged in piece-work and seasonal labour, as well as dockers, lived. Its insanitary conditions were observed by both social reformers and fictional commentators. Hector Gavin, in his *Sanitary Ramblings* (1848) provided a detailed description of the area. His work set out to show how little had been done to remedy conditions since Southwood Smith had exposed them in the Fourth Annual Report of the Poor Law Commissioners, 1838, and since Edwin Chadwick, on the instruction of the House of Lords, had set up his full-scale inquiry into the sanitary conditions of the working class, reporting comprehensively in 1842.

Hector Gavin, a lecturer in forensic medicine and public health at Charing Cross Hospital, was extremely active in the Health of Towns Association set up by Lord Ashley, Southwood

Smith and Lord Normanby in 1844, with the aims of implementing Chadwick's ideas on sanitary reform. Gavin published *Unhealthiness of London, and the Necessity of Remedial Measures* in 1847, and followed this with *Sanitary Ramblings* in 1848. In 1849, he was appointed Medical Inspector for the parishes of Bethnal Green and Shoreditch, where he used his intimate knowledge of the local sanitary conditions in combatting the serious outbreak of cholera in 1849. By visiting houses in areas likely to be infected, he was able to discover and treat many cases of cholera in their early stages. These early reforming movements were consolidated by the Metropolitan Board of Works, set up in 1855, and minimum standards of sanitation, public health and housing were formulated piece-meal, and finally consolidated into the Public Health Act of 1875. But the area about which Gavin wrote remained notorious throughout the nineteenth century. Its criminal rookery, The Old Nichol, and the demolition and rebuilding which were carried out in the district are central to Arthur Morrison's novel, *A Child of the Jago*, 1896.

For Gavin, see R.S. Roberts: 'Re-Readings. GAVIN, H., *Sanitary Ramblings. Being Sketches and Illustrations of Bethnal Green. A Type of the Conditions of the Metropolis and Other Large Towns* (1848)', *East London Papers*, 8, 1965, pp. 110-18.

Hector Gavin, Sanitary Ramblings. Being Sketches and Illustrations of Bethnal Green. A Type of the Conditions of the Metropolis and Other Large Towns, *London, 1848, pp. 42-4; 79-81.*

This district exceeds all those which have gone before it in filth, disease, mortality, poverty, and wretchedness; it abounds with the most foul courts, and is characterised by the prevalence of the greatest nuisances, and perennial foulness. Unlike the last district, there are several gardens in it resembling those already described, but infinitely surpassing them in everything degrading to our civilization. For many years this district has been notorious as the hot-bed of epidemics. This is easily explained, when the foulness of the streets, the dense crowding in some parts, and the nearly total absence of drainage and house-cleansing, are considered. The drainage, in fact, is characteristic of primitive barbarism; the drains are very near the surface, and some of the houses are built over them; the streets are perpetually covered with the most offensive foetid mud; the population is very dense, as many as 30 persons residing in a single house — 57 houses had a population of 580 persons. In about half a mile square of these houses and streets 30,000 persons are congregated; the houses are generally of the worst class, and four-roomed, but great numbers resemble, in many respects, those in the worst parts of the Old Town of Edinburgh — a class of houses common to the French, and which they were the cause of introducing into both places. The houses built by the French refugees are all several storied, and have large rooms on each floor, with a common staircase; the houses are, without exception, let out in rooms; each room contains a family, with a bed common to all; generally it is a work-room as well as a dwelling-room. Ventilation in these rooms is in the most defective state; the atmosphere is most oppressive, and loaded with unhealthy emanations; it is a common practice to retain the fœcal remains in the rooms, in order to avoid exposure, and the perfect nastiness of, the common privies. The parochial medical officer has not seen, and does not know of, one water-closet in the whole district. All the tenements in Greengate-gardens are unfit for human habitation; they are much under the level of the neighbouring road, and are very damp; they smell most offensively. There are great numbers of low public-houses and beer-shops in this district; all these are crowded with lodgers, and thus become great nuisances, and sources of disease and immorality. Since several streets have been pulled down by the Railway Company, there has been much overcrowding; so much so, that not a habitation or lodging can be had in the neighbour-hood, and some persons are, even now, in opposition to the law, residing in cellars, because they can find no place else to reside. The poor inhabitants generally prefer any kind of abode to the workhouse. The occupations of the inhabitants are chiefly weaving and shoe-making; hawkers, toy-makers, and cabinet-makers, abound here, and the women wind silk and cotton. Those small manufactures which are carried on here are chiefly prepared in the prospect of being sold to the ready-money shops, or on specu-lation. The earnings of the population of this district are very low and precarious, their habits most irregular, and generally intemperate — to-day an unexpected 'stroke of luck' supplies them with means to indulge their appetites with dainties and abundance — tomorrow sees them deprived of the most inferior kinds of sustenance. No pruor [sic] forethought prevents them from living on the best, when they can, or restrains their ill-regulated appetites. Their common food consists of potatoes and bread, and butcher's meat of a very inferior quality. Numerous

201

chandlers' shops are in the habit of supplying this inferior kind of food, and of receiving goods as pledges for its payment; these pledges are sold at the end of a month, if unredeemed. Moral debasement and physical decay, naturally enough, accompany the utter defiance of all the laws of health, and the complete disregard of all the characteristics of civilization. Such a population always supply our courts with criminals, our gaols with convicts, our charities with paupers, and our hospitals with the sick and diseased; and impoverish the honest, labouring poor, by the heavy poor-rates to which they give rise.

WILLOW-WALK, I. — There is one stand-tap to four houses in this court, but there is no receptacle for refuse; there is a cowshed in it. The houses are two-roomed, and let at 3s. at week. None of the inhabitants earn 10s. a week.

GREENGATE-GARDENS, 2, 3. — These gardens are divided into 'three walks'; the first, the middle, and third. The first contains eight houses, which are in a most wretched condition, planted on the clay, and without drainage of any kind. One of them has a cesspool, which is not emptied more than once in three years; the others have three privies, which are full, and most disgustingly offensive. The houses contain two rooms on the ground floor, and are let at 3s.6d. per week. The average earnings of the inhabitants are 6s. per week. One water-tap is common to five houses; three houses are without any water supply, and the occupants require to obtain it at the 'Green-Gate' public-house. In the middle walk the greatest dirtiness and filthiness prevail; all the privies are full, and have not been emptied for at least four years; many are overflowing, and the contents spread over the yard; all kinds of refuse and garbage are thrown in front of the houses, for want of dust-bins; holes are dug in the earth to receive the slops; collections of dung and manure abound in some places. 2s. 6d. a week are paid for these houses, and the average earnings are 6s. per week. The third walk is still more filthy than the rest; excrements are scattered about, all the privies are full and overflowing, and the soil desiccating in the sun. One standpipe, beside a dung-heap, is the only means by which 30 houses are supplied with water; of course quarrels for precedence and to ensure a supply are common. The whole of these gardens are in a condition alike disgusting and disgraceful. Being private property, they are never cleansed by the parish, but are left in a perpetual state of dirt and nastiness; they are excessively damp, and most noisome. The tenements, as has been remarked, are unfit for human habitation; disease is always common here; some of the worst cases of typhus fever were removed from this locality to the workhouse.

STROUT-PLACE, 4. — This place is always very dirty, from cattle going and returning to a cow-shed, the smell from which is frequently very offensive, and is much complained of.

CRESCENT-PLACE, 5. — One pump in the centre of the crescent, communicating with a sunk tank supplied from the main, supplies all the 25 houses.

SOMERSET-BUILDING, 6. — The drainage is imperfect, the drains being stopped. A tap supplies every two houses, which are two and three-roomed.

CRABTREE-ROW, 7. — The privies at the back of Somerset-buildings abut on the street, and are only separated by a boarding; the surface drainage flows into street-gutter, and stagnates there, and the soil from the privies oozes into the main road. At the south-end of these buildings all kinds of garbage, putrefying remains of fish, and every kind of refuse, are deposited by the public, to the great annoyance and injury of the occupants. Opposite to this row there is a very large triangular open space, which has been made by the removal of numerous gardens and houses similar to those described under the head of Greengate-gardens — a removal at once beneficial to the neighbourhood and the occupants, as it is the only open space in this densely-populated district. But although the houses have been swept from the ground, the holes attached to the privies and cesspools were only partially filled up; a considerable quantity of night-soil, therefore, remains mixed up with the ground and refuse on the surface; in addition, being waste ground, and quite open, it is largely made use of to deposit all kinds of dirt, garbage, and excrementitious matter, which are allowed to dry in the sun. After rain (which stagnates, on account of the level), and in warm weather, a very offensive odour arises from this place; it is greatly complained of in the neighbourhood as a resort for all the reprobate characters in the vicinity on Sundays, who there gamble, fight, and indulge in all kinds of indecencies and immoralities. The passers-by on Sundays are always sure to be subjected to outrage in their feelings, and often in their persons. The enclosing of the space would be considered 'a great blessing'.

PRIVIES AND CESSPOOLS
'The deficient number of privies in the poorer quarters of towns,

and the large number of inhabitants resorting to them, deprives them of any right to be considered private, and render it absolutely necessary for the safety of the public health, that some alteration should be made in the law regarding them.' — (Second Rep. Com. Health of Towns.)

It is scarcely possible to conceive the utter degradation of the human mind which permits it, at least, to tolerate the disgusting offensiveness of these abominable nuisances, which exist in the form of common privies, in the poorer neighbourhoods. One open necessary for numerous families, and for 20, 30, or 50 persons, is surely most objectionable, but it is quite a common occurrence. It is true that Bethnal-green is not so bad as Sunderland, where there is only one necessary for every 76 persons, but there is a vast amount of moral degradation entailed upon the inhabitants by their being compelled to make use of such a scanty number of such filthy receptacles ...

The generality of the privies in this parish are full, and most offensive, great numbers are overflowing. The cesspools attached are, in the majority of instances, in no better condition. Many of the privies are wooden sheds erected over holes from which a surface hollow conducts off the fluid refuse to some other part of the ground. Many are most dilapidated, and some are dangerous to make use of. In numerous instances the soil has infiltrated the walls, percolated through them, and spread itself over the surface of the neighbouring yard; the soil has likewise percolated through the walls, and into the houses, and in some instances, the floors have been saturated, and have been rendered very quagmires of filth; the flooring, in such cases, has become rotten. In numerous instances, the inhabitants have piled either in their yards, or in their houses, or in the alleys fronting the houses, collections of dust and cinders, to conceal from the eye the soil which has oozed from the neighbouring privies or cesspools.

The soil from the privies and cesspools is very rarely removed, it is an expensive process, and its occurrence is reckoned on as a disgusting event, necessary to be postponed as long as possible. The landlords of the poorer tenements very rarely indeed remove the contents of the cesspools or privies, and often neglect to do so, till compelled by the devastations which the exhalations from the soil produce, in the form of fever, and alarmed lest their property should get a bad name, and be thus rendered untenantable. The poor, left to rot in their filth, sometimes attempt to rid themselves of this nuisance, and fancy they effect it by burying the soil in their yards. Not unfrequently it happens that the supply of water to such houses is by a well in these yards; the water necessarily becomes tainted, and a slow or active poison according to the amount of soil which has percolated into it; the poor inhabitants who have gardens near or attached to their dwellings, generally manure the ground with the soil from their privies. Not only do the poor find the removal of night soil an expensive process but even those inhabiting the better class of houses and public institutions are known to remove the soil from their privies and bury it in their gardens. Often this burying consists in merely sprinkling earth over the surface of the soil so as to conceal it from sight. In some parts of the parish the privies of whole rows of houses drain into black ditches, and thus render these ditches horrible nuisances; the effects of such modes of dealing with animal refuse are daily exemplified, — head-ache, indigestion, nausea, loss of appetite, debility, pallor, wasting, diarrhoea, dysentery, cholera, fever and zymotic diseases, in a malignant form, are the every day consequences, and whenever an epidemic attacks a place, those localities, where such abominations exist, suffer the most; the influenza in Bethnal-green has chiefly exhausted its virulence in prostrating and destroying the unfortunate inhabitants of such filthy abodes. While there has been little increase in the usual mortality in the healthy, and clean streets, the mortality has been quintupled in the unhealthy and dirty streets. These dwellings are indeed reservoirs of pestilence, that only require the match to be applied to cause enormous destruction of life. In some places, as in Shacklewell-street, food cannot be retained a single night without becoming tainted, and leather rapidly becomes covered with green mould.

The disgusting and abominable state of the open and common privies, proves a source of much disease and domestic discomfort in another way; women and children find these places so repulsive that they avoid them, and retain, in their ill-ventilated rooms, their refuse; the utensils are seldom emptied on account of the trouble thereby occasioned; the air of the rooms, therefore, becomes most offensive, and deleterious, and the walls absorb the emanations, and render the abode permanently unhealthy.

The nearly total want of efficient house drainage, and the general absence of sewers, necessitate, to some extent, the present state of things. This is proved by the fact that in the *new buildings* in Hackney-road, duly provided with house drainage, water closets are attached. Probably there are more water-closets to these few houses than in all the 13,000 houses in the parish. Certainly there are not fifty water-closets for the 82,000 inhabitants.

The present customary method of emptying cesspools and privies by hand labour, and removing the soil by cartage, is excessively offensive, and occasionally the cause of serious accidents. The expense, moreover of the removal of the soil in this way, acts as an insurmountable obstacle to the riddance of this pestilential refuse from the dwellings of the poor. When it is considered that the usual cost of cleansing cesspools in London, is 1*l* each time, and that the rents of the dwellings of the poor range from 1s. to 3s. 6d. and 5s. a week, it can readily be understood, that the poor cannot cleanse their cesspools and privies, and that the landlords consider the expense very oppressive, and consequently neglect the operation. In the evidence of Mr Beek before the metropolitan Sanitary Commission some contradictory evidence is given, to the effect that the expense of emptying the cesspools of common tenements varies, probably, from 7s. to 10s.; but that if the man who does the work is allowed to come to the house and charge, he will charge perhaps four or five times that amount. He states, likewise, the average cost of cleansing to amount to 15s. but that that is not allowing the nightman to use his own discretion about it. It is, therefore, clear that the average as stated by the nightmen themselves, of £1 is more near the truth. But besides the expense, the offensiveness of the operation causes the process to be much neglected. Science, certainly, has made rapid progress in presenting us with chloride of manganese. A waste product of the manufacture of chlorine; procured in very large quantities (probably 160 tons a day,) and at present applied to no useful process, and consequently very cheap. This agent almost immediately destroys the disgusting odour of night soil and other animal substances in a state of putrecence, even when used in very small quantities, such as a pint to about a ton, in winter; and would consequently remove two difficulties in the way of riddance of the soil by the process of hand labour and cartage, namely: the offensiveness and the danger. But when conjoined with the new method of flushing and cleansing cesspools by means of the common fire engine and hose, the remaining difficulty, namely — the expense is surmounted, the expense is only one-sixth that of the old process.

28

Dickens's periodical, *Household Words*, maintained a sustained concern with the living conditions of Londoners. Like Gavin, its correspondent, Henry Morley [see p. 85-6], visited the infamous area of Bethnal Green:

Unsigned article [Henry Morley], 'The Quiet Poor', Household Words, IX, 15 April 1854, pp. 201-6.

I obtained leave to visit the inhabitants of a parochial district in Bethnal Green, remarkable for its poverty, for the struggles made by its inhabitants to keep out of the workhouse, and for the small number of the offences brought home to their doors.

The little district of which I speak, small as it is, contains the population of a country town. To judge by the eye I should imagine that it covers ground about a quarter of a mile wide, and a quarter of a mile long. It is composed wholly of narrow courts and lanes, with a central High Street or Church Street of shops — itself a miserable lane. Although the houses are for the most part but cottages, with two floors and a cellar, there are crammed together in them fourteen thousand people. In the whole quarter there is not one resident whom the world would call respectable; there are not more than about half-a-dozen families able to keep a servant; and there is not one man I believe able to tenant a whole house. The shopkeepers who make a little outside show, fare indoors little better than their neighbours. As a general rule, each room in each house is occupied by a distinct family; they are comparatively wealthy who afford to rent two rooms; but, generally, as the families enlarge, the more they require space, the less they can afford that costly luxury. The natives of this parish chiefly subsist upon potatoes and cheap fish, buying sprats when they are to be had, and in default of them sitting down to dine on potatoes and a herring. They earn money as they can, and all are glad to work hard when there is work for them to do. The majority of the men are either weavers, or they are costermongers and hawkers. These two classes occupy, speaking generally, different portions of the neighbourhood; the weavers earn a trifle more, and hold their heads up better than their neighbours: they are the west end people of the district. The whole place is completely destitute of sewerage; one sewer has been made in a street which forms part of its boundary; it has its share in that, but nothing more. The houses all stand over cesspools; and, before the windows, filth, dead cats, and putrid matter of all sorts run down or stagnate in the open gutters. How do people, who are quiet people, live in such a place?

From a wretched lane, an Egypt watered by a muddy Nile, I turned into a dark house like a catacomb, and after some hazardous climbing reached a chamber in which there were more people than things. Two women sat at work with painful earnestness before the latticed window, three childen shivered round an empty grate. Except the broken chairs on which the women sat, there was no seat in the room but an old stool. There was no table, no bed. The larder was the windowsill, its store a couple of potatoes. In one corner was a confused heap of many-coloured rags, in another corner were a few battered and broken jugs and pans; there was a little earthen teapot on the cold bars of the grate, and in the middle of the room there was a handsome toy. I saw a household and its home. The father had been some months dead, the mother expected in two or three days to receive from God another child. She had four, and 'Have you lost any?' I asked, looking down into the Egypt out of doors. 'I have lost nine!'

This woman and her sister were at work together on cloth-tops for boots; each woman could make one in about four hours, and would receive for it threepence, out of which sum she would have expended three farthings on trimming or binding, and a fraction of a farthing upon thread. She had parted with her furniture piece by piece during the last illness of her husband. I talked to the children, and began to pull the great toy by the string: a monkey riding on a cock. As the wheels rolled, it made music, and up scrambled the fourth child, a great baby boy. 'His grandmother gave him that,' the mother said. They had sold their bed, their clothes, but they had kept the plaything!

We traced the current of another Nile into another Egypt. These Niles have their inundations, but to their unhappy Egypts such floods only add another plague. In summer time the courts and lanes are rich with exhalation, and in autumn their atmosphere is deadly. When May comes round the poor creatures of this district, pent up as they are, feel the spring blood leaping faintly within them, and are not to be restrained from pressing out in crowds towards the green fields and the hawthorn blossoms. They may be found dancing in the tea-gardens of suburban public-houses, rambling together in suburban meadows, or crawling out to the Essex marshes. That is the stir made by the first warm sunshine of the year, and after that the work goes on; the warm weather is the harvest time of the hawkers and costermongers, who at the best suffer severely during winter.

The summer heat lifts out of the filthy courts a heavy vapour of death, the overcrowded rooms are scarcely tenantable, and the inhabitants, as much as time and weather will permit, turn out into the road before their doors. The air everywhere indeed is stifling, but within doors many of the cottages must be intolerable. I went into one containing four rooms and a cellar, and asked, 'How many people live here?' They were counted up for me, and the number came to six and twenty! The present clergyman of this district — whose toil is unremitting in the midst of the vast mass of sorrow to which he is called to minister — dwells upon wholesome ground outside the district. Within it, there is not a parsonage or any house that could be used as one, and if there were — what man would carry wife or children to a home in which they would drink poison daily? The pastor is very faithful in the performance of his duty; liberal of mind, unsparing of toil; and, although the reward of his office is as little as its toil is great, and he is forced to take new duties on himself to earn a living, yet I know that he pours out his energies, his health, and all the money he can earn beyond what suffices for a frugal maintenance, upon his miserable people. We have need to be thankful that the Church has such sons. The Reverend Theophilus Fitzmumble may be a canon here, a master there, a rector elsewhere, and a vicar of Little Pogis, with a thousand a year for the care of a few hundred farmers and farm labourers who rarely see his face. Fitzmumble may be a drone, the thousand a year paid for his ministration at Little Pogis might be better paid to a man who has daily to battle with, and to help such misery as that of which I speak in Bethnal Green. But let us, I repeat, be thankful that Fitzmumble is not the whole Church. It has sons content to labour as poor men among the poor, whose hearts ache daily at the sight of wretchedness they cannot help; whose wives fall sick of fevers caught at the sick beds of their unhappy sisters. Of such ministers the tables are luxurious, for they who sit at meat know that their fare is less by the portion that has been sent out to the hungry; such men go richly clad in threadbare cloth, of which the

nap is perhaps represented by small shoes upon the feet of little
children who trot to and fro in them to school.

But, though the incumbent of this parochial district about
which I speak, is truly a Christian gentleman, he has his body to
maintain alive, and dares not remain too long in the poison bath
of his unsewered district during the hot summer days. He visits
then only the dying, and they are not few. 'I have seen,' he said,
'a dead child in a cellar, and its father dying by its side, a living
daughter covered with a sack to hide her nakedness when I went
in, the rest all hungry and wretched, furniture gone, and an open
sewer streaming down into a pool upon the floor.' Again he said,
'I have seen in the sickly autumn months a ruined household
opposite the back premises of a tripe and leather factory, which is
a dreadful nuisance to its neighbours; it emits a frightful stench,
and lays men, women, and children down upon sick beds right
and left. In this room opposite the place, I have seen the father of
the family and three children hopelessly ill with typhus fever, and
the eldest daughter with malignant small pox, while the mother,
the one person able to stir about, sat on a chair in the midst of
them all deadened with misery. The place by which this household was being murdered has been several times indicted and
fined as a nuisance. Every time this has occurred, the proprietors
have paid the fine and gone on as before; they regard such fine-
paying as only a small item in their trade expenses.'

The people in this black spot of London all strive to the last to
keep out of the workhouse. The union workhouse planted in a
region that is crammed with poor, must be managed strictly, or
there will be fearful outcry about keeping down the rates. Are the
poor people in the wrong for keeping their arms wound about
each other? There is not a house, a room, — of all I visited the
other day, I did not see one room, — in which there was not sickness. Talk of the workhouse, and the mother says, in effect, 'who
would nurse Johnny like me? Oh, I could not bear to think that
he might die, and strangers cover up his face!' Johnny again cries
for his mother, or if he be a man, he says that he would die naked
and in the streets, rather than not give his last words to his wife.

But, somebody may say, This is sentimentality. The poor have
not such fine feelings. They get to be brutalised. Often it is so;
but, quite as often certainly, they are refined by suffering, and
have depths of feeling stirred up within them which the more
fortunate are only now and then made conscious of in themselves. I went into one room in this unhappy place — this core of

all the misery in Bethnal Green — and saw a woman in bed with a three weeks infant on her arm. She was still too weak to rise, and her husband had died when the baby was three days old. She had four other children, and she panted to get up and earn. It eased her heart to tell of her lost love, and the portion of her story that I here repeat was told by her, in the close narrow room, with a more touching emphasis than I can give it here; with tremblings of the voice and quiverings of the lip that went warm to the hearts of all who listened: —

'The morning before my husband died,' she said, 'he said to me, "O Mary, I have had such a beautiful dream!" — "Have you, dear?" says I; "do you think you feel strong enough to tell it me?" — "Yes", says he, "I dreamt that I was in a large place where there was a microscopic clock" (he meant a microscope), "and I looked through it and saw the seven heavens all full of light and happiness, and straight before me, Mary, I saw a face that was like a face I knew." "And whose face was it, love?" says I. — "I do not know", says he; "but it was more beautiful than anything I ever saw, and bright and glorious, and I said to it, Shall I be glorified with the same glory that you are glorified with? And the head bowed towards me. And I said, Am I to die soon? And the head bowed towards me. And I said, Shall I die to-morrow? And the face fixed its eyes on me and went away. And now what do you think that means?" — "I do not know," says I, "but I think it must mean that God is going to call you away from this world where you have had so much trouble, and your suffering is going to be at an end, but you must wait His time, and that is why the head went away when you said, shall I die to-morrow?" — "I suppose you are right," says he, "and I don't mind dying, but O Mary, it goes to my heart to leave you and the young ones" (here the tears spread over the poor woman's eyes, and her voice began to tremble). "I am afraid to part with you, I am afraid for you after I am gone." — "You must not think of that," says I, "you've been a good husband, and it's God's will you should go." — "I won't go, Mary, without saying good bye to you", says he. "If I can't speak, I'll wave my hand to you," says he, "and you'll know when I'm going." And so it was, for in his last hours he could not speak a word, and he went off so gently that I never should have known in what minute he died if I had not seen his hands moving and waving to me Good-bye before he went.'

Such dreams and thoughts belong to quiet poverty. I have told this incident just as I heard it; and if I were a daily visitant in Bethnal Green, I should have many tales of the same kind to tell.

The people of this district are not criminal. A lady might walk unharmed at midnight through their wretched lanes. Crime demands a certain degree of energy; but if there were ever any harm in these well-disposed people, that has been tamed out of them by sheer want. They have been sinking for years. Ten years ago, or less, the men were politicians; now, they have sunk below that stage of discontent. They are generally very still and hopeless; cherishing each other; tender not only towards their own kin, but towards their neighbours; and they are subdued by sorrow to a manner strangely resembling the quiet and refined tone of the most polished circles.

By very different roads, Bethnal Green and St James's have arrived at this result. But there are other elements than poverty that have in some degree assisted to produce it. Many of the weavers have French names, and are descended from French emigrants, who settled hereabouts, as many of their countrymen settled in other places up and down the world after the Revocation of the Edict of Nantes; and at that time there were fields and market gardens near the green of Bethnal. There are here some runlets of the best French blood, and great names may be sometimes met with. The parish clerk, who seemed to have in him a touch of Spanish courtesy, claims to be a descendant from Cervantes. The literary spirit still works in him; for I found his table covered with papers and tickets relating to a penny lecture — twopence to the front seats — that he had been delivering on Nineveh, Palmyra, Babylon, and other ancient cities, illustrated with a little panorama that he had. His lecture had drawn crowds, seventy had been turned from the doors, and he was preparing to repeat it. Then there is a poor fellow in the parish named Racine, who declares that he can prove his descent from Racine the dramatist. There is a Lesage too, to be met with, and many other men whose names are connected with ideas of noble race or noble intellect. The daughters of these handloom weavers dress their hair with care, and will not let themselves be seen in rags. The mothers of the last generation were often to be seen in the old French costumes, and to this day hundreds work in such glazed attics as were used by their forefathers across the sea. Little as they earn, the weaver-households struggle to preserve a decent poverty and hide their cares. They must have some pleasures too. In two or three parts of the parish, there are penny balls; there is a room also for penny concerts, and there is a penny circus, 'with a complete change of riders'. These places are all quietly and well conducted; but are chiefly supported by the surrounding localities.

The fathers of these families lived when their parents could afford to them the benefit of dame schools. How courteously and sensibly they often talk, and with what well chosen words, I was amazed to hear. A doll-maker, dying of consumption, who certainly believed in long words too devoutly, but who never misapplied them, talked in periods well weighed and rounded, that were in admirable contrast to the slip-slop gossip of my dear friend Sir John Proaser. 'One of the weavers', said the clergyman of the district (the Reverend Mr Trivett), 'asked me to lend him Calvin's Institutes, and when I told him that mine was a black letter copy, he said that he should not mind that in the least. Another asked once for the Colloquies of Erasmus, and one who was unmarried and working with his brother, so that he had some shillings to spare, wanted to know what it would cost to get a copy of Smith's Wealth of Nations.'

I mentioned just now a doll-maker — him I found roasting himself by a large fire — a man wasted and powerless — discussing on what day he should go into Guy's Hospital. There was a heap of bran in a corner, used for doll-stuffing and for a children's bed also, no doubt. Here, as elsewhere, however large the family collected in one room, I never saw more than a single bed. Sleeping places were made usually on the floor. One woman, rich in half-a-dozen chairs, showed me with triumph how she made a first-rate bedstead by putting them artfully together. Before the doll-maker's bran sat a boy at a stool, with a pile of broken tobacco-pipe at his side, and some paste and strips of paper. Each bit of paper as he pasted it he screwed round a fragment of tobacco-pipe. These were, perhaps, to be doll's bones, the basis of their arms and legs. At a deal table near the window a mother, who tottered with ill-health, and a daughter about seventeen years old, were measuring some lengths of calico. The calico was to be cut up for doll's bodies, or skins. The cutting out of bodies requires art and skill. The girl many days before had pricked her thumb, the result was that it had gathered, and was in a poultice. 'She is the only one of us, except me, able to make the bodies,' said the poor father, 'and you see —' He pointed to the crippled thumb, and the mother looked down at it in a maze of sorrow. They looked to its recovery for bread.

In another house I saw a room swept of all furniture, through the distress that such a pricked thumb had occasioned, and two other homes I saw made wretched by the accidental wounding of the husband's hand.

In one of them, an empty room rented at half-a-crown a-week, there stood a woman all by herself. She stood because she did not possess a chair and told us that they — she and her husband — had that morning got some work. They had been living on their furniture for twelve weeks, because her husband, who was a carpenter, had hurt his hand. She had failed to get work until the day before, when she obtained a pair of stays to make, a chance job, for which she would receive fourpence. She was a young woman who would have been pretty if she had been better fed. Alas, for the two young hearts failing there together, for the kisses of the thin and wasted lips that should be full with youth and pleasure! 'You earn so little here, and could have a beautiful cottage in the country for the price of this room in Bethnal Green; — you scarcely could be worse off if you went into the country.' They had done that, but the law of settlement had forced them back again on Bethnal Green.

Why should I make the readers' hearts as heavy as my own was made by the accumulation of these evidences of woe heaped up over woe? I saw families in cellars with walls absolutely wet; in dismantled rooms covered with dust and cobwebs, and containing nothing but a loom almost in ruins; or striving to be clean. One I found papering and whitewashing his home, having obtained means to do so from his landlord after seven years of neglect. In another house a neighbour had dropped in to tea in a company dress of old black satin with plenty of cherry-coloured ribbons. The daughter of that house made elaborate and very pretty fringe-tassels at fourteen pence for a hundred and forty-four of them. The father of that house had been two weeks dead. Everywhere I found present sickness, and in many places recent death. Only in one place I found sullen despair, and there the room was full of people — there was no fire in the hearth, and there was no furniture, except a bed from which a woman was roused who spoke hoarsely and looked stupidly wild with ragged dress and hair disordered. She may have been drunk, but she could have sat as she was to Lebrun for a picture of despair. 'Why,' she was asked, 'do none of your children come to school?' — 'No money.' — 'But you need pay nothing, — only wash and send them.' — 'I can't wash them; — no fire.'

We went into a cellar shared by two families: — the rent of a room or cellar in this district is commonly two shillings a-week. One half of this room was occupied by a woman and four children, who had also a husband somewhere working for her; her division contained many bits of furniture and quite a fairy-land of ornaments upon the mantelpiece. The other woman was a widow with a son nineteen years old. They had nothing but a little deal table and two broken chairs; but there were hung up against the wall two coloured pictures in gilt frames, which her son, she said, had lately given her. Perhaps they were a birthday gift; certainly, cheap as they may have been, they were the fruit of a long course of saving; for the poor woman, trembling with ill-health, and supporting her body with both hands upon the little table, said, that her son was then out hawking, and that she expected him in every minute in hope that he might bring home three-halfpence to get their tea.

Account was made of the earnings of a whole lane, and they were found to average threepence farthing a day for the maintenance of each inhabitant, both great and small. There was, I think, one in about six positively disabled by sickness. The dearness of everything during the last winter had been preventing hawkers and others from making their small purchases and sales; the consequence was to be seen too plainly in many a dismantled room. The spring and summer are for all the harvest time, but some were already beginning to suspect that 'the spring must have gone by,' for their better times used to begin early in March, and there is still no sign of them. All were, however, trusting more or less that, in the summer, they would be able to recover some of the ground lost during a winter more severe than usual. None seemed to have a suspicion of the fate in store, of the war-prices and causes of privation that probably will make for them this whole year one long winter of distress. It is not only in the dead upon the battle-field, or among the widows and orphans of the fallen, that you may see the miseries of war. Let any one go, five months hence, among these poor people of St Philip's, Shoreditch (that is the right name of this region of Bethnal Green), when they find that they have lost not their spring only, but their summer, — let them be seen fasting under an autumn sun in their close courts and empty rooms, starved by hundreds out of life as well as hope, and he will understand, with a new force, what is the meaning of a war to the poor man.

Something I have neglected to say concerning the dismantled

rooms. The absent furniture and clothing has not been pawned, it has gone to a receiving-house. The district is full of miserable people preying upon misery who lend money on goods under the guise of taking care of them, and give no ticket or other surety. It is all made a matter of faith, and an enormous interest is charged for such accommodation in defiance of the law.

And another miserable truth has to be told. The one vice with which misery is too familiar is well-known also here; for on the borders of this wretched land, which they must give up hope who enter, there is a palace hung round outside with eight or ten huge gaslights — inside brilliantly illuminated. That is the house of the dragon at the gate — there lives the gin devil.

What is to be done? Private charity must look on hopelessly when set before an evil so gigantic. Here is but a little bit of London, scarcely a quarter of a mile square, we look at it aghast, but there is other misery around it and beyond it. What is to be done? So much drainage and sewerage is to be done, is very certain. All that can be done is to be done to change the character of a Bethnal-Green home. The Society for Improving the Dwellings of the Poor makes nearly five per cent. on its rooms for families, though it fails commercially when taking thought for single men. The Society professes pure benevolence, and no care about dividends. Let it abandon that profession, abide by it certainly as a guiding idea, but let it take purely commercial ground before the public, and let its arm be strengthened. They who are now paying from five to seven pounds a-year for a filthy room or cellar, will be eager enough to pay the same price for a clean and healthy lodging. Let model lodging-houses for such families be multiplied, let them return a percentage to their shareholders; and since the society is properly protected by a charter, let all who would invest a little money wisely look into its plans. I see the need of this so strongly that I shall begin to inquire now very seriously into its affairs, and I exhort others to do the same, with a view to taking shares, if they be found a safe and fit investment.

Private and direct charity may relieve individuals, and console many a private sorrow in this part of London, but it cannot touch — such charity to the extent of thousands of pounds cannot remove — the public evil. Associations for providing any measure of relief are checked by the necessity for charters to protect themselves against the present unjust laws of partnerships.

And, after all, the truth remains, that the people are crowded together in a stagnant corner of the world. They are all poor together; no tradesman or employer living among them finds them occupation; they ramble about and toil their lives away painfully to earn threepence farthing a-day; while the same people shifted to other quarters in the country, would find men contending for the possession of their labour, glad to give two or three shillings daily for a pair of hands. The people of the parish hang together like a congealed lump in a solution that needs to be broken up and stirred in with the rest.

Half the men here would be hailed with chants of joy by the manufacturers were they to turn their back upon their handlooms and march to the aid of steam in Preston. I do not say, Send them to Preston, for in that town one misery can only be relieved because another has been made, but there are very many parts of England in which labour is wanted sorely, and would earn fair pay. Employers in those parts of England should be made fully aware of the existence of such parishes as this, in which hardworking, earnest, quiet people struggle in the dark. Such parishes are banks on which cheques may be drawn to any amount for the capital that can be made of honest labour.

There is room for many of these people in large provincial towns, and in small towns and rural districts. The abolition of the Law of Settlement — a horrible evil and an absolutely frightful cruelty, fully discussed last year in this journal — will remove the chief obstacle to such an attempt to break up little lumps of social misery. The abolition of that law is promised to the country, and whoever strives to make the promise null or to postpone its fulfilment, strives practically — whatever his intent may be — to perpetuate or to prolong some of the worst pains that vex both flesh and spirit of our labourers. When the migrations of the poor cease to be watched with narrow jealousy, as will be the case when this bad law is dead, no corner of our social life in London, or in England, need stagnate or putrify. There need be no longer six-and-twenty people in a cottage, upon ground that does not find fit work for six. Change will be then possible for Bethnal-Green. It may remain the home of poverty and toil, but it may cease to be the home of want.

29

The suburbs did not suffer from the same immediate problems of overcrowding and poor sanitation as did the worst inner-city areas. But Dickens, in his fiction, shows an awareness of the problems caused by the displacement of the inhabitants of the old rookeries, speaking, particularly in *The Old Curiosity Shop*, *Dombey and Son* and *Our Mutual Friend*, of the tracts of 'suburban sahara', with their shoddy, speculative building, that spread on the fringes of the metropolis. This theme was taken up in articles in *Household Words*. 'A Suburban Connemara', moreover, alludes to the London mounds of dust and dirt which are central to *Our Mutual Friend*.

The *Household Words* contributors' book ascribes this article to T.M. Thomas, but this would seem to be a misrecording for William Moy Thomas (1828-1910), a prolific journalist and writer, who contributed a number of articles for *Household Words*, mostly on topics of current social interest.

Unsigned article [William Moy Thomas], 'A Suburban Connemara', Household Words, *II, 8 March 1851, pp. 562-5.*

... though I am a Manchester man, I know the City as well as any Londoner. I know every court and alley of it, and can make short cuts, and find the nearest way from any one part of that great labyrinth to another. I confess I am not so well acquainted with the suburbs. I had always a favourable impression of the northern side of London, from the pretty villas and cottages which I had remarked on each side of the line, on coming up by the North-Western Railway. Therefore, having lately found it advisable to transfer my business altogether to Watling Street, City, I resolved to seek in that quarter for a residence for myself and family. Another reason induced me to select that spot. My goods are coming up continually by the North-Western Railway; and having some commissions in the West Riding, who send up parcels by the Great Northern line, I wished to be somewhere between Battle Bridge and Euston Square: in order, occasionally, to give an eye to my consignments at both stations. With this purpose I procured a new map, on a large scale, in order to see all the Victoria Crescents and Albert Terraces thereabouts.

I drew out my pocket-compasses, measured the line, reduced it one half; and, on finding the unknown locality, brought one point of the dividor's plumb upon a spot which I at once read off from the map as 'Agar Town'. Looking more minutely, I observed that the particular point of the district indicated, was 'Salisbury Crescent'. I could not repress an exclamation of satisfaction, as Oxford and Cambridge Crescents also met my eye. Without further delay, I struck a half-mile circle; and as I observed therein several streets and terraces bearing the names, Canterbury, Winchester, Durham, Salisbury, &c., I concluded that this was (as it eventually turned out to be) Church property; and, as a lover of order and decency, I congratulated myself on the felicitous idea that had suggested to me that neighbourhood; for I felt this circumstance to be a guarantee of an orderly and well-regulated estate.

From these high-sounding names, however, I had some misgivings that the houses in that neighbourhood might be of too expensive a class for a man of moderate means. Still, I resolved to proceed there, and reconnoitre, in the hope of finding a decent little place, at a moderate figure. So, with my map in my hand, I rode down to King's Cross, and proceeding along the old Pancras Road, entered the King's Road, which is the boundary of the property I was seeking. I had not gone far beyond a large building, which I found was the St Pancras Workhouse, when I observed a woman and a number of ragged children drawing a truck. The truck contained a table, two or three old chairs, and some kitchen utensils, with a large bundle of bed-clothes tied up in a patchwork quilt. The entire strength of the company was exerted to draw the truck up the steep pathway of a turning on the right-hand side of the road, in which they succeeded at length; and the woman, struggling, with her hair about her face, and her bonnet hanging round her neck, the truck moved on, aided by the vigorous pushing of her young family behind. The pathway was some feet above the road, which was a complete bog of mud and filth, with deep cart-ruts; the truck, oscillating and bounding over the inequalities of the narrow pathway, threatened every moment to overturn with the woman, her family, and all her worldly goods.

There was something so painfully picturesque in the little group, and so exciting in the constant apprehension of an accident, that I could not help following. For a time, however, a special Providence seemed to watch over the party. I began to give up all fear of a mishap; when, suddenly, the inner wheel encountered a small hillock of dust and vegetable refuse at the door of a cottage, and finally shot its contents into the deep slough of the roadway. The woman turned back; and, having well thumped the heads of her family, seated herself upon the heap of ashes which had been the cause of her misfortune, to vent the rest of her rage in abuse of a miscellaneous character.

A dustman happening to pass at the time, helped the children to restore the chattels to the righted truck.

'How fur have you to go?' he asked.

'Oh! not fur', said she, 'only to one of them cottages yonder. It's very aggravatin, arter draggin' them goods all the way from Smithses Rents, and all along that there nasty road, all right; just to upset when one's got here! This ain't no woman's work, this ain't; only my husband's got a job this mornin', and we was obliged to move out afore twelve; which is the law, they says.'

'What is the name of this place?' I asked.

'This here, sir?' replied the woman; 'why, Hagar Town.'

'Agar Town?' I exclaimed, with astonishment, remembering how clean and promising it had appeared upon the map. 'Do you mean to say that I am really in Agar Town?'

The dustman, who by this time had finished his job, and who sat upon the pathway smoking a short black pipe, with his legs dangling over the road, like a patient angler by a very turbid stream, ventured to join the conversation, by answering my question.

'You're as nigh,' said he, 'to the middle o' Hagar Town as you vell can be.'

'And where,' said I, 'is Salisbury Crescent?'

'There's Salisbury Crescent!'

I looked up, and saw several wretched hovels, ranged in a slight curve, that formed some excuse for the name. The doors were blocked up with mud, heaps of ashes, oyster-shells, and decayed vegetables.

'It's a rum place, ain't it?' remarked the dustman. 'I am forced to come through it twice every day, for my work lays that way; but I wouldn't, if I could help it. It don't much matter in my business, a little dirt, but Hagar Town is worse nor I can abear.'

'Are there no sewers?'

'Sooers? Why, the stench of a rainy morning is enough fur to knock down a bullock. It's all very well for them as is lucky enough to have a ditch afore their doors; but, in gen'ral, everybody chucks everythink out in front and there it stays. There used to be an inspector of noosances, when the choleray was about; but, as soon as the choleray went away, people said *they* didn't want no more of that suit till such times as the choleray should break out agen.'

'Is the whole of Agar Town in such a deplorable state as this?' I asked.

'All on it! Some places, wuss. You can't think what rookeries there is in some parts. As to the roads, they ain't never been done nothink to. *They* ain't roads. I recollect when this place was all gardeners' ground; it was a nice pooty place enough then. That ain't above ten or twelve year ago. When people began to build on it, they run up a couple o' rows o' houses oppersite one another, and then the road was left fur to make itself. Then the rain come down, and people chucked their rubbidge out; and the ground bein' naturally soft, the carts from the brick-fields worked it all up into paste.'

'How far does Agar Town extend?' I asked.

'Do you see them cinder heaps out a yonder?'

I looked down in the distance, and beheld a lofty chain of dark mountains.

'Well,' said the Dustman, 'that's where Hagar Town ends — close upon Battle Bridge. Them heaps is made o'breeze; breeze is the siftins of the dust what has been put there by the conteractor's men, arter takin' away all the wallyablcs as has been found.'

At this point, the woman who had been combing her hair, arose, and the truck resumed its perilous journey. The dustman waited, and saw it arrive at its destination, in safety; whereupon the dustman having smoked his pipe, departed. As I had, by this time, given up all intention of seeking a residence in that neighbourhood, I continued my researches, like Dr Syntax, simply in search of the picturesque.

Crossing another bridge — for the canal takes a winding course through the midst of this Eden — I stood beside the Good Samaritan public-house, to observe the houses which the dustman had pointed out, with the water 'a flowin' in at the back doors'. Along the canal side, the huts of the settlers, of many shapes and sizes, were closely ranged. Every tenant, having, as I was informed, his own lease of the ground, appeared to have disdained to imitate his neighbour, and to have constructed his abode according to his own ideas of beauty or convenience. There were the dog-kennel, the cow-shed, the shanty, and the elongated watch-box, styles, of architecture. To another, the ingenious residence of Robinson Crusoe seemed to have given his idea. Through an opening was to be seen another layer of dwellings, at the back: one, looking like a dismantled windmill; and another, perched upon a wall, like a guard's look-out on the top of a railway carriage. The love of variety was, everywhere, carried to the utmost pitch of extravagance. Every garden had its nuisance — so far the inhabitants were agreed — but, every nuisance was of a distinct and peculiar character. In the one, was a dung-heap; in the next, a cinder-heap; in a third, which belonged to the cottage of a costermonger, were a pile of whelk and periwinkle shells, some rotten cabbages, and a donkey; and the garden of another, exhibiting a board inscribed with the words 'Ladies' School', had become a pond of thick green water, which was carefully dammed up, and prevented from flowing over upon the canal towing-path, by a brick parapet.

Continuing my way until I came within the shadow of the great cinder-heaps of Mr Darke, the contractor, I turned off at Cambridge Crescent, to make the hazardous attempt of discovering a passage back into the Pancras Road. At the corner of Cambridge Crescent are the Talbot Arms Tea Gardens, boasting a dry skittle-ground, which, if it be not an empty boast, must be an Agar Town island. The settlers of Cambridge Crescent are almost all shopkeepers — the poorest exhibiting in their ragpatched windows a few apples and red-herrings, with the rhyming announcement, 'Table-beer, Sold here.' I suspect a system of barter prevails — the articles sold there comprehending, no doubt, the whole of the simple wants of the inhabitants; a system, perhaps, suggested by the difficulty of communication with the civilised world.

A stranger in these parts immediately attracts the attention of the neighbourhood; and if he be not recognised for an Agarite, is at once set down for a 'special commissioner', about to report to some newspaper upon the condition of the inhabitants. I met no one having the air of a stranger, except an unlucky gentleman, attempting to make a short cut to the London and York Railway station; and a postman, vainly inquiring for Aurora Cottage. There were Bath, and Gloucester, Roscommon, Tralee, and Shamrock Cottages; but Aurora Cottage, being probably in some adjoining street, was entirely unknown to the mud-bound inhabitants. The economy of space which I had observed from

the bridge, was also apparent here. Every corner of a garden contained its hut, well stocked with dirty children. The house of one
family was a large yellow van upon wheels, thus raised above
high mud-mark. This was the neatest dwelling I had observed. It
had two red painted street-doors, with bright brass knockers, out
of a tall man's reach, and evidently never intended for knocking
— the entrance being by steps at the head of the van; indeed, I
suspect that these doors were what the stage managers call
'impracticable'. The interior appeared to be well furnished, and
divided into bed-room and sitting-room. Altogether, it had a
comfortable look, with its chimney-pipe smoking on the top; and
if I were doomed to live in Agar Town, I should certainly like
lodgings in the yellow van.

As I proceeded, my way became more perilous. The footpath,
gradually narrowing, merged at length in the bog of the road. I
hesitated; but, to turn back was almost as dangerous as to go on.
I thought, too, of the possibility of my wandering through the
labyrinth of rows and crescents until I should be benighted; and
the idea of a night in Agar Town, without a single lamp to guide
my footsteps, emboldened me to proceed. Plunging at once into
the mud, and hopping in the manner of a kangaroo — so as not
to allow myself time to sink and disappear altogether — I found
myself, at length, once more in the King's Road.

30

In 1850, Dickens published an article by R.H. Horne on the
sifters who obtained their living from the London dustheaps. The
piece is a blend of fact with a melodramatic cinders-to-riches
fiction of lost title deeds found among the rubbish, restoring an
annuity to their owner, who rewards the finders with their hearts'
desire, a cottage by the dust-heap: an unrealistic romance which,
none the less, may well have laid the imaginative foundations
with which Dickens plays in *Our Mutual Friend.*

The composition of these dustheaps, and the associations
which they would have held for the readers of *Our Mutual Friend,*
are comprehensively discussed by Harvey Peter Sucksmith, 'The
Dust-heaps in *Our Mutual Friend*', *Essays in Criticism,* XXIII, 1973,
pp. 206-12.

Unsigned article [R.H. Horne], 'Dust; or Ugliness Redeemed',
Household Words, *I, 13 July 1850, pp. 380; 382; 383.*

A Dust-heap of this kind is often worth thousands of pounds. The present one was very large and very valuable. It was in fact a large hill, and being in the vicinity of small suburb cottages, it rose above them like a great black mountain. Thistles, groundsel, and rank grass grew in knots on small parts which had remained for a long time undisturbed; crows often alighted on its top, and seemed to put on their spectacles and become very busy and serious; flocks of sparrows often made predatory descents upon it; an old goose and gander might sometimes be seen following each other up its side, nearly mid-way; pigs routed round its base, — and, now and then, one bolder than the rest would venture some way up, attracted by the mixed odours of some hidden marrow-bone enveloped in a decayed cabbage-leaf — a rare event, both of these articles being unusual oversights of the Searchers below.

The principal ingredient of all these Dust-heaps is fine cinders and ashes; but as they are accumulated from the contents of all the dust-holes and bins in the vicinity, and as many more as possible, the fresh arrivals in their original state present very heterogeneous materials. We cannot better describe them, than by presenting a brief sketch of the different departments of the Searchers and Sorters, who are assembled below to busy themselves upon the mass of original matters which are shot out from the carts of the dustmen.

The bits of coal, the pretty numerous results of accident and servants' carelessness, are picked out, to be sold forthwith; the largest and best of the cinders are also selected, by another party, who sell them to laundresses, or to braiziers (for whose purposes coke would not do so well); and the next sort of cinders, called the *breeze*, because it is left after the wind has blown the finer cinders through an upright sieve, is sold to the brick-makers.

Two other departments, called the 'soft-ware' and the 'hard-ware', are very important. The former includes all vegetable and animal matters — everything that will decompose. These are selected and bagged at once, and carried off as soon as possible, to be sold as manure for ploughed land, wheat, barley, &c. Under this head, also, the dead cats are comprised. They are, generally, the perquisites of the woman searchers. Dealers come to the wharf, or dust-field, every evening; they give sixpence for a white cat, fourpence for a coloured cat, and for a black one according to her quality. The 'hard-ware' includes all broken pottery, — pans, crockery, earthenware, oyster-shells, &c, which are sold to make new roads.

'The bones' are selected with care, and sold to the soap-boiler. He boils out the fat and marrow first, for special use, and the bones are then crushed and used for manure.

Of 'rags', the woollen rags are bagged and sent off for hop-manure; the white linen rags are washed, and sold to make paper, &c.

The 'tin things' are collected and put into an oven with a grating at the bottom, so that the solder which unites the parts melts, and runs through into a receiver. This is sold separately; the detached pieces of tin are then sold to be melted up with old iron, &c.

Bits of old brass, lead, &c., are sold to be melted up separately, or in the mixture of ores.

All broken glass vessels, as cruets, mustard-pots, tumblers, wine-glasses, bottles, &c, are sold to the old-glass shops.

As for any articles of jewellery, — silver spoons, forks, thimbles, or other plate and valuables, they are pocketed off-hand by the first finder. Coins of gold and silver are often found, and many 'coppers'.

Meantime, everybody is hard at work near the base of the great Dust-heap. A certain number of cart-loads having been raked and searched for all the different things just described, the whole of it now undergoes the process of sifting. The men throw up the stuff, and the women sift it.

These Dust-heaps are a wonderful compound of things. A banker's cheque for a considerable sum was found in one of them. It was on Herries and Farquhar, in 1847. But banker's cheques, or gold and silver articles, are the least valuable of their ingredients. Among other things, a variety of useful chemicals are extracted. Their chief value, however, is for the making of bricks.

From all that has been said, it will have become very intelligible why these Dust-heaps are so valuable. Their worth, however, varies not only with their magnitude (the quality of all of them is much the same), but with the demand. About the year 1820, the Marylebone Dust-heap produced between four thousand and five thousand pounds. In 1832, St George's paid Mr Stapleton five

hundred pounds a year, not to leave the Heap standing, but to
carry it away. Of course he was only too glad to be paid highly for
selling his Dust.

31

Henry Mayhew also describes the river men who fish for
drowned bodies, and whose livelihood provides the melodramatic opening chapter to *Our Mutual Friend.*

The details of Mayhew's writings did not feed directly into
much mid-century fiction, although the stress on personality and
individuality among the 'characters' of the poor may well owe
much to him. His brother Augustus (1826-75) helped him gather
material, and the brothers Mayhew incorporated some of it
wholesale into *Paved With Gold* (1857: issued in parts: published
in book form in 1858 under Augustus's name alone). Augustus
Mayhew's *Kitty Lamere* (1855) was also based on the *Morning
Chronicle* survey.

For Henry Mayhew, see p. 163. For the relationship of
Mayhew's writings to *Our Mutual Friend,* see Harland S. Nelson,
'Dickens's *Our Mutual Friend* and Henry Mayhew's *London Labour
and the London Poor*', *Nineteenth Century Fiction*, XX, 1965, pp. 207-
22.

Henry Mayhew, London Labour and the London Poor, *London,
1861-2, II, pp. 149-50.*

The dredgerman and his boat may be immediately distinguished
from all others; there is nothing similar to them on the river. The
sharp cutwater fore and aft, and short rounded appearance of the
vessel, marks it out at once from the skiff or wherry of the water-
man. There is, too, always the appearance of labour about the
boat, like a ship returning after a long voyage, daubed and filthy,
and looking sadly in need of a thorough cleansing. The grappling
irons are over the bow, resting on a coil of rope, mixed with the
mud of the river. The ropes of the dredging-net hang over the
side. A short stout figure, with a face soiled and blackened with
perspiration, and surmounted by a tarred sou'wester, the body

habited in a soiled check shirt, with the sleeves turned up above
the elbows, and exhibiting a pair of sunburnt brawny arms, is
pulling at the sculls, not with the ease and lightness of the water-
man, but toiling and tugging away like a galley slave, as he scours
the bed of the river with his dredging-net in search of some
hoped-for prize.

The dredgers ... are the men who find almost all the bodies of
persons drowned. If there be a reward offered for the recovery of a
body, numbers of the dredgers will at once endeavour to obtain
it, while if there is no reward, there is at least the inquest money
to be had — beside other chances. What these chances are may
be inferred from the well-known fact, that no body recovered by a
dredgerman ever happens to have any money about it, when
brought to shore. There may, indeed, be a watch in the fob or
waistcoat pocket, for that article would be likely to be traced.
There may, too, be a purse or pocket-book forthcoming, but
somehow it is invariably empty. The dredgers cannot by reasoning or argument be made to comprehend that there is anything
like dishonesty in emptying the pockets of a dead man. They consider them as their just perquisites. They say that any one who
finds a body does precisely the same, and that if they did not do
so the police would. After having had all the trouble and labour,
they allege that they have a much better right to whatever is to be
got, than the police who have had nothing whatever to do with it.
There are also people who shrewdly suspect that some of the
coals from the barges lying in the river, very often find their way
into the dredgers' boats, especially when the dredgers are
engaged in night-work; and there are even some who do not hold
them guiltless of, now and then, when opportunity offers,
smuggling things ashore from many of the steamers coming from
foreign parts. But such things, I repeat, the dredgers consider in
the fair way of their business.

One of the most industrious, and I believe one of the most skilful and successful of this particular class, gave the following
epitome of his history.

Father was a dredger, and grandfather afore him; grandfather was a dredger and a fisherman too. A'most as soon as
I was able to crawl, father took me with him in the boat to
help him to pick the coals, and bones, and other things out
of the net, and to use me to the water. When I got bigger
and stronger, I was sent to the parish school, but I didn't

like it half as well as the boat, and couldn't be got to stay
two days together. At last I went above bridge, and went
along with a fisherman, and used to sleep in the boat every
night. I liked to sleep in the boat; I used to be as comfortable as could be. Lor bless you! there's a tilt to them boats,
and no rain can't git at you. I used to lie awake of a night in
them times, and listen to the water slapping ag'in the boat,
and think it fine fun. I might a got bound 'prentice, but I
got aboard a smack, where I stayed three or four years, and
if I'd a stayed there, I'd a liked it much better. But I heard
as how father was ill, so I com'd home, and took to the
dredging, and am at it off and on ever since. I got no
larnin', how could I? There's on'y one or two of us dredgers
as knows anything of larnin', and they're no better off than
the rest. Larnin's no good to a dredger, he hasn't got no
time to read; and if he had, why it wouldn't tell him where
the holes and furrows is at the bottom of the river, and
where things is to be found. To be sure there's holes and
furrows at the bottom. I know a good many. I know a
furrow off Lime'us Point, no wider nor the dredge, and I
can go there, and when others can't git anything but stones
and mud, I can git four or five bushel o' coal. You see they
lay there; they get in with the set of the tide, and can't git
out so easy like. Dredgers don't do so well now as they used
to do. You know Pelican Stairs? Well, before the Docks was
built, when the ships lay there, I could go under Pelican
Pier and pick up four or five shilling of a morning. What
was that tho' to father? I hear him say he often made 5l.
afore breakfast, and nobody ever the wiser. Them were fine
times! there was a good livin' to be picked up on the water
them days. About ten year ago, the fishermen at Lambeth,
them as sarves their time 'duly and truly' thought to put us
off the water, and went afore the Lord Mayor, but they
couldn't do nothink after all. They do better nor us, as they
go fishin' all the summer, when the dredgin' is bad, and
come back in winter. Some on us down here [Rotherhithe]
go a deal-portering in the summer, or unloading 'tatoes, or
anything else we can get; when we have nothin' else to do,
we go on the river. Father don't dredge now, he's too old for
that; it takes a man to be strong to dredge, so father goes to
ship scrapin'. He on'y sits on a plank outside the ship, and
scrapes off the old tar with a scraper. We does very well for

all that — why he can make his half a bull a day [2s 6d]
when he gits work, but that's not always; howsomever I
helps the old man at times, when I'm able. I've found a
good many bodies. I got a many rewards, and a tidy bit of
inquest money. There's 5s 6d. inquest money at Rother-
hithe, and on'y a shillin' at Deptford; I can't make out how
that is, but that's all they give, I know. I never finds anything on the bodies. Lor bless you! people don't have any-
think in their pockets when they gits drowned, they are not
such fools as all that. Do you see them two marks there on the
back of my hand? Well, one day — I was on'y young then — I
was grabblin' for old rope in Church Hole, when I brings up a
body, and just as I was fixing the rope on his leg to tow him
ashore, two swells comes down in a skiff, and lays hold of the
painter of my boat, and tows me ashore. The hook of the
drag went right thro' the trowsers of the drowned man, and
my hand, and I couldn't let go no how, and tho' I roared
out like mad, the swells didn't care, but dragged me into
the stairs. When I got there, my arm, and the corpse's shoe
and trowsers, was all kivered with my blood. What do you
think the gents said? — why, they told me as how they had
done me good, in towin' the body in, and ran away up the
stairs. Tho' times ain't near so good as they was, I manages
purty tidy, and hasn' got no occasion to holler much; but
there's some of the dredgers as would holler, if they was
ever so well off.

32

Mary Carpenter (1807-77), the daughter of a Unitarian minister,
spent her life caring for the welfare and education of deprived
young people, including juvenile offenders. In 1846, she founded
a particularly successful ragged school in Bristol; in 1854, she
established Red Lodge, the first girls' reformatory school in
England.

Her book *Reformatory Schools* (1851) was an instant success. It
emphasises that since deprived and delinquent children are
indeed children, one should treat them as such. She demands

schooling, rather than incarceration: free day schools for the poor; industrial schools for young vagrants and beggars, and boarding reformatory schools, under voluntary management, for convicted children who would otherwise be sent to prison. Her policies marked the beginning of a movement which helped to change public attitudes to young offenders. On 10 December 1851, Carpenter convened a public conference on juvenile delinquency. Her incorporation of the picture of a pickpocket in her book *Juvenile Delinquents* (1853) shows the continuing relevance of the types described in *Oliver Twist*. More broadly, the range of issues touched on in both *Reformatory Schools* and *Juvenile Delinquents* joins with, for example, the existence of the Select Parliamentary Committee on Criminal and Destitute Children and the public discussion which attended it to show that the ignorance and quasi-vagrancy of Jo, in *Bleak House*, is neither exaggerated nor atypical.

See Trevor Blount, 'Poor Jo, Education, and the Problem of Juvenile Delinquency in Dickens's *Bleak House*', *Modern Philology*, 62, 1964-5, pp. 325-39. For Mary Carpenter, see Jo Manton, *Mary Carpenter and the Children of the Streets*, London, 1976.

Mary Carpenter, Juvenile Delinquents, *London, 1853, pp. 50-3.*

We have hitherto been considering juvenile delinquents as forming a large class; — although this has been subdivided for the sake of convenience, we have still regarded them as constituting masses of individuals, though typified by single instances, and we have thus derived some general idea of the features which mark the class in its varied aspects. Yet we cannot reform whole classes as such; we may indeed adopt such general plans as, wisely formed and executed, may produce a very perceptible effect on the whole, by removing causes of evil, and applying remedial measures. The work of reformation is an individual work; for every one must bear his own moral burden, and by his own works shall each one stand or fall. The soul of each one must be acted on singly, and for its own sake. We shall, therefore, in this chapter endeavour to gain an insight into the actual condition of individuals of the class, and shall take various 'single captives', who, from the solitude of their cells, shall tell their own mournful tales.

The first is one of the gang of transported pickpockets in Preston Gaol; he was not one of the most daring, and there does not appear to be any culpable neglect on the part of his parents; his is a case which is probably a very common one. William Thompson says,

At the age of 14, I was sent to the factory. At length I went strolling about the railway, instead of looking for work, watching the trains come in, very often getting three or four jobs in a day, receiving from three pence to six pence for each parcel. I very soon spent it, then returned home, and told my mother I had been looking for work all day. I went on in this way for a time, notwithstanding all that was said to me; work I would not, though I had the offer of several places. If my mother said any thing to me I would run away from home, and not show my face for a week. Then I had lodgings to pay, and clothing and food to find, how I was to do it I did not know, my mind was not given to work. I met a companion of mine, he showed me some money, I asked him where he got it? He said he had picked a lady's pocket in St Anne's Square, *I thought it very clever of him*, so we went and got something to eat, paid our lodgings, and went to bed, and I got into bad company from that time. Thus we went on for a long time, one thing led to another, at length *the police knew me quite well from seeing me always among bad characters.* At last, I and another were apprehended in St Anne's Square, on suspicion of pocket-picking, and *sent to Salford prison for a month.*

Is it not evident that a boy in the condition here described by himself, is not likely to be reformed by a month's confinement? Whether it would not have been a blessing to himself and to society, had he then been withdrawn from his career of vice, the subsequent history will show.

'I was again taken up, and sentenced to two months in Salford; when my time was up, and I was restored to liberty again, I soon forgot all my good resolutions I had formed during my imprisonment. I was soon taken again for the same offence, and got two months; when the time expired, my mother came to meet me at the gate, and tried to get me to go to work, *but I would not go.* I again took to my former wicked life, *and went on worse than before.* I went to Stockport fair, where I got £4; then I took all the fairs and races within

231

ten miles round Manchester, getting £3 or £4 at every place, sometimes more, till I came to Rochdale, then I was sent to Salford for fourteen days. I was not long out, when I was taken in Market Street, and sent back for three months. I was taken again, and got one month; when I came out I led just the same life for about six months, when I was taken again in Shud Hill, and sent back for three months more. When I came out, the fever was very bad in Manchester, and I was confined to my bed; I was soon removed to the fever ward, and the fourth week I was sent home in a very weak state. A many of my companions had gone off at this time with the fever. They were not missed, *plenty rising up as fast as they died.* I was not long at my old game before I was taken up and sentenced to one month's imprisonment; when I came out I went to Leeds fair and stayed a week with some friends; I then went to Ripon hirings, and got £25; I then came to Manchester, and soon spent it all.' Mr Clay computes that at the age of 20, when this narrative was written, this young man had mulcted the public during five years of as much as £1800!

What a fruitless conflict has the law, with all its ponderous machinery, its active and vigilant agents, its denouncing bench of magistrates, here waged against a boy! He defies it all, and by his acts challenges it to do its worst, — it cannot change *his will,* which, with the elasticity of youth, rises more strong and resolute after each encounter, which reveals to him its powers. At first he was only idle and disobedient; then led away by a cleverness which promised to relieve him from the fruits of that disobedience; then he is taught, by a month's confinement only, that the once dreaded gaol is not so much to be feared; he was 'soon taken up again', and during a two months' seclusion he appears to have formed some 'good resolutions', which passed away like the morning dew, and he soon had the same punishment again. He does not now appear to have even a temporary remorse, for his mother met him at the gate, entreating him to go to work; but even in those first moments of new liberty he would not yield to parental love, and 'went on worse than before'. He plunges into a bolder career, and undertakes regular plundering expeditions, alternating his time between the gaol and the enjoyment of unlawful booty. Heaven then sends him a warning in a dangerous malady, but his heart is too hardened to listen to the voices of his numerous companions, who, swept off by the same fever, thus spoke to him from the grave. He continued the same fearful 'game' unchecked! And this is the life of a youth who has not reached the term fixed by the law for the commencement of manhood! What is his maturer life to be, when its commencement has been so ripened in crime? This young man is one of thousands! Shall Christians not try if they have not a force more persuasive, more powerful to subdue them than the law?

33

Prostitution, as opposed to the theme of the fallen and unfortunate woman, enters only on the margins of the Victorian novel: in, for example, the figures of Mary Barton's aunt Esther; of Nancy in *Oliver Twist*; Alice Marwood in *Dombey and Son*; the fate of Martha Endell and Little Em'ly in *David Copperfield*; and the moral descent of Carry Brattle in Trollope's *The Vicar of Bullhampton* and of Mercy Merrick in Wilkie Collins's *The New Magdalen*.

Dickens worked actively for the rehabilitation of prostitutes, supporting the plan launched by Angela Burdett Coutts, in 1846, for a 'Home for Homeless Women'. As the letter addressed by Dickens to potential inmates of this home indicates, the aim was to train them in housewifely and responsible duties so that, as emigrants, they would make fit wives for future colonial workers.

The article published anonymously by Dickens in *Household Words* in 1853 ['Home for Homeless Women', *Household Words*, 23 April 1853, pp. 169-75], when Urania Cottage had been in existence for five years, showed that the policy of the home had shifted somewhat from its original rehabilitatory function, and now admitted girls whose unprotected status made them vulnerable to the economic temptations of prostitution, or who had already been in trouble for minor infringements of the law. As has frequently been noted, Dickens's ten-year involvement with Miss Coutts's home does not seem to have changed his presentation of prostitutes in any way, although, as Michael Slater has put it: 'such prostitutes as did come into the Home would have been likely to conform to Dickens's idea of them as inwardly tormented by shame and remorse' (Michael Slater, *Dickens and Women*, London, 1983, p. 344).

See: Charles Dickens, *Letters from Dickens to Angela Burdett Coutts 1841-1865*, edited by Edgar Johnson, London, 1953; Paul McHugh, *Prostitution and Victorian Social Reform*, London, 1980; Keith Nield, ed., *Prostitution in The Victorian Age: Debates on the Issue from 19th Century Critical Journals*, Westmead, Hants, 1973; Judith R. Walkowitz, *Prostitution and Victorian Society*, Cambridge, 1980.

Charles Dickens, 'An Appeal to Fallen Women', Letters from Charles Dickens to Angela Burdett Coutts 1841-1865, edited by Edgar Johnson, London, 1953, pp. 98-100.

You will see, on beginning to read this letter, that it is not addressed to you by name. But I address it to a woman — a very young woman still — who was born to be happy and has lived miserably; who has no prospect before her but sorrow, or behind her but a wasted youth; who, if she has ever been a mother, has felt shame instead of pride in her own unhappy child.

You are such a person, or this letter would not have been put into your hands. If you have ever wished (I know you must have done so at some time) for a chance of rising out of your sad life, and having friends, a quiet home, means of being useful to yourself and others, peace of mind, self-respect, everything you have lost, pray read it attentively and reflect upon it afterwards.

I am going to offer you, not the chance but the *certainty* of all these blessings, if you will exert yourself to deserve them. And do not think that I write you as if I feel myself very much above you, or wished to hurt your feelings by reminding you of the situation in which you are placed. God forbid! I mean nothing but kindness to you, and I write as if you were my sister.

Think for a moment what your present situation is. Think how impossible it is that it can ever be better if you continue to live as you have lived, and how certain it is that it must be worse. You know what the streets are; you know how cruel the companions you find there are; you know the vices practised there, and to what wretched consequences they bring you, even while you are young. Shunned by decent people, marked out from all other kinds of women as you walk along, avoided by the very children, hunted by the police, imprisoned, and only set free to be imprisoned, over and over again — reading this

very letter in a common jail you have already dismal experience
of the truth.

But to grow old in such a way of life, and among such company — to escape an early death from terrible disease, or your
own maddened hand, and to arrive at old age in such a course —
will be an aggravation of every misery that you know now, which
words cannot describe. Imagine for yourself the bed on which
you, then a terrible object to look at, will lie down to die. Imagine
all the long, long years of shame, want, crime, and ruin that will
arise before you. And by that dreadful day, and by the judgment
that will follow it, and by the recollections you are certain to have
then, when it is too late, of the offer that is made to you now,
when it is NOT too late, I implore you to think of it and weigh it
well.

There is a lady in this town who from the windows of her
house has seen such as you going past at night, and has felt her
heart bleed at the sight. She is what is called a great lady, but she
has looked after you with compassion as being of her own sex and
nature, and the thought of such fallen women has troubled her in
her bed.

She has resolved to open at her own expense a place of refuge
near London for a small number of females, who without such
help are lost for ever, and to make a HOME for them. In this
home they will be taught all household work that would be useful
to them in a home of their own and enable them to make it comfortable and happy. In this home, which stands in a pleasant
country lane and where each may have her little flower-garden if
she pleases, they will be treated with the greatest kindness: will
lead an active, cheerful, healthy life: will learn many things it is
profitable and good to know, and being entirely removed from all
who have any knowledge of their past career will begin life afresh
and be able to win a good name and character.

And because it is not the lady's wish that these young women
should be shut out from the world after they have repented and
learned to do their duty there, and because it is her wish and
object that they may be restored to society — a comfort to themselves and it — they will be supplied with every means, when
some time shall have elapsed and their conduct shall have fully
proved their earnestness and reformation, to go abroad, where in
a distant country they may become the faithful wives of honest
men, and live and die in peace.

I have been told that those who see you daily in this place

believe that there are virtuous inclinations lingering within you, and that you may be reclaimed. I offer the Home I have described in these few words, to you.

But, consider well before you accept it. As you are to pass from the gate of this Prison to a perfectly new life, where all the means of happiness, from which you are now shut out, are opened brightly to you, so remember on the other hand that you must have the strength to leave behind you all old habits. You must resolve to set a watch upon yourself; to be gentle, patient, persevering, and good-tempered. Above all, to be truthful in every word you speak. Do this, and all the rest is easy. But you must solemnly remember that if you enter this Home without such constant resolutions, you will occupy, unworthily and uselessly, the place of some unhappy girl, now wandering and lost; and that her ruin, no less than your own, will be upon your head, before Almighty God, who knows the secrets of our breasts; and Christ, who died upon the Cross to save us.

In case there should be anything you wish to know, or any question you would like to ask about this Home, you have only to say so, and every information shall be given to you. Whether you accept or reject it, think of it. If you awake in the silence and solitude of the night, think of it then. If any remembrance ever comes into your mind of any time when you were innocent and very different, think of it then. If ever your poor heart is moved to feel truly, what you have been, and what you are, oh think of it then, and consider what you may yet become.

Believe me that I am indeed,
your FRIEND.

Part Three
The Agricultural Poor

34

Disraeli's *Sybil* dealt with problems of agricultural as well as industrial hardship, for, as Martin Fido puts it:

The plight of the agricultural labourer could not be ignored in a social novel composed in 1844 for publication in 1845. Rick-burning had flared up again in 1841, and 1843-4 saw the greatest outburst of agricultural incendiarism since the Swing riots of 1830. Disraeli had to offer some explanation of this rural unrest to his readers. (Martin Fido, 'The Treatment of Rural Distress in Disraeli's *Sybil*', *The Yearbook of English Studies*, 5, 1975, pp. 153-63.)

His position was a slightly embarrassing one, since the Young England faction which he supported wanted the landed interest to provide a focal point for the country's revival. Perhaps for this reason, rural distress does not feature very prominently within the novel, and, unlike the urban labourers, no farm-workers are characterised in any detail. The three-tiered structure — the landlord who leased a farm to a tenant who in his turn employed casual or weekly labour — is assumed to be familiar to the reader, but its contribution to poverty is not examined. Nor, despite the opposition to the New Poor Law which he maintained throughout his parliamentary career, does Disraeli develop the remarks made in Book III, Chapter 2 about outdoor relief. Fido draws the conclusion that Disraeli is playing safe, unwilling to antagonise his party's landed supporters.

As Fido shows, Disraeli's picture of the village of Marney is cobbled together from elements in Chadwick's *Report*.

Edwin Chadwick (1800-90), sanitary reformer, trained as a lawyer, and became a close friend and disciple of Jeremy Bentham. Preoccupied with the idea of eradicating disease, in 1832 he accepted an assistant commissionership on the Poor Law commission, which was just beginning its work. Assiduous in collecting facts and suggesting remedies, he became a chief commissioner the following year, and, also in 1833, he was involved in the commission investigating the conditions of factory children, the results of which eventually led to the passing of the Ten-Hour Act. The first Sanitary Commission was appointed at his instigation in 1839 and its notorious report (1842), exposing appalling conditions and suggesting means for their improvement, became a textbook for sanitary reform throughout the country.

Report on the Sanitary Condition of the Labouring Population of Great Britain, *by Edwin Chadwick 1842, edited with an introduction by M. W. Flinn, Edinburgh, 1965.*

(a) Report of Mr Gilbert, acting as Assistant Commissioner for Devon and Cornwall, recording that he found that open drains and sewers were the most common cause of malaria, pp. 80-1.

In Tiverton there is a large district, from which I find numerous applications were made for relief to the Board of Guardians, in consequence of illness from fever. The expense in procuring the necessary attention and care, and the diet and comforts recommended by the medical officer, were in each case very high, and particularly attracted my attention.

I requested the medical officer to accompany me through the district, and with him, and afterwards by myself, I visited the district, and examined the cottages and families living there. The land is nearly on a level with the water, the ground is marshy, and the sewers all open. Before reaching the district, I was assailed by a most disagreeable smell; and it was clear to the sense that the air was full of most injurious malaria. The inhabitants, easily distinguishable from the inhabitants of the other parts of the town, had all a sickly, miserable appearance. The open drains in some cases ran immediately before the doors of the houses, and some of the houses were surrounded by wide open drains, full of all the animal and vegetable refuse not only of the houses in that part, but of those in other parts of Tiverton. In many of the houses, persons were confined with fever and different diseases, and all I talked to either were ill or had been so: and the whole community presented a melancholy spectacle of disease and misery.

Attempts have been made on various occasions by the local authorities to correct this state of things by compelling the occupants of the houses to remove nuisances, and to have the drains covered; but they find that in the present state of the law their powers are not sufficient, and the evil continues and is likely so to do, unless the legislature affords some redress in the nature of sanitary powers. Independently of this nuisance, Tiverton would be considered a fine healthy town, situate as it is on the slope of a hill, with a swift river running at its foot.

It is not these unfortunate creatures only who choose this centre of disease for their living-place who are affected; but the whole town is more or less deteriorated by its vicinity to this pestilential mass, where the generation of those elements of disease and death is constantly going on.

Another cause of disease is to be found in the state of the cottages. Many are built on the ground without flooring, or against a damp hill. Some have neither windows nor doors sufficient to keep out the weather, or to let in the rays of the sun, or supply the means of ventilation; and in others the roof is so constructed or so worn out as not to be weather tight. The thatch roof frequently is saturated with wet, rotten, and in a state of decay, giving out malaria; or other decaying vegetable matter.

(b) Mr John Fox, medical officer of the Cerne Union, reported on the housing conditions of Dorsetshire agricultural labourers, pp. 82-3.

These cases (of diarrhoea and common fever) occurred in a house (formerly a poor-house) occupied by nearly 50 persons on the ground-floor; the rooms are neither boarded nor paved, and generally damp; some of them are occupied by two families. The upstairs rooms are small and low, and separated from each other by boards only. Eleven persons slept in one room. The house stands in a valley between two hills, very little above the level of the river, which occasionally overflows its banks, and within a few yards of it. There is generally an accumulation of filth of every description in a gutter running about two feet from its front, and a large cesspool within a few feet behind. The winter stock of potatoes were kept in some of the day-rooms, and generally put away in a wet state. The premises had not been white-limed during three years; in addition to this state of things, the poor were badly fed, badly clothed, and many of them habitually dirty, and consequently typhus, synochus, or diarrhoea, constantly prevailed. No house-rent was paid by the occupants. Many, under more favourable circumstances, were clean and tidy, and if their wages were sufficient to enable them to rent a decent cottage, I have no doubt they would soon regain their lost spirit of cleanliness. In this same parish I have often seen the springs bursting through the *mud* floor of some of the cottages, and little channels cut from the centre under the door-ways to carry off the water, whilst the door has been removed from its hinges for the children to put their feet on whilst employed in making buttons. Is it surprising that fever and scrofula in all its forms prevail under such circumstances?

It is somewhat singular that seven cases of typhus occurred in one village heretofamed for the health and general cleanliness of its inhabitants and cottages. The first five cases occurred in one family, in a detached house on high and dry ground, and free from accumulations of vegetable or animal matter. The cottage was originally built for a school-room, and consists of one room only, about 18 feet by 10, and 9 high. About one-third part was partitioned off by boards reaching to within three feet of the roof, and in this small space were three beds, in which six persons slept; had there been two bedrooms attached to this one day-room, these cases of typhus would not have occurred. The fatal case of typhus occurred in a very small village, containing about sixty inhabitants, and from its locality it appears favourable to the production of typhus, synochus, and acute rheumatism. It stands between two hills, with a river running through it, and is occasionally flooded. It has extensive water meadows both above and below, and a farm-yard in the centre, where there is always a large quantity of vegetable matter undergoing decomposition. Most of the cases of synochus occurred under circumstances favourable to its production. Most of the cottages being of the worst description, some mere mud hovels, and situated in low and damp places with cesspools or accumulations of filth close to the doors. The *mud floors* of many are much below the level of the road, and in wet seasons are little better than so much clay. The following shocking case occurred in my practice. In a family consisting of six persons, two had fever; the mud floor of their cottage was at least one foot below the lane; it consisted of *one* small room only, in the centre of which stood a foot-ladder reaching to the edge of the platform which extended over nearly one-half of the room, and upon which were placed two beds, with space between them for one person only to stand, whilst the outside of each touched the thatch. The head of one of these beds stood within six inches of the edge of the platform, and in the bed of one of my unfortunate patients, a boy about 11 years old, was sleeping with his mother, and in a fit of delirium jumped over the head of his bed and fell to the ground below, a height of about seven feet. The injury to the head and spine was so serious that he lived a few hours only after the accident. In a cottage fit for the residence of a human being this could not have occurred. In many of the cottages, also, where synochus prevailed, the beds stood on the ground-floor, which was damp three parts of the years; scarcely one had a fireplace in the bed-room, and one had a single small pane of glass stuck in the mud wall as its only window, with a large heap of wet and dirty potatoes in one corner.

(c) Report from Robert Weale, Assistant Poor Law Commissioner, p. 86. He records

instances of the condition of large proportions of the agricultural population in the counties of Bedford, Northampton, and War-wick. The medical officer of the Woburn union states, in respect to Toddington, that:

'In this town fever prevailed during the last year, and, from the state of the dwellings of the persons I called on, this could not be wondered on. Very few of the cottages were furnished with privies that could be used, and contiguous to almost every door a dung heap was raised on which every species of filth was accumulated, either for the purpose of being used in the garden allotments of the cottagers, or to be disposed of for manure. Scarcely any cottage was provided with a pantry, and I found the provisions generally kept in the bed-rooms. In several instances I found whole families, comprising adults and in fact children with their parents, sleeping in one room.'

35

In writing *Yeast*, Charles Kingsley was strongly influenced by his brother-in-law, Sidney Godolphin Osborne (1808-89), rector of Bryanston-cum-Durweston, near Blandford, in Dorset. Osborne, despite his clerical profession was far more interested in medicine, surgery and microscopic investigation than in religion. Throughout his life, he campaigned against the conditions in which agricultural labourers lived, writing books, pamphlets and hundreds of letters, many of which were published in *The Times*. As a general rule, his letters were granted some importance: printed in large type and frequently complemented by a leading article commenting on their contents. He provided Alfred Austin, one of the Assistant Poor Law Commissioners, with evidence on conditions in Dorset. The publicity which Osborne attracted made him unpopular: 'labourers, farmers, landowners alike regarded his action as pestilent interference' (Michael White, introduction to *The Letters of Sidney Godolphin Osborne*, I, p. xii). Godolphin did not confine himself to agricultural matters: he also contributed ideas on Free Trade, education, the government of the Church of England, the Crimean War, women's rights, the cattle plague and cholera. Charles Kingsley stayed with Osborne in April, 1844, and was moved to write to his wife:

I never will believe that a man has a real love for the good and the beautiful except he attacks the evil and the disgusting the moment he sees it. Therefore you must make up your mind to see me, with God's help, a hunter out of abuses till the abuses cease — only till then. The refined man to me is he who cannot rest in peace with a coal mine, or a factory, or a Dorsetshire peasant's house near him in the state in which they are. (*Charles Kingsley: His Letters and Memories of his Life*, edited by his wife, I, p. 121.)

(a) Alfred Austin, The Assistant Poor Law Commissioners' Reports on the Employment of Women and Children in Agriculture, *1843, pp. 19-25.*

With regard to lodging, there is no difference between that of the women who labour in the fields and the women of the same class who do not. The want of sufficient accommodation seems universal. Cottages generally have only two bed-rooms (with very rare exceptions); a great many have only one. The consequence is, that it is very often extremely difficult, if not impossible, to divide a family so that grown-up persons of different sexes, brothers and sisters, fathers and daughters, do not sleep in the same room. Three or four persons not unfrequently sleep in the same bed. In a few instances I found that two families, neighbours, arranged so that the females of both families slept together in one cottage and the males in the other; but such an arrangement is very rare, and in the generality of cottages I believe that the only attempt that is or that can be made to separate beds, with occupants of different sexes, and necessarily placed close together from the smallness of the rooms, is an old shawl or some article of dress suspended as a curtain between them. At

Stourpain, a village near Blandford, I measured a bed-room in a cottage consisting of two rooms, the bed-room in question upstairs, and a room on the ground-floor in which the family lived during the day. There were eleven in the family: and the aggregate earnings in money were 16s. 6d. weekly (Dec. 1842), with certain advantages, the principal being the father's title to a grist of a bushel of corn a-week, at 1s. below the market price, his fuel carted for him, &c. They had also an allotment of a quarter of an acre, for which they paid a rent of 7s. 7d. a-year. The following diagram shows the shape of the room and the position of the three beds, A, B, C, it contained. The room was ten feet square, not reckoning the two small recesses by the sides of the chimney, about 18 inches deep. The roof was the thatch, the middle of the chamber being about seven feet high. Opposite the fire-place was a small window, about 15 inches square, the only one to the room.

Bed A was occupied by the father and mother, a little boy, Jeremiah, aged 1½ year, and an infant aged 4 months.

Bed B was occupied by the three daughters, — the two eldest, Sarah and Elizabeth, twins, aged 20; and Mary, aged 7.

Bed C was occupied by the four sons, — Silas, aged 17; John, aged 15; James, aged 14; and Elias, aged 10.

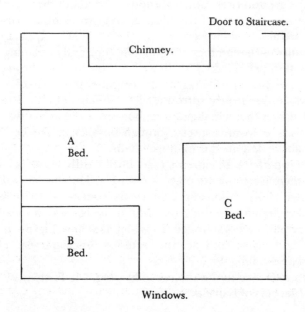

There was no curtain, or any kind of separation between the beds.

This I was told was not an extraordinary case; but that, more or less, every bed-room in the village was crowded with inmates of both sexes, of various ages, and that such a state of things was caused by the want of cottages.

It is impossible not to be struck, in visiting the dwellings of the agricultural labourers, with the general want of new cottages, notwithstanding the universal increase of population. Everywhere the cottages are old, and frequently in a state of decay, and are consequently ill adapted for their increased number of inmates of late years. The floor of the room in which the family live during the day is always of stone in these counties, and wet or damp through the winter months, being frequently lower than the soil outside. The situation of the cottage is often extremely bad, no attention having been paid at the time of its building to facilities for draining. Cottages are frequently erected on a dead level, so that water cannot escape; and sometimes on spots lower than the surrounding ground. In the village of Stourpain, in Dorsetshire, there is a row of several labourers' cottages, mostly joining each other, and fronting the street, in the middle of which is an open gutter. There are two or three narrow passages leading from the street, between the houses, to the back of them. Behind the cottages the ground rises rather abruptly; and about three yards up the elevation are placed the pigsties and privies of the cottages. There are also shallow excavations, the receptacles apparently of all the dirt of the families. The matter constantly escaping from the pigsties, privies, &c., is allowed to find its way through the passages between the cottages into the gutter in the street, so that the cottages are nearly surrounded by streams of filth. It was in these cottages that a malignant typhus broke out about two years ago, which afterwards spread through the village. The bed-room I have above described is in one of them.

This is perhaps an extreme case; but I hardly visited a cottage where there were any attempts at draining. The dirt of the family is thrown down before or behind the cottage; if there is any natural inclination in the ground from the cottage, it escapes; if not, it remains till evaporated. Most cottages have pigsties joining them; and these add to the external uncleanliness of the labourer's dwelling.

With reference to the subject of lodging, Mr Phelps, an agent of the Marquis of Lansdowne, says —

I was engaged in taking the late census in Bremhill parish, and in one case in Studley I found 29 people living under one roof; amongst them were married men and women, and young people of nearly all ages. In Studley it is not at all uncommon for a whole family to sleep in the same room. The number of bastards in that place is very great; the number of unmarried women is greater than that in the neighbouring places. I don't think this state of things is attributable to the women working in the fields, but more to the want of proper accommodation in the cottages.

The Hon. and Rev. *S. Godolphin Osborne*, rector of Bryanston, near Blandford, in Dorsetshire, says —

To say nothing of the physical injury done to himself (the labourer) and family from the want, in most instances, of anything like proper drainage without his dwelling, and the foul air which they are compelled to breathe from the too confined space of the dwelling within, from infancy to puberty his children for the most part sleep in the same room with his wife and himself; and whatever attempts at decency may be made (and I have seen many most ingenious and praiseworthy attempts), still there is the fact of the old and young, married and unmarried, of both sexes, all herded together in one and the same sleeping apartment. Within this last year I saw, in a room about 13 feet square, three beds: on the first lay the mother, a widow, dying of consumption; on the second two unmarried daughters, one 18 years of age, the other 12; on the third a young married couple, whom I myself had married two days before. A married woman of thorough good character told me, a few weeks ago, that on her confinement, so crowded with children is her one room, they are obliged to put her on the floor in the middle of the room, that they may pay her the requisite attention: she spoke of this as to her the most painful part of that her hour of trial. I do not choose to put on paper the disgusting scenes that I have known to occur from this promiscuous crowding of the sexes together. Seeing, however, to what the mind of the young female is exposed from her very childhood, I have long ceased to wonder at the otherwise seeming precocious licentiousness of conversation which may be heard in every field where many of the young are at work together. Early robbed by circumstances of much of that purity which is her honour's safest guard, field-work lends a finish to the mischief.

Mr. *Spooner*, of Blandford, surgeon, says —

Generally the cottages are too small for the families living in them, and tend to produce and aggravate disease, from the inmates living so closely together. Two years ago typhus fever occurred in a neighbouring parish, which I attend; there was one cottage I attended which consisted of one room on the ground-floor, and two small bed-rooms upstairs. In this cottage lived an old man, with his wife, his two daughters, middle-aged women, and his son and wife, with three children, — in all ten individuals. The whole family had the fever, some of them very severely. The son's wife, with two of her children, were on a bed in an out-house; in the out-house was a well, and a large tub containing pigs' victuals, and was the general receptacle for everything. The floor was earthen, with no ceiling but the thatch of the roof. In the same village there were more than forty cases of typhus, and the spread of the disease must be attributed to the people living so densely packed together.

The clothing of women employed in field-labour would appear to be inadequate for their work, but the deficiency is not complained of by them. A change of clothes seems to be out of the question, although necessary not only for cleanliness but for convenience and saving of time. The upper parts of the under-clothes of women at work, even their stays, quickly become wet through with perspiration, whilst the lower parts cannot escape getting equally wet in nearly every kind of work they are engaged in, except in the driest weather. It not unfrequently happens that a woman, on returning home from work, is obliged to go to bed for an hour or two to allow her clothes to be dried. It is also by no means uncommon for her, if she does not do this, to put them on again the next morning nearly as wet as when she took them off. It does not appear that any ill consequences to the health have been observed by medical men to arise from this cause, unless rheumatism be partly attributable to it. The want of a change of working clothes, however, does not prevent the generality of working women having a better gown and other articles of dress for Sundays or holidays.

With reference to the question of clothing and linen for the family generally, a great change has been effected for the benefit of the labouring classes within these few years by the clothing clubs, which are excellently contrived for aiding the poor, and at the same time making such assistance depend upon their own exertions and good conduct, and for avoiding all the mischiefs of indiscriminate charity. I had an opportunity of examining the clothing club at Blandford, in Dorsetshire, and its arrangements and working appeared equally excellent. Any labouring family of good conduct was allowed to belong to it, subscribing 1d., 2d., or 3d. a-week, according to its size and other circumstances. At the end of the year, Christmas, these subscriptions are doubled by the donations of persons in a better position of life living in the neighbourhood. The subscribers are then entitled to purchase of the tradesmen appointed to supply the club, to the amount of their respective shares of the funds, any plain articles of dress or of household linen. The tradesman of the club, in consideration of the large sum of money thus laid out, and promptly paid at his shop, which in the Blandford club exceeded 2000*l.* last Christmas, supplies the best articles of the description wanted at a price rather lower than he could afford to sell them to the labourer dealing with him in the ordinary way. It is also an imperative rule of the club, that if any subscriber purchases with club money any article of dress or linen not of a plain and useful description, he ceases to be a member, as he also does upon any ill conduct. The effect of these clubs has been very great in increasing the linen and clothes of the labourers' families since their establishment.

The general conclusion as to the physical condition of women engaged in agriculture is, that it is better generally than those of the same class not so employed. The reason is evident; the means of the family are increased by her earnings; she has more food, if she be not better clothed and lodged. Her health is also better. I am now speaking of her own physical condition; the effects of her working at farm-labour upon her domestic economy, her husband and children, will be considered presently.

There are no very apparent effects upon the morality of women from their working in the fields; very frequently they are active, energetic, and well-disposed women, working from the sole desire of increasing the means of subsistence of the family, and personally undergoing the labour of their employment for that object. Their motive, being thus meritorious, is hardly consistent with any great degree of immorality. Instances of a want of chastity on the part of married as well as single women thus employed occur, but not more frequently, as far as I could ascertain, amongst them than amongst women of the same class who do not work at the same labour.

There is no doubt that the mixed employment of men and women in hay-making, and perhaps in the corn-harvest, tends to immorality. Hay-making is a season of comparative license; hard work is expected by the master; but if it is performed he overlooks conduct on the part of the work-people which he might not suffer to pass unnoticed at other times. Drink, and frequently food, is plentifully supplied to stimulate to work, and gaiety is promoted by every means. The topics of conversation and the language that is used amongst men and women, young and old, is described as coarse and filthy. That breaches of morality occur cannot be doubted; indeed there is plenty of evidence that they actually take place.

But one-half of the women and girls employed in the hay-field are never engaged in any other kind of farm-work, and the licentiousness of that season, as far as the women are concerned, would appear rather to proceed from those occasionally employed. Women who work the whole or the greater part of the year are too much accustomed to work in the company of men, and moreover are too much inclined to look upon their work in the serious light of an important part of their means of subsistence, to conduct themselves in a reckless manner at any particular season; and generally the testimony in favour of such women's good conduct is abundant. At other times of the year than the hay and corn harvests, no extraordinary licentiousness is generally imputed to women employed in farm-labour.

But there is a great difference of opinion upon the question of the conduct of women thus employed: I have adopted the opinion expressed by the greater number of persons with whom I conversed upon the subject. On the other hand, the clearly-expressed opinion of the Hon. and Rev. S.G. Osborne, whose experience is not confined to one district, and who, moreover, has devoted many years to understand and alleviate the condition of the agricultural poor, speaks strongly as to the immoral effects upon women of their working in the fields.

Their morality, however, appears to me to be that of women in general of the agricultural labouring class, and which cannot be considered as high. This is owing to their poverty, and to the habits they are accustomed to from their infancy, and to the want of proper education, to raise them above their sad condition. The morality of the agricultural labourer is a subject to which my inquiry did not extend, nor had I sufficient opportunities of making any satisfactory inquiry respecting it; but certain things forced themselves upon my attention, and amongst others the consequences of the want of accommodation in their dwellings for sleeping. The sleeping of boys and girls, young men and young women, in the same room, in beds almost touching one another, must have the effect of breaking down the great barriers between the sexes, — the sense of modesty and decency on the part of women, and respect for the other sex on the part of the men. The consequences of the want of proper accommodation for sleeping in the cottages are seen in the early licentiousness of the rural districts, — licentiousness which has not always respected the family relationship. It appeared to me that generally the accommodation for sleeping is such as necessarily to create an early and illicit familiarity between the sexes; for universally in the village where the cottages are the most crowded, there are the greatest number of illegitimate children, and also the greatest depravity of manners generally. On one considerable estate in Wiltshire, no family is allowed by the owner to occupy a cottage containing fewer than two bed-rooms. The morality and general good conduct of the labourers upon that estate are much superior to that above described. The want of proper accommodation for sleeping exists in the villages, rather than in detached cottages on the farms; and I believe that the more immoral of the women employed in agriculture, particularly the women only occasionally employed, as in hay-making and at harvest, are from neighbouring villages; and that the steady and better, and also the largest portion of the women regularly employed in the fields, are from the detached cottages, rather than the villages.

(b) Letter from the Hon. and Rev. S. Godolphin Osborne, *Rector of* Bryanston-cum-Durweston, Dorsetshire, The Assistant Poor Law Commissioners' Reports on the Employment of Women and Children in Agriculture, *1843, pp. 71-7.*

The moment in Chapter XIII, 'The Village Revel' of *Yeast,* where

251

Lancelot enters the village fair, owes much to Sidney Godolphin Osborne's description of 'statute fairs' in the *Reports on Agriculture*, 1843, but as Sheila Smith points out, Kingsley 'belittles the festivities witnessed by Lancelot by describing not a country town's hiring fair where a countryman would go on the serious errand of securing a job, but a village wake, a local parish feast' (*The Other Nation*, pp. 108-9).

My Dear Sir, — I have great pleasure in submitting to your attention the result of my observation upon the moral and physical condition of the women and children employed in agriculture.

I have now, for more than 11 years, been actively engaged as a clergyman in agricultural districts; for seven years I have acted as a magistrate and *ex-officio* guardian; my opportunity for observation in the matter in question has thus been great.

As to the physical effect of field-labour on women, whatever injury may result from it to their bodily health is, I think, purely accident. It cannot be denied that exposure to excess of wet or heat is, in many cases, prejudicial, as well to young unmarried women as to those who are wives and more advanced in years. To both classes there are seasons when the quiet and shelter of home would be preferable to exposure to the weather, and to fatigue of body abroad. That women will work too hard up to the hour of their confinement, and too soon afterwards, and that we frequently see serious injury following upon such imprudence, is very true; but I question, if no field-labour existed, whether the same imprudence would not be shown, though in some other form.

I have often known women hard at work at the washing tub, in their own or a neighbour's house, within a few hours of their delivery.

Occasional instances of severe illness occur from over-work in the gleaning season, both to the women and children: but, it must be remembered, this is employment of their own seeking, guided as to its extent by their own will; and as it is always a species of scramble, there is a jealousy in its performance, which, whether the end it seeks be considered praiseworthy or not, is productive of too great and too prolonged exertion at a season when the weather is most trying to the physical powers.

As to the reaping and binding corn; where a woman is thus employed, it is seldom as a hired servant of the farmer; but her husband, being paid by the acre, she works with him, and virtually *for him*. If she over-works herself it cannot fairly be said that the owner of the farm is to blame.

With regard to 'hoeing', or weed-picking, there is exposure to the weather, and perhaps weariness from many hours of stooping, but the women are in general clad for field-work, and I have never known any complaint of the severity of such work.

Hay-making is not severe work; it requires from the women no great exertion of manual strength, and does not generally commence so early in the day, and it is more subject to interruption than other harvest-work.

In dairy countries women are, I fear, often worked beyond their strength. Many of the operations in a large dairy require great muscular exertion, and the women are exposed to damp within doors, as well as to more or less wet without; but I cannot call to my mind any instance in which I have known serious injury to women so employed.

With regard to children, except for bird-keeping or watching cattle, &c., in the field, I do not think that very young children are often employed by farmers; but it frequently happens that a labourer takes wood-cutting, hedging, and thatching by the piece — he then has one or more of his children to assist him, or rather, I should say, to wait on him with his tools. I do not think the child is injured by the amount of labour required of him, but I have seen injury done to children from their having to go with their parent too great distances from home, especially when the circumstances of the parents have not permitted them to give their children sufficient and proper food.

As to bird-keeping, it may appear cruel that a child should have to pass some eight or ten hours a-day apart from all human society, its sole employment the frightening birds from the corn; but I have never yet had any reason to believe that the boys so employed in any way suffer injury from it. Towards the end of the day, they are, doubtless, anxious to return home, and their inquiries of passers-by as to 'what o'clock it is,' prove how gladly they watch for the hour that is to release them from their day's labour; but this, after all, is no more than any schoolboy feels, who is anxious for the hour when business for the day concludes, and he is released from his books and invited to his evening meal. That these juvenile watch-men do contrive to mix up amusement with their toil, no one who has observed their labyrinths cut in turf, or their carving on gates, trees, or sticks, can doubt; for my own part, I think the importance of their trust, and the knowledge that they are earning wages, goes far to lighten the effect of the monotony of their employment.

Bird-keeping is the earliest work at which boys are employed. Their next stage in labour is the watching cattle or poultry in the field; for this purpose more personal activity is required. Their next step in life is driving the plough, and assisting the carter in the stable, &c.; and then comes the actual holding plough, mowing, ditching, and the usual work of a regular farm-labourer.

I cannot say that, in my experience, I have ever known any of these stages of schooling in out-door employment to tax too heavily the physical powers of the age at which it is entered on, except in cases where, from the parents' neglect or poverty, the constitution has not been dealt fairly with in the way of food.

I have seen the effects of lace-making, straw-plaiting, and button-making, and I have no hesitation in saying that there are many diseases, directly proceeding from the confinement of young persons in crowded rooms, the keeping the body constantly in an unnatural position, and the incessant call upon the utmost power of the eye, which these trades require. Thousands of children of agricultural labourers are employed at these species of work. However much I am opposed to field labour for females, I must add that, in my opinion, there is infinitely less physical injury to be feared from it than from employments of the nature spoken of above.

As to the moral condition of the wives and children of agricultural labourers, I must at once affirm that it is far below what it ought to be, but it is not worse than, under the circumstances, we have a right to expect. The rent of a cottage, so constructed as to enable a labourer to rear his family with attention to the common decencies of life, is far beyond what his wages will allow him to give.

To say nothing of the physical injury done to himself and family from the want, in most instances, of anything like proper drainage without his dwelling, and the foul air which they are compelled to breathe from the too confined space of the dwelling within; from infancy to puberty, his children, for the most part, sleep in the same room with his wife and himself; and whatever attempts at decency may be made — and I have seen many most ingenious and praiseworthy attempts — still there is the fact of the old and young, married and unmarried, of both sexes, all herded together in one and the same sleeping apartment. Within this last year I saw in a room about 13 feet square three beds: on the first lay the mother, a widow, dying of consumption; on the second, two unmarried daughters, one 18 years of age, the other 12; on the third, a young married couple, whom I myself had married two days before. A married woman, of thorough good character, told me, a few weeks ago, that on her confinement, so crowded with children is her one room, they are obliged to put her on the floor in the middle of the room, that they may pay her the requisite attention. She spoke of this as, to her, the most painful part of that her hour of trial. I do not choose to put on paper the disgusting scenes that I have known to occur from this promiscuous crowding of the sexes together. Seeing, however, to what the mind of the young female is exposed from her very childhood, I have long ceased to wonder at the otherwise seeming precocious licentiousness of conversation which may be heard in every field where many of the young are at work together. Early robbed by circumstances of much of that purity which is her honour's safest guard, field-work lends a finish to the mischief.

Few persons will take a woman of known laxity of character as a domestic servant, but for out-door work it is rare to find any other qualification required, beyond punctuality to time and activity in the work undertaken; so that the worst characters in a parish are in general the chief leaders in the conversation, as they are the most accustomed to the different kinds of labour in the fields in which the women are employed. I once spoke to a rather wealthy farmer on the impropriety of giving so much beer to the young of both sexes employed in the hay fields, and the allowing unchecked the grossness of their conversation, and the indecency of many of their acts. His answer was to this effect: — 'Those young ones would never stick to their work if it was not for the beer I find them, and the fun they make for themselves.' I have no hesitation in affirming that field-work for women, let it be overlooked how it may, is liable to great moral abuse; that little overlooked, as it mostly is, it is one of the greatest sources of immorality that I know.

I know that every farthing that can be earned by any member of a labourer's family is of importance to him; but I also believe that the habits gained by this species of employment are of a nature directly leading to a course of life in which far more is eventually squandered in evil than was ever saved for good purposes.

When, too, as in the case of the hop-growing counties, the children of the agricultural labourers are mixed for weeks together with the population that yearly immigrates for the purpose of hop-picking, from London and other large towns, I can see no bounds to the mischief. I wish I could see a remedy for it which would stand any chance of general adoption.

I am well aware of the commonly received opinion, that children are taken too early from school to go to work; but the necessity laid on the parent of obtaining all the help he can towards the support of his family cannot be denied, and this it is that forces him to get them, as soon as he can, into regular employment.

For my own part, as soon as a boy is capable of taking any situation, which whilst it may afford him some wages at the same time initiates him into the calling by which he is in the end to gain his bread, and gradually inures him to that exposure to the weather which must form a part of his lot, I am glad to see him obtain one. Bird-keeping boys are not, however, removed from school altogether, but are generally 'out on leave' for this particular purpose: their education is interrupted, not ended.

The plough-drivers, and those whose strength and age enables them either to work regularly with their father, or take a regular situation on a farm, have in general arrived at a time of life when for many reasons I think it unadvisable to retain them in the day school.

Girls, when taken from school altogether, are mostly either sent to service, or needed at home to assist the mother in the care of the younger children and other household duties. If the parents are of good character I do not much regret this, as it is to be hoped they have been already well grounded at school in religious truth, been taught to read with ease to themselves, and probably to write and sum enough for the situation of life in which they are likely to be placed. If girls are well looked after at home, a few months there between leaving school and going into service is advantageous to them, as they thus pick up some knowledge of household work, and get some experience in the care of young children. If children, as is now usually the case, are, after leaving the day school, allowed to attend the Sunday school, further opportunity is afforded them of advancing in religious knowledge. I cannot but think that children are in most places kept at the day school as long as is advisable, but I am also strongly of opinion that they should be put to school at the earliest possible age. The system pursued at a good infant school gives to a child before it is seven years old as much knowledge as used to be obtained in the old day schools at the age of 12. Let a child on leaving an infant school at seven enter and continue in a good day school, say from two to three years: this, followed up by instruction in the Sunday school to the age of 13 or 14, and I imagine that the result will be, that enough of religious and general knowledge will have been obtained to lead the mind through life to profit by what it has already learned, and to seize every opportunity of procuring for itself more experience as well in spiritual as in secular things.

The habits of order and cleanliness, the habit of strict obedience maintained in every good infant school; the fact that the children are taken at the very earliest moment they can be taught anything, and instructed in a manner adapted to their age in things that shall profit them as well in this as the next world; the getting them away for so many hours from the crowded cottage, its impure air, and too often its unprofitable examples, — all this has made me feel from experience that the infant school, when it is well managed, is of all instruments in our hands one of the most powerful in improving the moral character of the poorer classes of society.

In some parishes there are evening schools for adults: they prove most useful, giving as they do opportunity to many young persons who wish to improve themselves of snatching an hour or two hours' instruction after their day's work; they should receive every encouragement.

There are also adult schools for young women, to which, after they have left the day school, they are admitted for a part of the day to learn the art of cutting out clothes, and the various species of needlework which may be required of them in 'good service': they are also further instructed in religious knowledge. Under proper management these schools are most valuable: without taking the young female entirely from home, thus permitting her there to acquire a practical knowledge of many things required in 'service', they still keep her under the eye of her superiors, within reach of the advice of those who are best qualified to advise, and this at an age when proper superintendence is most valuable, and a word of friendly advice from those she has been taught to love and respect will often rescue from habits tending to ruin. There can be no question but that the sooner young women can be fitted for and get out into service the better for them, and I know no way in which the higher classes can better direct their charity than in promoting every means of fitting the female children of the village poor for respectable service.

Let me now call your attention to one of the most destructive sources of evil to which the character of the young female is exposed in the agricultural districts. In many counties it is the custom to hire lads and girls for farm-work at what are called 'Statute Fairs', known amongst the poor as 'Staties', 'Mops' or 'Wakes'. Some second-rate country town is in general the scene of these assemblages: a few shows, a few stalls for the sale of toys, &c.; a good many itinerant singers and sellers of ballads, many of which are of the most obscene character; a certain number of fiddlers in a certain number of public-houses and beer-shops, comprise the chief attractions of the fair. The business part of it consists in the exhibition of a large number of young lads and girls, dressed in all the finery they can muster, that they may be seen, as they think, to the best advantage, and be hired on the spot by those masters or mistresses who come to such places to seek for servants. Apparent strength and health are the only requisites, with the exception of a professed knowledge to a greater or less degree of the duties of the situation for which they propose themselves. Mothers with a girl of bad character at home will often say, 'Well, she must go to the next staties, and as she is stout and healthy she'll be hired fast enough.' Accordingly such girls are cleaned and dressed up for the fair, are often at once hired, and as often within a few months have to appear on summons before a bench of magistrates, that the said hiring may, for some dishonest or profligate conduct, be terminated. Those only who have witnessed them can form any idea of the scenes of vice which these fairs become late in the day: I know no language of reproach too strong to apply to them, and I think one of the first duties of the legislator, who seeks to throw the protection of the law over the moral character of the young in country districts, will be either to put an end to, or at least appoint some efficient superintendence over, these fairs.

As to the crimes most common amongst the class we have been considering, wood-stealing is the most common overt act of crime they commit: it is practised in some districts to an immense extent by women and young children. The boys at an early age but too often take to turnip-stealing and poaching.

As a magistrate I have frequently found these crimes to originate in a great measure from circumstances of a local character. Where there is a poor straggling village, with few, if any, resident gentry, at a distance from any market at which fuel could be pur-

chased at a price within the poor man's means; where wages are
low and work difficult to be got — and these two things are in
general indicative of a population too large for the locality, which
again is a cause of house rent being high from the number of
dwellings being disproportioned to the population, — in such a
district I am not surprised if fuel and food are both obtained dis-
honestly.

We are too apt to forget that the poor are often so situated that
they have no market within their reach at which they can procure
many of the absolute necessaries of life, and this is especially the
case with regard to fuel. Unless they have a right of turf-cutting,
or the proprietors of woods will sell fuel on the spot, they are
often wholly without the means of procuring it honestly.

If a market for fuel is within the labourer's reach, I have never
found any difficulty in getting him to lay by, in small instalments
through the summer, sufficient money to purchase his winter's
stock of that article, but the expense of its carriage from any
distance is a complete bar to his obtaining it at all. From no
limited experience I can say, that the only way in which wood-
stealing can be successfully checked is by first placing fuel at a
fair price within reach of the poor man, and then showing a firm
determination to prosecute in every case in which the stealing it is
detected. There is, however, a very great disinclination on the
part of the farmers, generally speaking, to prosecute a labourer,
let him be discovered in what theft he may. This may arise from
the expense and trouble of a prosecution: it does, I know, often
arise from fear of injury to their property by the associates of the
criminal, or from himself, should he be acquitted, or only sentenced to some short term of imprisonment. I think, too,
instances might be found of this feeling arising from a cause
which you may gather from the following argument of a farmer:
— 'I know Will ——— is a thief; he has robbed me. He robs us all in
turn — something from one, something from another. However,
he has a large family: they cost us nothing now out of the rates;
but if we put him in prison we must put them in the union, and
that would cost us a pretty deal.' Whilst I trace the immorality of
the labouring classes to defective education, the want of means to
preserve decency in their families, and the temptations to
intemperance which are to be found in the manner in which the
beer-shop keepers, unchecked by legal interference, offer at every
hour of the day, and almost every hour of the night, all the
inducements likely to draw the labourer from home, and to fix

him in a love of drink and bad company, I trace much of the crime he commits to *absolute want.* I am satisfied that the law should, under any and every circumstance, be enforced against offenders when detected, and that every means should be used for their detection; but is it not the bounden duty of the higher and middling classes of society to endeavour at any cost to place the labourer, as far as possible, in such a condition as shall afford him the option of acquiring for himself and children right principles of action towards his fellow-men, and the means of obtaining by his own industry all that is necessary for his own and his children's support? The law must be held in respect; but who shall justify us in placing any of our fellow-creatures in a position in which, whilst they have little encouragement to do right, they have every temptation to do wrong.

With regard to the general condition of the agricultural labourer, I believe the public to be less informed, or worse informed, than about that of any other class of society. His most common vices are, it is true, pretty well known, for they have been exposed with no hesitating pens, have been officially proclaimed throughout the length and breadth of the land; but the hardships of his life at best, its temptations, the hindrances to its improvement, the scanty remuneration afforded for his hardest labour, the ingenious methods used to hold him in thraldom, permitting him neither to work where he likes, at the wages he could obtain, or to spend those he does obtain where he chooses; the manner in which he often sees the welfare of the beast he drives more valued than his own, and his own welfare often sacrificed to some caprice of his employer — threatened with the 'Union House' if he refuses them, his wages are settled by the combined interest or opinion of the employers around him, forced to pay an exorbitant rent for a dwelling in which he cannot decently rear his family: if he is single, he is to receive less for the sweat of his brow than if he was married; if he does marry, every ingenuity is used to make him feel that he is regarded as one about to increase the burdens of the parish, to say nothing of the ingenuity used to shift him into some other parish, — these are parts of his condition on which the public are not so well informed, or at least of which they seem to act in perfect ignorance. Let the charitable do what they will to increase the comforts and elevate the character of the poor of a parish, alas! but too often because Parish A is thus more favoured than parish B, it is made the pretext for raising the rent of the labourer's dwelling, and diminishing the amount of his wages.

I do, Sir, sincerely hope that this your present commission may be but the forerunner of one that shall thoroughly investigate the condition of the labourer — his moral, social, and physical condition. Let the public have *bonâ fide* evidence of the labourer's condition, and I feel confident the wonder will be, — not that this class of the community have from time to time shown a disaffected spirit, — not that evidence of their immorality, dishonesty, and extravagance abounded, — not that they are daily becoming more and more burdensome upon the poor-rates, but that they have borne so long the hardships of their condition, have not been urged to greater crimes — that any of them can at all, at the prices they have to pay for rent, fuel, and food, honestly support their families out of the wages they receive. I cannot say that their wives and children are subject to any physical injury from the nature of the employments in agriculture in which they engage, but I do assert, of the agricultural labourers as a class, that they have found fewer friends of any weight to contend for their rights in high places, and more enemies to their moral and physical improvement at their own doors, than any other class of society. Attachment to their superiors, respect for their employers, loyalty to their rulers, is fast passing away; they have found themselves made the subjects of experiments, the smart of which they have felt, but the intention of which they could not understand. Their education has occupied the mind of the public chiefly as a scene for party strife; their relief in age or sickness has been discussed in a philosophical tone, of which the most forbidding features were the only ones they could appreciate. Pamphlets on cottage husbandry, plans for cottage buildings, tracts on morality, treatises on economy, have been sent forth with no sparing hand; but in nine villages out of ten the cottage is still nothing but a slightly improved hovel, morality is borne down by the pressure of temptation on minds unfortified by education in good principles, and the wages of the stoutest and most industrious scarce find the coarsest food, the smallest sufficiency of fuel. In my opinion, unless those above them soon determine to give up some of their own luxuries, that they may give to the labourer such wages as shall enable him to rear his family in comfort in a dwelling in which decency can be preserved, and within reach of a school, and a church in which he and his may be taught the learning fitted for their station here, and tending to place them in the way to heaven hereafter —

unless some great effort is made to obtain these objects, our peasantry will become not the support they should be to the country, but a pregnant source of all that can tend to subvert its best institutions.

Yours truly,

S. GODOLPHIN OSBORNE.

To Alfred Austin, Esq.,
Assistant Poor Law Commissioner.

(c) Letter to The Times, *24 August 1846,* The Letters of S.G.O.: A Series of Letters on Public Affairs Written by the Rev. Lord Sidney Godolphin Osborne and Published in 'The Times' 1844-1888, *edited by Arnold White, 2 vols, London, 1891, I, pp. 14-19.*

In London, I believe, there are persons appointed to inspect the markets, and see that unwholesome food is not offered for sale. Newgate has one or more officials whose duty it is to take care that the meat of diseased or improperly killed animals is not sold as food for anything above the grades of a dog or pig. There is a clerk of the fish market, whose nose is supposed to be ever ready and keen to hunt out fish unfit for human food. It may then be fairly assumed, that our laws contemplate the protection of the people's health, so far at least as they establish the principle that the sale of unwholesome food is illegal.

The Act of Parliament known as the 'Vagrant Act', makes the lodging in the open air, without 'visible means of subsistence', penal; here I think we may assume that the law considers every subject of the realm to have shelter and subsistence honestly within reach. There are certain laws in existence directed against the practice of master manufacturers being retailers of goods to their workmen; the evident aim of the law being to secure to the workman liberty of choice in the market at which he purchases the necessaries of life, to protect him from anything like a compulsion to buy where he would be afraid to question the quality or price of the things he needs. Surely, Sir, if it is illegal to offer for sale unwholesome meat in London, to act the truckmaster in Lancashire, although there may be no express enactments to that effect, it is no unfair presumption to say that the *animus* of the law is against such practices wherever practised.

I am this day returned from a visit to a neighbourhood, in which I found meat which would be condemned in Newgate

Market, sold to the labouring poor — in which whole families are living in unroofed houses, without any but invisible means of subsistence; the wages of at least nine out of ten of the labourers in husbandry being paid to them in the shape of goods sold to them by their masters, including meat of the above character.

The parish of Ryme is situated in Dorsetshire, but only divided from Somerset by a brook; it belongs almost entirely to the Duchy of Cornwall; its population is about 200; according to the poor-rate of 1840, its acreage was 978, rented at the sum of 1,108*l.*; about rather more than a third of the parish is arable. Two or three years ago a report was made to the union board of the wretched state of the cottages in this parish; a friend favoured me with a copy of it, and means were found to bring it before the council of the Duchy. To their credit be it said, steps have been taken to in some measure mitigate the disgraceful state of the dwellings on their property; six or eight new cottages are either built or are in progress; and some of the old hovels have been destroyed. Though I cannot say much for the substantial nature of the new buildings, they are worthy of all praise, as planned to favour the observation of the common customs of decent life; they have good garden grounds, and are let at a moderate rent. I cannot but hope that in a few years' time the few shameful specimens of dwellings that still exist may also be destroyed, and new ones, fit for human beings, erected in their stead. It is painful, Sir, to see, that where the proprietary of an estate do thus, however late, endeavour to do their duty to those who till the ground on it, their tenantry should be allowed to go on in a course of treatment of the labourer which I can only characterise as most wicked and unjust. I was not content to inquire of the labourers themselves as to their condition, but I took no common pains to trace out the truth of their assertions, by obtaining the statements of educated persons in the higher grade of life, who, living on the spot, were, by their professions or business, brought into a thorough acquaintance with the system to which I would now draw attention.

In the parish of Ryme, with one or two exceptions, the wages of able-bodied married men are 7s. a week; those of single men and lads, from sixteen to twenty-five or more years of age, are from 2s. 6d. to 6s. The mowing and harvest afford about two months of task work, at which about 10s. a week is earned, besides the allowance of a gallon of cider a day, but the hours then worked are from five in the morning to seven in the evening.

The pay for mowing barley is 1s. 6d. an acre; for reaping and binding wheat 6s. an acre, the men finding their own tools. When doing day work the men get about two pints of cider a day; but this is stuff of an inferior quality; it is made on the farms, and costs the farmer but little. At day work they are expected to be on the farm, if the light will permit, at least twelve hours a day. There are no privileges of any kind whatever, that I could discover, afforded by the masters to the men. Thus far, Sir, I have only told of men working for the tenantry of the Prince of Wales for ten months of the year at 7s. a week, having to pay 1s. out of it for the rent of a cottage, and therefore, as it would appear, having only 6s. to bring home to buy food and clothing; for the cider drunk in the field may spur them on to work harder, but it is of no use to their families at home. But now comes the worst part of my story; they are paid almost entirely on the truck system; for a bushel of best wheat they pay 7s. the bushel, which is 56s. the quarter; for first tailings they pay 6s. the bushel, *i.e.* 48s. the quarter; for second tailings 5s. the bushel, *i.e.* 40s. the quarter. If wished for, I shall be happy to supply a sample of this grist, when any judge will at once say it is charged at least 1s. a bushel too much. Now, Sir, I would have you bear in mind, that, having to pay 1s. rent, the labourer needing a bushel of grist a week, and having to pay 6s. for it, his wages being only 7s., he is left wholly without money to buy anything else. In justice to the farmer, I will put the 1s. overcharge for the grist against the cider he gives in the field. But the farmer makes butter and cheese; there are of these articles inferior qualities, for which there would be no market did not the labourer prove a customer. These, then, are taken by such men as may have children or wives at work on the farm, in lieu of their wages. The cheese is made of skim-milk, is of the colour and hardness of chalk, smells perfectly sour, but is charged for at 3½d. a pound. The butter is charged at 10d. a pound, is on the average good, but it does again and again occur, that firkins returned by the salesmen as unfit for the market are sold to the men at a price above the market price of good butter. In the neighbouring parish of Yetminster, a tradesman informed me of one farmer who sold his labourers soap and candles; and here let me say I am speaking of large and apparently well-to-do farmers, renting, some of them, 400*l.* a year.

We have found, Sir, that there is a 'tailing' as it were of cheese and butter; but what will the public think of a tailing of meat? Three days before I was at Ryme a sheep with the staggers was killed, 'just afore he died', and sold to the labourers of one of the principal farmers at 4d. the pound. When ewes die in lambing, or as the men express it 'are killed afore they are *cold* dead', the men are sold the meat at 2½d. One woman, who had some of a *giddy sheep* at 4d. the pound, a few days ago, said she would have no more of this 'breeding ewe mutton,' for it made her husband ill. It will happen on a dairy farm that a cow will die diseased. There is a complaint called the 'quarter evil', which seems to me the only purveyor of beef to the poor in these parts. When an animal has time, in dying of this disease, to have its throat cut, it is retailed at 2½d. the pound to the labourers. In one instance we had the positive evidence of the man who found it dead, that a sheep's throat was then cut; it was not quite cold, and the meat sold as above. It may be said, are the men compelled to take these things? They answer this question in various ways, but one, I think, will give the sense of all the rest: — 'They just tell us they can't afford the money to pay us, and therefore axes of us to take the gristing and the cheese of them; many of us must soon get in debt to them, and then you see, Sir, we must go on. As to the dead animals, they just says, "We can't be expected to take the whole loss," and they then tells us as we should take some of it off their hands. There may be from twelve to a score of such sheep in the year on my master's farm. 'Tis the only meat we ever sees.' Knowing that there was a most respectable and humane man farming largely a few miles off, and that he is rather a fancy sheep breeder, I asked of a man what Mr P. did with his animals that were so diseased? The answer was, 'They be given to the dogs and pigs.' As to wages paid in money, I think you would be puzzled to find any one man who had drawn 2*l.* in any one year; by the help of clothing clubs, and an occasional job at draining out of the parish, they are alone enabled to get clothes. As a specimen of what life still is in some instances, and was generally for many years, I went into the cottage of a man who it was found had stolen some of his master's wheat. I found the woman, with two of the children, eating a few unwholesome potatoes and some bread; a child, of nine years of age, dead, in a coffin close to them; the only ascent to the bedroom by a broken ladder; the roof so dilapidated that it rains down on the bed. They had five children, all young; she was close to her confinement; the husband earning 7s. paying 6s. for a grist of tailings, of which I procured a sample, and defy any one to say it is worth 5s.; the whole building unfit for any human being to live in. Who can wonder that they steal their master's corn? As to drunkenness, the whole system of payment in cider encourages it.

On one side of Ryme is Yetminster, on the other side is Closworth, in Somersetshire; in the former the cottages belong, for the most part, to the parish or to small proprietors. In the latter they are, with the whole parish, the property of a nobleman of known large landed possessions [Lord Portman]. Your Commissioner made a faint attempt to describe one place in Yetminster in which sixty souls dwell. I went all over it. It is in all truth the very cesspool of everything in which anything human can be recognised — whole families wallowing together at night on filthy rags, in rooms in which they are so packed, and yet so little sheltered, that one's wonder is that the physical existence can survive, as it does, the necessary speedy destruction of all existing moral principle. What matters it that they are the refuse of the parish? It is a refuse pregnant with an eternal life, that requires a care and a preparation for its future birth, which the circumstances of such a place utterly forbid. In a Christian land, divided by law into districts and parishes, professedly each charged with the expense of a moral apparatus, calculated to protect the bodies of the people from the assaults of hunger or violence, their souls from ignorance and heathenism, a vast — almost roofless — manufactory of misery, and nursery for vice is allowed to rear its smoke-blackened walls in the very midst of a landscape in which the eye may trace the existence of the mansions and parks of the wealthy, charged to see justice done the body; churches, telling of the existence of an order of men whose duty it is to preach the plain truth boldly, that God will not have the poor oppressed in body or in soul.

If Closworth, the other parish of which I have spoken, is, as I am informed, no worse than two-thirds of the Somerset villages, I can only say that Dorset, bad as it is, I am convinced can show few such specimens of miserable existence. It is no argument to say that most of these wretched, damp, decaying, confined, glassless hovels are the property of little lifeholders. I admit it to be a very general case, though not true in this instance. No one can travel through these districts and not see how every atom of waste ground is seized on for the erection of these dens; but you may go for miles, you may make what inquiry you will, and you will find that those who draw incomes from the soil not only will not, and have not, until lately in a few instances, built any cottages, but they have perseveringly pursued the system of cottage destruction. Hence it is, the dwellings of the peasantry must be thus planted by themselves on the wastes, or they must become the prey of those who, having little lifeholds, built cabins on them to let at exorbitant rents.

The potato crop is a failure throughout the whole district; I do not believe a third will be fit for food. This is of no small importance, for the only money the poor man can draw to purchase clothing is from the potatoes, either by their sale, or by their consumption enabling them to make shift with a grist once in two instead of every week.

Secondary Works

Literary Studies

Aydelotte, William O., 'The England of Marx and Mill as Reflected in Fiction', *Journal of Economic History*, Supplement VIII, 1948, pp. 42-58

Bergmann, Helena, *Between Obedience and Freedom: Women's Role in the Mid-Nineteenth Century Industrial Novel*, Gothenburg, 1979

Blainey, Ann, *The Farthing Poet: A Biography of Richard Hengist Horne 1802-1884*, London, 1968

Bland, D.S., '*Mary Barton* and Historical Accuracy', *Review of English Studies*, 1, 1950, pp. 58-60

Blount, Trevor, 'Poor Jo, Education, and the Problems of Juvenile Delinquency in Dickens's *Bleak House*', *Modern Philology*, 62, 1964-5, pp. 325-39

———, 'Dickens's Slum Satire in *Bleak House*', *Modern Language Review*, LX, 1965, pp. 340-51

Bodenheimer, Rosemarie, '*North and South*: A Permanent State of Change', *Nineteenth-Century Fiction*, 34, 1979, pp. 281-301

———, 'Private Grief and Public Acts in *Mary Barton*', *Dickens Studies Annual: Essays on Victorian Fiction*, 9, 1981, pp. 195-216

Brantlinger, Patrick, 'The Case against Trades Unions in Early Victorian Fiction', *Victorian Studies*, 13, 1969, pp. 37-52

———, 'Bluebooks, the Social Organism, and the Victorian Novel', *Criticism*, 14, 1972, pp. 328-44

———, *The Spirit of Reform: British Literature and Politics, 1832-1867*, Cambridge, Mass., 1977

———, 'Tory Radicalism and "The Two Nations" in Disraeli's *Sybil*', *Victorian Newsletter*, 41, 1972, pp. 13-17

Browning, Elizabeth Barrett, *Letters of Elizabeth Barrett Browning Addressed to Richard Hengist Horne, With Comments on Contemporaries*, edited by S.R. Townshend Mayer, 2 vols, London, 1887

Butwin, Joseph, '*Hard Times*: The News and the Novel', *Nineteenth-Century Fiction*, 32, 1977, pp. 166-87

Carnall, Geoffrey, 'Dickens, Mrs Gaskell, and the Preston Strike', *Victorian Studies*, 8, 1964, pp. 31-48

Cazamian, Lewis, *The Social Novel in England, 1830-1850: Dickens, Disraeli, Mrs Gaskell, Kingsley*, translated by Martin Fido, London, 1973

Chaloner, W.H., 'Mrs Trollope and the Early Factory System', *Victorian Studies*, 4, 1960, pp. 159-66

Chapman, Raymond, *The Victorian Debate: English Literature and Society*, London, 1968

Chitty, Susan, *The Beast and the Monk: A Life of Charles Kingsley*, London, 1974

Colby, Robert, *Fiction with a Purpose: Major and Minor Nineteenth Century Novels*, Bloomington, 1967

Collin, D.W., 'The Composition of Mrs Gaskell's *North and South*', *Bulletin of the John Rylands Library*, 54, no. 1, 1971

Colloms, Brenda, *Charles Kingsley: The Lion of Eversley*, New York, 1975

Craig, David, 'Fiction and the Rising Industrial Class', *Essays in Criticism*, 17, 1967, pp. 64-74

———, *The Real Foundations: Literature and Social Change*, London, 1974

Craik, W.A., *Elizabeth Gaskell and the English Provincial Novel*, London, 1975

Dickens, Charles, *The Speeches of Charles Dickens*, edited by K.J. Fielding, Oxford, 1960

Dunn, Richard, 'Dickens and Mayhew Once More', *Nineteenth-Century Fiction*, 25, 1970, pp. 348-53

Easson, Angus, *Elizabeth Gaskell*, London, Boston and Henley, 1979

Edelstein, T.J., 'They Sang "The Song of the Shirt": The Visual Iconology of the Seamstress', *Victorian Studies*, 23, 1980, pp. 183-210

Fido, Martin, 'The Treatment of Rural Distress in Disraeli's *Sybil*', *The Yearbook of English Studies*, 5, 1975, pp. 153-63

———, '"From His Own Observation": Sources of Working-class Passages in Disraeli's *Sybil*', *Modern Languages Review*, 72, 1977, pp. 268-84

Fielding, K. J., '*Hard Times* and Common Things', in *Imagined Worlds*, edited by Maynard Mack and Ian Gregor, London, 1968

Fielding, K.J. and Smith, Anne, '*Hard Times* and the Factory Controversy: Dickens vs. Harriet Martineau', *Nineteenth-Century Fiction*, 24, 1970, pp. 404-27

Frykstedt, Monica Correa, '*Mary Barton* and the *Reports of the Ministry to the Poor*: A New Source', *Studia Neophilologica*, LII, 1980, pp. 333-6

———, 'The Early Industrial Novel: *Mary Barton* and its Predecessors', *Bulletin of the John Rylands Library*, 63, 1980, pp. 11-30

Gallagher, Catherine, *The Industrial Reformation of English Fiction: Social Discourse and Narrative Form 1832-1867*, Chicago and London, 1985

Gaskell, Elizabeth, *Letters of Mrs Gaskell*, edited by J.A.P. Chapple and Arthur Pollard, Manchester, 1966

Gérin, Winifred, *Elizabeth Gaskell: A Biography*, Oxford, 1976

Gill, Stephen, 'Price's Patent Candles: New Light on *North and South*', *Review of English Studies*, 27, 1976, pp. 313-21

Haberman, Melvyn, 'The Courtship of the Void: The World of *Hard Times*', in *Worlds of Victorian Fiction*, edited by Jerome H. Buckley, Cambridge, Mass., 1975

Hamilton, Robert, 'Disraeli and the Two Nations', *Quarterly Review*, 288, 1950, pp. 10-15

Himmelfarb, Gertrude, *The Idea of Poverty: England in the Early Industrial Age*, New York, 1984

Hopkins, Annette, *Elizabeth Gaskell: Her Life and Work*, London, 1952

House, Humphry, *The Dickens World*, London, 1941

Howard, David, Lucas, John and Goode, John, *Tradition and Tolerance in Nineteenth Century Fiction*, London, 1966

Humphreys, Anne, *Travels into the Poor Man's Country: the Work of Henry Mayhew*, London, 1977

James, Louis, *Fiction for the Working Man, 1830-1850: A Study of the Liter-

ature Produced for the Working Classes in Early Victorian England, London, 1963

Keating, P.J., *The Working Classes in Victorian Fiction*, London, 1971

Kestner, Joseph, *Protest and Reform: The British Social Narrative by Women 1827-1867*, London, 1985

Kettle, Arnold, 'The Early Victorian Social-Problem Novel', in *From Dickens to Hardy*, edited by Boris Ford. Vol. 6 of *The Pelican Guide to English Literature*, London, 1958

Kingsley, Charles, *Charles Kingsley: His Letters and Memories of his Life*, edited by his Wife, 2 vols, London, 1877

Kovačević, Ivanka, *Fact into Fiction: The Literature and the Industrial Scene, 1750-1850*, Leicester, 1975

——, and Kammer, Barbara, 'Blue Book into Novel: The Forgotten Industrial Fiction of Charlotte Elizabeth Tonna', *Nineteenth-Century Fiction*, 25, 1970, pp. 152-73

Lansbury, Coral, *Elizabeth Gaskell: The Novel of Social Crisis*, London, 1971

Lucas, John, *Literature and Politics in the Nineteenth Century Novel*, London, 1971

——, *The Literature of Change: Studies in the Nineteenth Century Provincial Novel*, Sussex, 1977

Mayhew, Henry, *The Unknown Mayhew: Selections from the 'Morning Chronicle' 1849-1850*, edited and introduced by E.P. Thompson and Eileen Yeo, London, 1971

Melada, Ivan, *The Captain of Industry in Victorian Fiction, 1821-1871*, Albuquerque, 1970

Nelson, Harland S., 'Dickens's *Our Mutual Friend* and Henry Mayhew's *London Labour and the London Poor*', *Nineteenth Century Fiction*, XX, 1965, pp. 207-22

Pikoulis, John, '*North and South*: Varieties of Love and Power', *Yearbook of English Studies*, 6, 1976, pp. 176-93

Schwarz, Daniel R., *Disraeli's Fiction*, New York, 1969

Sharps, J.G., *Mrs Gaskell's Observation and Invention*, London, 1970

Slater, Michael, 'Dickens's Tract for the Times', *Dickens 1970*, edited by Michael Slater, London, 1970, pp. 99-123

——, *Dickens and Women*, London, 1983

Smith, David, '*Mary Barton* and *Hard Times*: Their Social Insights', *Mosaic*, 5, 1971, pp. 97-112

Smith, Sheila, 'Willenhall and Wodgate: Disraeli's Use of Blue Book Evidence', *Review of English Studies*, n.s.2, 1962, pp. 368-84

——, 'Blue Books and Victorian Novelists', *Review of English Studies*, 21, 1970, pp. 23-40

——, *The Other Nation: The Poor in English Novels of the 1840s and 1850s*, Oxford, 1980

Stonehouse, J.H., ed., *Catalogue of the Library of Charles Dickens from Gadshill*, London, 1935

Sucksmith, Harvey Peter, 'The Dust-heaps in *Our Mutual Friend*', *Essays in Criticism*, XXIII, 1973, pp. 206-12

Sussman, Herbert S., *Victorians and the Machine: Literary Response to Technology*, Cambridge, Mass., 1968

Tillotson, Kathleen, *Novels of the Eighteen-Forties*, London, 1956

Vicinus, Martha, *The Industrial Muse: A Study of Nineteenth Century British Working-class Literature*, London, 1974
Webb, Igor, *From Custom to Capital: The English Novel and the Industrial Revolution*, Ithaca, N.Y., 1981
Wheeler, Michael D., 'The Writer as Reader in *Mary Barton*', *Durham University Journal*, 67, 1974, pp. 92-106
Williams, Raymond, *Culture and Society: 1780-1950*, London, 1958
Wright, Edgar, *Mrs Gaskell: The Basis for Reassessment*, London, 1965

Social and Economic History

Ashton, T.S., *Economic and Social Investigations in Manchester, 1833-1933: A Centenary History of the Manchester Statistical Society*, Manchester, 1934
Backstrom, P.N., 'The Practical Side of Christian Socialism in Victorian England', *Victorian Studies*, 7, 1963, pp. 305-24
Briggs, Asa, *Chartist Studies*, London, 1959
———, 'Cholera and Society in the Nineteenth Century', *Past and Present*, 19, 1961, pp. 76-96
———, 'The Language of "Class" in Early Nineteenth Century England', in *Essays in Labour History*, edited by Asa Briggs and J. Saville, London, 1960
———, *Victorian Cities*, London, 1963
Bythell, Duncan, *The Handloom Weavers: A Study in the English Cotton Industry during the Industrial Revolution*, London, 1969
———, *The Sweated Trades: Outwork in Nineteenth-Century Britain*, New York, 1978
Cantor, Milton and Laurie, Bruce, eds., *Class, Sex, and the Woman Worker*, Westport, Conn., 1980
Chambers, J.D., *The Workshop of the World: British Economic History from 1820 to 1880*, London, 1961
Checkland, S.J., *The Rise of Industrial Society in England: 1815-1885*, London, 1964
Dutton, H.I., and King, J.E., *'Ten Per Cent and No Surrender': The Preston Strike, 1853-1854*, Cambridge, 1981
Dyos, H.J. and Wolff, Michael, eds., *The Victorian City: Images and Realities*, London and Boston, 1973
Finer, S.E., *The Life and Times of Sir Edwin Chadwick*, London, 1952
Grampp, William Dyer, *The Manchester School of Economics*, Stanford, 1960
Hammond, Barbara, and Hammond, L.J., *The Age of the Chartists, 1832-1854: A Study of Discontent*, London, 1930
Hearn, Francis, *Domination, Legitimation and Resistance: The Incorporation of the Nineteenth-Century English Working Class*, Westport, Conn., 1978
Hewitt, Margaret, *Wives and Mothers in Victorian Industry*, London, 1948
Hobsbawm, Eric J., *Labouring Men: Studies in the History of Labour*, London, 1964
Houghton, Walter E., *The Victorian Frame of Mind, 1830-1870*, London, 1966
Hutchins, B.L., *The Public Health Agitation, 1833-1848*, London, 1909

Longmate, Norman, *The Hungry Mills*, London, 1978

Mathias, Peter, *The First Industrial Nation*, London, 1969

McLachan, Herbert, 'Cross Street Chapel in the Life of Manchester', *Memoirs and Proceedings of the Manchester Literary and Philosophical Society*, 84, 1939-41, pp. 29-41

Perkin, Harold J., *The Origin of Modern English Society, 1780-1880*, London, 1972

Pinchbeck, Ivy, *Women Workers and the Industrial Revolution, 1750-1850*, New York, 1969

Roberts, David, *Paternalism in Early Victorian England*, New Brunswick, N.J., 1979

Smelser, N.J., *Social Change in the Industrial Revolution: An Application of Theory to the British Cotton Industry*, Chicago, 1959

Thomas, M.W., *The Early Factory Legislation: A Study in Legislation and Administrative Evolution*, Leigh-on-Sea, Essex, 1948

Thompson, E.P., *The Making of the English Working Class*, London, 1966

——, 'Time, Work-Discipline, and Industrial Capitalism', *Past and Present*, 38, 1967, pp. 56-97

Treble, James H., *Urban Poverty in Britain, 1830-1914*, London, 1978

Vicinus, Martha, 'Dark London', *Indiana University Bookman*, 12, 1977, pp. 63-92

Viner, Jacob, *The Role of Providence in the Social Order: An Essay in Intellectual History*, Princeton, N.J., 1972

Ward, J. Trevor, *The Factory Movement, 1830-55*, London, 1962

Wiener, Martin J., *English Culture and the Decline of the Industrial Spirit, 1850-1980*, Cambridge, 1981

Wohl, Anthony, *The Eternal Slum: Housing and Social Policy in Victorian London*, London, 1977

Index